C000195254

A Transport Travelogue of Britain 1948-1972, By Road, Rail and Water

Combined edition

CASH
PHILLIPS
A 47
A 46
A 6
REFUGE
ASSURANCE COMPY LTD
WHITE HART
Schweppes
BLACKBIRD RD
CREMALT
LOAF
from all Good Bakers
4
WINNS CAFE
LUNCHEONS
MAIL
GILBEY'S GIN
TAILORING
FURNITURE REMOVALS
EBO 960

A Transport Travelogue of Britain 1948-1972, By Road, Rail and Water

Combined edition

Cedric Greenwood

First published in 2018 as six volumes in the 'Recollections' series as Nos 70-74 and 94
Combined edition first published in 2019

British Library Cataloguing in Publication Data

A catalogue record for this book is available from the British Library.

ISBN 978 1 85794 505 8

Silver Link Books
Mortons Media Group Limited
Media Centre
Morton Way
Horncastle
LN9 6JR

Tel/Fax: 01507 529529
email: sohara@mortons.co.uk
Website: www.nostalgiacollection.com

Printed and bound in the Czech Republic

All the pictures were taken by the author unless otherwise credited. Some appeared previously in the same author's *Merseyside: The Indian Summer* (Silver Link Publishing, 2007) and *Echoes of Steam and Vintage Voltage* (Silver Link Publishing, 2015).

Half title: **SLEDDALE** The railway from Whitby to Middlesbrough runs through the Cleveland Hills and this was the view from a diesel multiple unit train passing through Sleddale between Commondale and Kildale stations on 18 June 1970. The early DMUs of the mid-1950s had glazing in the partitions between the passenger saloons and the driving cabs, affording passengers this view along the route ahead. All later DMUs have had opaque panels that block this view.

Page 2: **LEICESTER** The Clock Tower was the hub of the city's 22-mile tramway system and the most complex network of tracks in Britain with tramcars passing both ways on three sides of the Victorian Gothic clock tower of 1868 and radiating in four directions, along High Street, Humberstone Gate, Gallowtree Gate and Belgrave Gate. Here the trams mingled with motor traffic on three A-class trunk routes that passed through this junction: the A6 (London to Carlisle), the A46 (Grimsby to Bath) and the A47 (Great Yarmouth to Birmingham). A point duty policeman regulated the traffic at the pedestrian crossing in the foreground. The tramways were systematically replaced by motorbuses in 1947-49, but 10 of the 13 tram routes were still operating when this picture was taken in 1948. There are three crimson and cream tramcars and few motor vehicles in this picture; a 1948 Austin removals van is on the right.

Only the Clock Tower and the buildings on the left survive today but all the shops have changed owners and uses. The range of buildings across the background, including the White Hart Hotel, has been replaced by the stark, horizontal lines of a balconied, rectangular, modern shopping centre that appears to turn its back on its city centre location. This area is now part of the city centre pedestrian zone with restricted vehicular access on the left. *George Greenwood*

Title page: **ROTHERHITHE** The Thames spritsail barge, *May*, of Ipswich, sails up Limehouse Reach past the Surrey Commercial Docks at Rotherhithe on 23 September 1972, when she delivered 50 tons of Portland stone from Dorset to London for the restoration of St Paul's Cathedral. This was the last known freight trip by a Thames sailing barge, albeit with the help of her auxiliary motor. All other Thames barge trade under sail alone finished in 1970.

These barges, with their large, russet sails, were a characteristic feature of London River and the ports and creeks of Kent, Essex and Suffolk. The derrick-like sprit held up the peak of the mainsail to keep the deck clear for working. Large leeboards on the sides could be lowered to prevent these shallow draught vessels drifting. They plied river and coastal trades in bulk cargoes like bricks, cement, coal, coke, grain, manure, timber and complete stacks of hay and straw. Some even brought coal from the Humber and Tyne and traded on the south and west coasts. Their flat bottoms allowed them to settle on beaches and the beds of creeks and rivers at low tide and load overside.

May was built at by J. & H. Cann at Harwich in 1891 for the Ipswich grain trade to London. In 1964 she was sold to Tate & Lyle's Silvertown Lighterage Services to carry 50-ton sugar freights to the isle of Wight. In 1974 Tate & Lyle berthed her at St Katharine's Dock, London, for charter and barge racing and sponsored her trip to Canada and back as deck cargo to take part in the 1976 Olympic Games. *May* has won many races in her time. In 2010 she was sold to private owners and is now berthed at Pin Mill on the River Orwell in Suffolk.

Contents

Introduction 7

1 South-east England: Kent, London and Sussex

Kent 16
County of London 45
Sussex 57

2 South and South-west England: Wessex to Cornwall

Hampshire 69
Dorset 73
Buckinghamshire 74
Berkshire 75
Oxfordshire 77
Gloucestershire 91
Devon 93
Cornwall and Isles of Scilly 106

3 Eastern and Midland Counties: Norfolk to Cheshire

Norfolk 112
Cambridgeshire 114
Lincolnshire 115
Northamptonshire 123
Leicestershire 124
Warwickshire 125
Staffordshire 127
Shropshire 131
Nottinghamshire 133
Derbyshire 134
Cheshire 135

4 Lancashire: Widnes to Furness

South Lancashire 166
Liverpool 174
Burnley, Preston and Southport 192
Blackpool and Fleetwood 198
Lancaster and Morecambe 211
Furness 215

5 Yorkshire to the Border

Yorkshire 220
Westmorland 246
Cumberland 260
County Durham 269
Northumberland 271

6 Wales, Man and Scotland

Glamorgan 274
Merioneth 281
Denbighshire 284
Flintshire 286
Caernarvonshire 288
Isle of Man 291
Dumfries-shire 308
Midlothian 309
Lanarkshire 312
Inverness-shire 328
Aberdeenshire 330

Acknowledgements and References 331

Index 334

PRESTON A wet day on Preston station, strategic junction of Lancashire's railways, on 24 November 1962. This is the south end of Platform 13 on the east side of the station with a Southport train in the bay Platform 12. The Stanier Class 4 2-6-4 tank engine, which had brought the train in, is waiting to be released by another engine taking the four-coach train out as the 11.30am departure for Southport. The two parcels trolleys are standing beside an old wooden telephone booth on the corner of the building; this was a survivor of the 'call offices' that appeared in shops, post offices and railway stations in the 1880s and '90s before they appeared on the streets in about 1900. The Preston-Southport service closed in 1964 and the whole of this side of Preston station, which served mainly the former East Lancashire Railway route to Accrington, Colne and Todmorden, was demolished in 1971-73 and made into a car park; the reduced train services were re-routed into the remaining platforms.

Introduction

When we turn the calendar back to the mid-20th century and look through these photographs of the British transport scene in that period, we see Britain in happier, less hurried and more civilised times. Certainly the transport scene was more varied and interesting than it is today. In these pictures, taken from 1948 to 1972, we are looking at Britain in the twilight of the steam age, the industrial age, horse haulage, canal freight, electric tramways and trolleybuses, ocean liners and paddle steamers, Thames spritsail barges and Clyde steam 'puffers'.

After the trade slump of the 1920s and '30s and the 1939-45 war, the period 1948-54 was a time of recovery and full employment, a boom time for British industry, ports, public transport and home improvements. The period 1949-51 saw all-time peak passenger loadings on our buses, trains, ferries and excursion steamers. The wartime shortage of new cars, buses and coaches meant that pre-war vehicles remained on the road longer. It also led to overcrowding on 14-coach trains and long queues for buses and coaches. After the de-rationing of petrol in 1950 and the resumption of car production for the home market, patrons of public transport turned their thoughts to private transport. From its peak in 1950 patronage of public transport went into a long, slow decline – and then it was boom time for the car makers. All cars, lorries and buses on our roads were British-built and we could always identify a town by the shape and colour of its buses and trams alone.

Through the 1950s we led the world with our engineering, shipbuilding, merchant fleet, commerce, exports, prestige and in almost every other respect. Everything we used was made in Britain. We had more material prosperity, mutual trust and respect and a general sense of security and stability than we had ever known before – or have ever known since. Children and hitch-hikers could travel safely anywhere in Britain on their own. Stress, fast foods and obesity were unknown. Unemployment was at its lowest rate on record: the national unemployment rate was 1 per cent in 1951 compared with 4.1 per cent today.

In the rural areas we left our doors, cars and bicycles unlocked. We did not spend money on six-lever locks and there were no security cameras in the streets, shops, buses or railway stations. There was mutual trust, children respected their elders and everyone respected public servants such as the school teacher, the bus conductor, the shopkeeper and the policeman.

The vintage years were from 1948 to 1954. This was something of a golden age for Britain, for society, industry, public transport, BBC radio and the British film industry … before the motorcar and television changed people's habits and outlook. The cinema was the most popular form of entertainment and London film studios turned out their best films in that period. My favourites were *The Third Man* (1949), *The Blue Lamp* (1950), *Pool of London* (1950), *The Titfield Thunderbolt* (1952), *Forbidden Cargo* (1954), *The Love Match* (1954), *The Maggie* (1954) and *The Long Arm* (1956). All these were in superb quality black and white, except *The Titfield Thunderbolt*., an early British colour film. These films and many others of that era not only give an insight into British character of the period but also include some fine, professional shots of shipping, railways, tramways, motorbuses, trolleybuses and motorcars (especially those black Humber and Wolseley police cars) – vessels and vehicles mostly pre-war in origin. The character actors in these films could not be found today.

After we had recovered from the war the national spirit rose to the occasion to enjoy the Festival of Britain in 1951 and the coronation of Queen Elizabeth II in 1953 – but it was not quite the golden age we are inclined to remember. The period between those two highlights was marred by a remarkable succession of disasters within a span of 14 months.

In a typical British smog at Chatham on 4 December 1951 a bus mowed down a column of Royal Marine cadets, aged eight to 15, killing 23 and injuring 17. Many ships were disabled in a prolonged Atlantic storm in January 1952 and the American cargo liner *Flying Enterprise*, dangerously listing, keeled over and sank 42 miles off Falmouth after a 13-day epic salvage bid and a 300-mile tow by the Falmouth tug *Turmoil*, the 10 passengers and 40 crew having been rescued by other ships. The day the *Flying Enterprise* went down 23 people were killed when a London to Dublin airliner crashed over Snowdonia in the same gale. Our popular king, George VI, who shared our wartime experiences at first hand, died in February 1952, plunging the nation into deep mourning; radio and television closed down except for news bulletins. At the height of the summer holidays in August 1952, Lynmouth was destroyed by a torrent of flood water off Exmoor, killing 34 people. A prototype jet fighter aircraft crashed and killed 26 people at Farnborough Air Show on 6 September 1952. Our worst train crash occurred at Harrow & Wealdstone on 8 October 1952, when 112 people were killed and 340 injured in a pile-up of three trains. On 25 January 1953 the Canadian Pacific liner *Empress of Canada* burned out and capsized in dock at Liverpool. Over the weekend of 31 January and 1 February 1953 the Stranraer-Larne ferry *Princess Victoria* sank in a storm, drowning 128 people, and the same northerly, 80mph gale combined with a high spring tide in the North Sea to flood 160,000 acres along the east coast from Grimsby to Deal; 275 people were drowned or died of exposure, 18,476 people were made homeless, and farmers lost a total of 12,000 sheep, 2,400 cattle, 520 pigs and countless poultry.

Our total review period, 1948-72, was not only a zenith but also a time of change in the fortunes of Britain, the transport scene and the environment. The second half of the 1950s saw the first sign of things to come: the rise of 'angry young men', football hooliganism, vandalism and race riots. The growth of television and motoring led to the decline of cinemas, theatres, dance halls and public transport. Prolonged strikes coupled with growing competition started a long, steady rundown of our coal mines, steel works, heavy engineering, shipbuilding and textile mills. In 1956 the press began to campaign against the insidious spread of 'subtopia': housing estates, concrete roads, lamp posts and advertising hoardings across the countryside. Sixty years later the Government, with no sustainable population policy, is still urging more subtopia.

In 1959 the Ministry of Transport opened Britain's first stretch of motorway and downgraded the railway electrification programme to mainly one of dieselisation – just as it did again in 2017. The Transport Minister of 1959-64, Ernest Marples – he of the Marples, Ridgeway road construction company – was only too happy to pilot Britain's motorway network while rubber-stamping most of the amputations to the railway network recommended by his appointed chairman of British Railways (1961-65), Dr Richard Beeching. The construction of motorways and associated urban concrete viaducts (euphemistically called 'flyovers') catered to mass motoring and ever bigger lorries – at great cost to the nation in terms of road maintenance, noise and air pollution, the loss of good public transport, the massacre of wildlife and the destruction of our roadside heritage such as old buildings, bridges, milestones and cast-iron finger posts by errant drivers. Our big towns have been rearranged to cope with the transitory motorcar yet now we have gridlock and we breathe poisoned air. The old A-class trunk roads we knew in the 1950s are hard the follow across country today as they have been sidetracked by new roads, broken up into little bits and renumbered.

The cold wind of change blew through Britain in the 1960s. When the tramcars had gone the demolition gangs moved in and the old townscapes began to come down. Developers and town planners destroyed more of our townscapes than the Luftwaffe ever did and conspired to maximise rents and rates (now 'council tax') with bleak-looking tower blocks of offices and flats. The 1960s was the worst decade in the history of British architecture. The surviving buildings of that decade are now regarded as the ugliest in town. Their shoddy workmanship means that many have not survived the turn of the century and even some concrete 'flyovers', which were raised as prestige projects, have been demolished as unnecessary blots on the townscape.

Discipline was relaxed at home and at council schools and grammar was cut out of English lessons, which has resulted in the errant ways of children and the slovenly misuse of English language to this day.

The 1970s was the decade of greatest changes from the old familiar elements of our way of life: we switched to the 24-hour clock, decimal currency and metric weights and measures as a prerequisite to joining the European Economic Community. Finally the comprehensive reorganisation of local government in 1974-75 re-drew the map of British counties.

Our trade, industry and ports continued to decline to a nadir in the 1980s. In 1984 unemployment reached a record of 3,248,000, or 11.9 per cent, and by the end of that decade most of our coal mines, heavy engineering works, shipbuilding yards, textile mills and docks had closed down. So ended generations of experience, skill and pride. Then began a slow, belated process of modernisation, mechanisation, containerisation and revival for the surviving industries and ports and we have even seen the reopening of closed railways and stations in both commercial and preservation modes. I feel privileged to have witnessed 1948-54, but the 1960s, '70s and '80s is not a period I should like to live through again. Coincidentally, the years 1963 to 1991 were the tram-forsaken years in Britain, but since then we have seen a renaissance of tramways too.

Let's look at the changes in transport over that period. The British love of the sea was expressed in promenade piers and paddle steamer excursions, an era that lasted from the mid-19th century to the mid-20th century. Many paddle steamers were lost in Royal Navy service in the two world wars, but piers and sea excursions were still popular after 1945 and new paddle steamers were built for the Bristol Channel, the Firth of Clyde and Loch Lomond until 1953. The British climate, mass motoring and foreign holidays saw the excursion trade wane from the late 1950s onward. Most of the paddle steamers dated from the 1920s and '30s, they were getting to a pensionable age and operations were becoming uneconomic. No more excursion steamers were built and many piers, lacking that patronage, succumbed to rot, rust and closure. Another aspect of the British way of life was ending. The last paddle steamer in regular commercial service plied the Humber ferry in 1978.

Around 1960 the traditional two-man, front-engine, rear-entrance, 56-seat bus began to be replaced by the longer, one-man, front-entrance, rear-engine vehicle. The 77-seat Leyland Atlantean, introduced in 1958, represented a radical evolution in motorbus design over the 50 years since the pioneer Edwardian motorbuses, but little has changed in the last 60 years as the Atlantean was the model for the buses we still ride today.

The second half of the 20th century was also a period of economies and cuts in public transport as the number of passengers continued to decline. The larger-capacity buses ran less often and the late 1960s and early '70s saw the transition from two-man bus crews to one-man operation with the anomaly of the driver collecting the fares from larger payloads than formerly collected by the conductor!

This period also saw the transition from steam to diesel traction on our railways and the closure of 41 per cent of the post-war railway route mileage through the 1950s '60s and '70s (before, during and after Beeching). In 1962 BR divested itself of its 'common carrier' obligation to carry anything anywhere, the stunted railway system could not collect or deliver as much of the residual freight, and road haulage overtook the railways as the major freight mover.

The newly nationalised railways were saddled with a debt to the government for the price paid to buy them from the private companies for nationalisation. They also had to pay for a new bureaucracy that grew fourfold by 1962 in reverse proportion to the number of productive railwaymen, and for chairman Beeching on a higher salary than the prime minister! The new administration priced themselves out of the freight business in favour of road haulage and deliberately ran down services on the lines they wanted to scrap. Closures were based on contentious accounting that ignored the contributory traffic from the secondary and branch lines to the main lines and the potential for the economies of light rail principles. The railways also had to pay for constant reorganisation and a succession of unnecessary corporate identity schemes.

The Government never regarded our railways as an essential public service and has always demonstrated a bias in favour of road transport. Thus it has run down the safest and most economic mover of passengers and freight and invested in what has proved to be the most dangerous and environmentally damaging form of transport for this small and overcrowded island.

Following the Beeching closures of the 1960s the independent Policy Studies Institute reported that (1) only half of the passengers used the replacement buses, which were 'an inadequate alternative' in terms of comfort, frequency and reliability', (2) car ownership doubled in areas stripped of their railways and (3) 83 per cent of the people in those areas curtailed or stopped their leisure activities.

The Government short-sightedly closed many railways and stations we now wish we had retained for the growing population. Some lines and stations have been reopened to cope with the new housing that has since developed and for diversion routes. The Okehampton route between Exeter and Plymouth was closed in 1968, leaving only the route along the vulnerable sea wall at Dawlish as the way west. The biggest single closure was the ex-Great Central main line between London, Rugby, Leicester, Nottingham and Sheffield, which was curtailed north of Aylesbury in 1969. It had been opened in 1899 as a high-speed main line built to continental loading gauge for a future link between the industrial north of England and a Channel Tunnel. The Great Central had links with the Metropolitan Railway, the South Eastern Railway and the first Channel Tunnel Company, all under the same chairman, Sir Edward Watkin. This new line connected at Sheffield with the GCR's Manchester-Sheffield main line, which was electrified in 1954 … but closed in 1981. This leaves only the Hope Valley line linking those two great industrial conurbations. The Channel Tunnel opened in 1994 with a high-speed route only to London. As a result of these short-sighted closures and the reduced scope of franchised services from St Pancras we are now faced with traffic saturation of the roads and railways and grossly expensive, high-speed railway schemes from London to midland and northern England and Scotland.

BR not only *closed* railways. Within our period the Southern Region completed its DC third rail electrification to the Kent coast by 1959-62 and to Southampton and Bournemouth by 1967. The Midland Region opened its 25,000-volt AC electrification from Euston to Manchester London Road (then renamed Piccadilly) in 1966. Work continued to electrify the main line north of Crewe to Liverpool and Glasgow.

Transport is as important to a developed and densely populated country like Britain as water, electricity, health and education, but transport has always taken a back seat in government priorities. The British Transport Commission was set up in 1948 to coordinate canals, railways, lorries and buses, but because of changes of government the BTC was split up into separate boards in 1953 and they were abolished in 1962, having made no progress towards coordination of the transport modes. Since the late 1950s the Government has favoured roads and private cars, has never had a long-term, integrated transport policy, and invests less than half as much in public transport as France and Germany. As a result Britain now has more cars per head of population than any other European country and our train fares are the dearest in Europe.

Now let me take you back to the period 1948 to 1954, that 'Indian summer' of the old order before all these changes.

For local travel most people used the bus or tram. In those post-war years **private cars** were relatively scarce because wartime petrol rationing lasted till 1950. Most cars were Austin, Ford or Morris, built at Birmingham, Dagenham and Oxford. Others included Hillman and Standard of Coventry and Vauxhall of Luton. Police preferred black Humbers made in Coventry and Wolseleys made in Birmingham. These cars of the 1930s and '40s all had distinctive designs, unlike today, and were all the more distinctive because of their relative scarcity on the roads in the post-war period. Foreign cars were rarely seen here at that time.

Buses and trams were much more a part of our everyday life and a key element of the street scene. Many of the **buses**, like the cars, dated from the 1930s owing to the wartime shortage of materials and the consequent shortage of new vehicles.

At the beginning of our review period all buses and coaches were British with chassis and engines mainly by AEC, Albion, Bedford, BMMO, Bristol, Crossley, Daimler, Dennis, Foden, Guy and Leyland, each make of engine with its own identifiable sound. The main coachbuilders were Alexander, Burlingham, Crossley, Eastern, East Lancashire, Leyland, Massey, Metropolitan Cammell, Northern Counties, Park Royal, Roe, Weymann and Willowbrook; again you could identify the coachbuilder by the style. These are now all extinct bus builders except Alexander, Dennis and East Lancashire. The rest disappeared from the bus scene in the late 20th century succession of amalgamations, succeeded by foreign companies in a global market. Many of our new buses and all our new trams are built abroad and shipped to Britain.

In the mid-20th century our buses and trams had an innate good sense of practical and aesthetic design and simple, tasteful paint schemes. They not only complemented the townscape but enhanced it; they were friendly faces in the street scene. Reliability and efficiency were high in public services and we were proud of our corporation buses and trams. There were 97 towns and cities in Britain with their own municipal bus services in Britain in 1950 and they showed pride in the turnout of their vehicles with their coats of arms and uniformed staff.

Buses had the engine at the front, the entrance and staircase at the back with an open loading platform on the rear nearside corner. This arrangement together with the high floor two steps up from the road gave a more congenial, panoramic view from the lower saloon without the front staircase and luggage rack that mask the view today. The driver sat in a half-width cab partitioned off from the lower saloon and the conductor helped passengers on and off the platform and regulated the number of passengers to the limit of the seating and standing capacity. He also collected the fares as the bus was on its way, using a strapped-on leather cash bag and a hand-held wooden ticket rack with card tickets, coloured according to price, or a strapped-on ticket machine that printed tickets off a roll of paper. We saw more double-deckers on town and country services than today because of the high patronage.

Every self-respecting town and city had its own off-street bus station for interurban and country services. Many bus stations have been sold by new owners at big profits for shopping redevelopments and those bus services now terminate on the streets.

Electric tramcars, which served the more densely populated towns and cities, were invariably double-deckers and double-ended with staircases and dual-purpose platforms for the driver and conductor at each end so that they could reverse on the spot at the terminus or at any crossover en route without having to turn the vehicle around. The seats had reversible backrests that the conductor flipped over for the return journey. Both buses and trams had cushioned leather or moquette seating from the 1930s to the 1950s, more comfortable than the hard padded seating in modern buses and trams, although some of the older tramcars built before 1930 still had wooden seats, at least in the smoking saloon upstairs.

The tramways of the early and mid-20th century were part of the townscape. They were integrated into the fabric of the city, the grooved rails flush with the granite setts, the electric overhead wires suspended by span wires from iron 'rosettes' on the walls of the buildings or from ornate traction poles that doubled as street lamp posts. These traction poles with brackets reaching out to the middle of the road remained as street lamps anything up to 30 years or more after the closure of the tramways. The presence of those gleaming still ribbons through the streets gave you the feeling that a tramcar was always imminent, whereas a bus stop flag was not as assuring. For electric traction buffs it was an endless source of fascination to see a city with what the Americans called 'street railways' and to watch those sparking, hissing trolley wheels, skids or bow collectors passing along the underside of the overhead wires to conduct the power to the electric motors.

The ground trembled as the umpteen-ton tramcar approached along the street with dignity and noble bearing, steady on its course. As you walked out to the tracks in the middle of the road to meet it, a great range of mechanical hardware –

lifeguards, truck frames, springs, axle boxes, wheels and bogie shackles – pulled up beside you and the pleasant aroma of ozone and warm lubricating oil wafted up from the traction motors. To surmount all this running gear you had to climb two steps to the end platform and another step into the lower saloon, and passengers sitting upstairs looked down on the roofs of the passing buses. This combined with the smooth motion of the bogie cars on eight wheels and steel rails to make us feel that this was the most superior way to travel.

The very longevity of the electric rail vehicle made trams appear old-fashioned and obsolete in the brave new world of post-war recovery. Many tramcars still in service in the 1950s were built in the 1920s and those in Glasgow dated back to 1900. Putting new buses on the public road was the cheaper option to new trams costing 2½ times as much to buy abroad and renewing the rails and electric infrastructure neglected during the war. Consequently buses were also cheaper to extend to new housing estates. Town councillors and the travelling public compared the new buses on the market with shabby-looking trams up to 50 years old. Did they consider modern trams, the quality of ride and air quality, did they compare the maintenance costs of diesel engines and electric motors or did they consider whether the very longevity of trams, combined with their larger passenger capacity and much lower maintenance costs, made them the cheaper option to a diesel bus with no more than eight to 20 years of working life?

Many factors were against the tramways: the wartime backlog of maintenance, the post-war shortage of British manufacturers and spare parts, the increased cost of power after the municipal power supplies were nationalised under the state electricity boards, political changes on city councils and vested interests in oil, rubber and motor industries – all these factors drove the change-over from trams to buses. In the brave new world of the 1950s it was deemed 'modern' to have diesel buses for a change from the 'old trams'. Motorists, including city councillors (most of whom probably never used public transport) blamed the trams for traffic congestion by loading in the middle of the road, but the congestion grew worse after the trams had gone. Loading islands and traffic management options were not considered.

Most of the smaller British tramway systems had succumbed to motorbuses and cars in the 1920s and the economic depression in the 1930s combined with the cost of replacing the tracks laid at the turn of the century. After the 1939-45 war Britain still had 32 tramways left, in whole or in part. New tramcars entered service at Sheffield, Leeds, Blackpool, Sunderland, Glasgow and Aberdeen, but one by one the remaining systems were closed from 1945 to 1962, while Belgium, Holland, Germany and Austria were busy rebuilding and developing their bombed-out tramways into the progressive modern systems of today.

Without forethought we exchanged a transport system based on home-made steel and home-produced electricity for a transport system based on imported rubber and fuel oil. Birmingham, Leeds, Liverpool and Glasgow abandoned many miles of roadside and median strip tramway reservations while the substitute buses added to the road traffic and were less reliable than the trams in fog, snow and ice.

Two British interurban tramlines or light railways from the 1890s have survived right through to today. The 11-mile **Blackpool and Fleetwood line** and the 18-mile **Manx Electric Railway** from Douglas to Ramsey were the only two tramways still running through the 30-year hiatus from the last street tramway closure at Glasgow in 1962 to the first new-generation tramway at Manchester in 1992. The interesting coincidence here is that the leading promoters and construction companies of the Manx coast line then crossed the sea to the Fylde coast of Lancashire and took 43 Manxmen and their families with them to build and operate the Blackpool & Fleetwood Tramroad Company, which they opened in 1898 – within the same gestation period as the MER (1893-99).

The Fleetwood line was absorbed by Blackpool Corporation in 1920 and is now the sole remaining line of the Blackpool tram system. The original crossbench trolleycars and so-called 'box' cars of the Fleetwood line were virtually identical to the crossbench cars and 'winter saloons' that still run on the Ramsey line. John Cameron was general manager and secretary of the Fleetwood line, which was consistently the most profitable tramway in Britain. He was previously a consultant to the Douglas & Laxey Coast Electric Tramway and Snaefell Mountain Railway (1894-95) and general manager of the Manx Northern Railway (1879-94), which was the cheapest worked railway anywhere in the British Isles.

Both these lines were interurbans by the American definition as they carried mail and freight as well as passengers, but this other traffic disappeared early in the second half of the 20th century, although the MER still has vans for merchandise and parcels if required. The light railway style of route of these two lines has been adopted for the new-generation British tramways installed at Manchester in 1992, Sheffield in 1994, Birmingham and Wolverhampton in 1999, Croydon in 2000, Nottingham in 2004 and Edinburgh in 2014, all with many miles of segregated tracks, traffic management and compatibility with pedestrian zones.

If we compared contemporary tramcars

and motorbuses through the generations, the tramcars were always in advance in their design and performance, but because of their longevity the tramcars were generally older. The ultra-smooth, quiet ride on these up-to-date tramways is in contrast to the execrable ride on noisy, diesel motorbuses on today's badly maintained roads, and makes us wonder why we ever changed mode in the first place. The transition from tram to bus in Glasgow in 1957-62 was most marked for me. The ride by bus was rough and one wondered what was progressive about this change-over. You couldn't write or read, take photographs of the street scene or ride on the open platform with safety on a moving bus as we did on a tramcar. If you switched to a tram on one of the remaining lines it was to experience civilised transport again. We lost a great asset with a potential for development.

The **trolleybus,** a cross between a tram and a motorbus, was pioneered in 1911 and developed in the 1920s and early '30s to replace the inter-war tramway closures. While we still have trams and motorbuses in Britain today, we have no trolleybuses; they last ran in 1972. These were hybrid vehicles, electric buses with overhead pickup like trams except that they had twin trolleypoles tapping twin overhead wires, the second pole completing the electric circuit to source through the copper wires instead of rails. This required double overhead rigging and more traction poles to hold it up. It also required more power substations than the trams because of the extra rolling resistance of rubber tyres on asphalt roads compared with steel wheels on steel rails, particularly when starting from stops, and they could not coast with the power off like trams. The original trolleybuses were described as 'railless' or 'trackless cars', a name perpetuated in the Teesside Railless Traction Board until 1968.

Trolleybuses lacked the noise and vibration of motorbuses; they moved stealthily with only a mild hum from their electric motors and the swish of trolleys on the overhead wires, clicking through the junctions. They climbed hills easily and as quickly as on the level, which is why they lingered in Bradford. Running on rubber tyres over asphalt they were quieter than the trams but not as smooth riding. The complexity, maintenance and limitations of the overhead wires were the cause of their demise. Diesel buses replaced them all. Trolleybuses in working museums at Lowestoft, Sandtoft (near Scunthorpe) and Dudley testify to their quiet, fume-free operation and here again we wonder why we abandoned them.

Bus and tram journeys in Britain were quicker and more pleasant in mid-century than today because the conductor collected the fares while the vehicle was in motion between stops and there were fewer motorcars and signal stops and no diversions around pedestrian zones or one-way streets. We queued in an orderly file at the stop and quickly boarded the vehicle. The driver and conductor looked smart in full uniform and the conductor was usually a sociable, cheerful character, who called out the name of the next stop, kept his passengers entertained with his patter and counted out your change from the fare paid to the money tendered – as distinct from just dropping a pile of change in your hand as drivers do today.

Yes, travel around Britain was very different in the 1950s. Few of us could afford a car and most of us went on long journeys and holidays by steam train or motor coach and the journey was part of the pleasure, which is hardly the lot of the motorist today.

The **railway** companies that existed from the grouping before nationalisation in 1948 also had road vans for collection and delivery at the railheads and owned canals, docks, hotels and short sea ferries,. The hotels and ferries were then nationalised too but later sold to private enterprise. Despite nationalisation, staff, rolling stock and practices on the railways remained largely unchanged through the 1950s and we still called the railways by their old names: the Southern, the Great Western, the London & North Eastern and the London Midland & Scottish, the last two usually known by their initials, the LNER and the LMS. The old railway company stocks of tickets were still being issued in rural backwaters into the 1960s. The railways were still essentially the same 'big four' at the time of these photographs, but they were then actually British Railways' Southern, Western, Eastern, North Eastern, Midland and Scottish Regions.

The stations in steam days were architectural buildings with ample canopies, booking offices, waiting rooms, parcels offices, station masters, clerks, porters and signalmen, not forgetting the coal yard, goods yard and warehouse. The country stations were particularly pleasant with gardens tended by the staff between trains and plenty of seats, both under cover and out in the fresh air and sunshine. The booking clerk took only a few seconds to pull a pre-printed ticket from the rack, punch it in the date stamp and issue your change – all much quicker than today's computers. As you waited on the platform a succession of goods trains and parcels trains thundered through.

The railway carriages were painted in the more simple but tasteful colours that blended with town and country better than the psychedelic paint schemes of today's train operators. There was the mid-green of the Southern Railway and Region, the 'chocolate' and cream of the Great Western, also used by BR on Western Region expresses, the scumbled 'varnished teak' of the LNER, the early BR standard mid-red and cream and the deep crimson of the LMS, which succeeded the red and cream as standard for most BR loco-hauled trains. These were tasteful mono-colour and bi-colour paint schemes, offset with black and yellow lining, yellow lettering and numerals and brass door handles. The trains were not repainted in BR blue or blue/grey until around 1970.

When your train arrived it was anything from six to 14 coaches long with a guard's/luggage van at one end for large luggage, prams, bicycles, motorcycles, small merchandise and baskets of racing pigeons under supervision of the guard. Even the Southern Electric suburban trains had a short luggage section in each set of cars. The passenger coaches on long-distance trains had side corridors giving access through sliding doors to cosy, wood-lined compartments, furnished with seats facing each other on each side of the panoramic windows and landscape pictures on the walls under the luggage racks. There were also saloon coaches with a central gangway and the seats facing each other across tables corresponding with the windows, like dining cars. Local stopping trains were usually of non-corridor, compartment stock. All the seats were cushioned and had unobstructed window views of the passing scene with the windowsills at elbow level – an innate sense of practical design. When we ride these coaches on preserved steam railways today we contrast them with the hard-padded, airline-style seating in the claustrophobic, sardine-tin coaches on modern inter-city trains with the windowsills at shoulder level and the headrests – set too far back, ergonomically, to rest on – partly masking the window view from the seats behind.

The steam locomotive on the head of your train barked and hissed as it blasted its way out of town in a volcanic cloud of black smoke and white steam and gathered speed, the exhaust echoing against bridges and lineside buildings, leaving a wonderful aroma of steam, smoke and cylinder oil over the town. We galloped through the countryside at a cruising speed of, say, 70mph and the irregular patchwork of small, hedged and tree-lined fields was seen through the dancing telegraph wires slung from pole to pole along the railway bank and the clouds of steam drifting past the window, or obliquely across the landscape, according to the wind direction, accompanied by the rhythm of the bogie wheels drumming the joints between the 60-foot lengths of track.

We awakened the echoes through ample country town stations, their names spelt out legibly in large block capital letters on nameboards on the platform ends, complete with rock gardens, gas lighting, station offices, luggage trolleys, goods sheds and coal yards. We also glimpsed sparse, wooden, oil-lit platforms in areas of countryside with no apparent habitation nearby.

As we slowed for the next station the sound of clanking coupling rods and squealing flanges from the locomotive driving wheels echoed against lines of wagons in the sidings and was amplified by the station buildings and canopies as we slid alongside the platform. The stentorian, bass-baritone voice of the announcer on the station loudspeakers or the voice of a porter on the platform drifting past the window called out the name of the station and a list of all the stations where the train was going. We have arrived in mid-20th-century Britain.

In these pages we are looking at the British transport scene by road, rail and water in the period from 1948 to 1972, covering the heyday of public transport and the time when, in my view, our ships, ferries, excursion steamers, trains, tramcars and buses, many of them quite elderly, were at the acme of aesthetic good looks and character. In this travelogue we also see harbours, docks, railway stations, horse-drawn vehicles, steam road locomotives, lorries and private cars. I was interested in all these forms of transport, but not aviation. We must not omit the transport men, and in these pages we also meet Idris Jones, the East Kent bus and coach driver, Guthrie Pender and Lloyd Hicks, the Scillies inter-island ferrymen, Bill Sharpe, the Yorkshire signalman, and Joe Wilson, the Carnforth engine driver. How we envy them in their jobs retrospectively.

During the period under review I was living at Oxford, Wallasey, Herne Bay, Kendal and Southport as Dad's work with the Post Office Telephones and my work in weekly and evening newspapers moved me around the country.

I took most of these photographs on day cycle rides from home in the first half of the 1950s and on long-distance cycle touring holidays from 1957 onward. This is the best way to see the country, observe the details and meet the people. The bicycle also gives maximum flexibility when photographing or filming transport in towns with no kerbside parking and in the country with narrow lanes. I still don't own a car but I did own and drive a bus, a 1951 Wallasey double-decker, for 30 years; it's now in the Birkenhead transport museum.

I also travelled around the country by hitch-hiking, which was an accepted mode of travel. As I re-read my travel diaries today I am surprised how liberally we were disposed to hitch-hiking in those days, how readily drivers gave us a lift and went out of their way to help us. Hitch-hiking was then a safe and not uncommon form of travel, often quicker than travel by coach and sometimes quicker than the train.

Following previous acquaintance, I paid my last respects to the tramways at Liverpool in 1957, Leeds in 1959 and Sheffield in 1960 by hitch-hiking there and back from Herne Bay, Kent, at weekends when I had a Saturday off work.

I rode and photographed the last two lines of each system shortly before closure. I never attended tramway funerals; I preferred my last memories to be of normal service. I did each of the round trips to Liverpool and Leeds in two days, riding and photographing the lines on the Saturday afternoon and returning home on the Sunday. I hitched from Herne Bay to Sheffield *and back* one Saturday with time to ride and photograph the last two lines. It was the speed and mobility of hitch-hiking in those days that enabled me to do this. While on National Service at RAF Bircham Newton, Norfolk, in 1960-62, my pal Robin Hogg (a kindred spirit) and I spent every annual leave visiting the last remaining tramways at Blackpool and Glasgow and hitch-hiked there and back, in uniform in winter, in mufti and shorts in summer. We also went to the isle of Man via Fleetwood after a visit to Blackpool and before going on to Glasgow, all on the same holiday.

HITCH-HIKING was a common means of travel in the 1950s and '60s. Here, Miss Ruth Amos, from Margate, is a passenger in a 1957 Morris Commercial lorry at a fuel station on the A74 Carlisle-Glasgow trunk road in Lanarkshire on 21 May 1959. The fish merchant's lorry, on its way back home to Fife, took us exactly 100 miles from Kendal to Abington on our way that day from Skipton to Glasgow, part of a hitch-hiking and youth-hostelling holiday tour of Britain. In the background is a War Department railway 0-4-0 diesel shunter on a Pickford's low-loader.

Several pictures in this collection were taken on a 1,852-mile, 16-day hitch-hiking and youth hostelling tour of midland and northern England and Scotland with my wife-to-be, Ruth Amos, in May 1959. We had lifts for 1,606 miles in 52 private cars, 23 lorries and nine small vans. These lifts ranged from half a mile to 100 miles. We travelled 177 miles by public transport, including 42 miles by tram in Sheffield, Leeds and Glasgow, and we walked a total of 69 miles. We never booked overnight at a youth hostel or bed and breakfast guest house in advance; we simply found somewhere to stay wherever we were at the end of the day. Life was carefree and easy-going. That entire 16-day tour cost us less than £20 each in board, food and fares when we normally paid 10s 6d for bed and breakfast at a guest house, less at a youth hostel and 2s 6d for midday dinner. (There were then 20 shillings (s) in the pound and the national average weekly wage was £13 4s for men and £6 18s for women.)

In my time I have been to every county on the British mainland and cycled through most of them, from Kent to Cornwall and Sutherland, but this photographic survey is limited to areas where I have lived or spent some time on holidays and taken pictures of transport in the period under review. Thus there is scanty coverage of some parts of the country and some counties are not featured, but I think my selection of photographs is fairly representative of the British transport scene in the mid-20th century, when it was looking its best and had the most character.

A canal or railway enhances a landscape and when photographing a townscape I always waited for a bus or tram to animate the scene and give it some colour and local identity. I don't like close-up portraits of locomotives, vehicles or vessels; I like to stand back and show them in their setting. There are no telephoto views here because they distort the subject.

The publisher asked me for some street scenes, not necessarily with transport, that exude the character and atmosphere of the period, hence my pictures of Buxton, West Kirby and Wigan, all of which have some transport element but not much. He also asked me for some 'then and now' pictures for comparison or contrast and I have chosen the locations at Burnham Market in Norfolk, Ellesmere Port in Cheshire and Anderston Cross in Glasgow, where I have taken comparison views showing how the mid-20th century scenes have changed.

In this photographic peregrination we cover Britain region by region and county by county from south-east to north-west, from Kent west to Cornwall and north to Inverness-shire, the way the island was discovered and settled since prehistoric times; it is also my favourite direction of travel. We get a nice mixture of all forms of transport on our way across the country like this, which I think is preferable to sorting the ships, railways, buses, trams and others into separate sections. The pictures are sorted into six regions relating to one man's inevitably unequal photographic coverage of the country to give a roughly equal number of pictures in each part.

Remember that we are looking at Britain in 1948-72. I have used the **county names** as they were at the time of the photographs, before the reorganisation of local government in 1974-75. Those were the days when the isle of Wight and Bournemouth were in Hampshire, Abingdon was in Berkshire, Peterborough in Northamptonshire, Coventry in Warwickshire, Wolverhampton in Staffordshire, Wallasey in Cheshire, Coniston in Lancashire, Kendal in Westmorland, Tenby in Pembrokeshire, Llandudno in Caernarvonshire, Stranraer in Wigtownshire and Mallaig in Inverness-shire. That nomenclature is part of the nostalgia of the period.

Before 1974 the cities and county boroughs were all-purpose authorities, administratively independent of the counties, as they are today, but they were always regarded by the public, the press, the Post Office and the guidebooks as being part of those counties to which they belonged historically and geographically, such as Birmingham in Warwickshire, Liverpool in Lancashire, Newcastle in Northumberland and Glasgow in Lanarkshire.

Those counties were much older than the county councils set up in 1889-90, previously being designated areas under the rule of the civil and criminal judiciary and for collecting taxes and raising armies. The English counties originated under the rule of the Jutes, Saxons, Angles, Danes and Normans and were delineated by natural features like hill ridges and rivers. Kent, Essex and Sussex began as independent kingdoms. The Welsh counties were formed between medieval and Tudor times and the Scottish sheriffdoms were sorted into 33 counties by about 1800. The County of London was created in 1889 out of parts of Middlesex, Surrey and Kent and expanded in 1965 as Greater London, annexing parts of Essex and Hertfordshire as well.

My **photographs** – all those not credited – were taken over the period from 1948, when I was aged 10, to 1972, when I was 34 and losing interest in the modern transport scene. I include a few photographs Dad took for me and they are credited to George Greenwood (1900-95). I was with him when he took the black and white photographs with his glass plate camera. As my transport coverage of eastern Scotland in that period was so scanty I have invited a guest picture from an old friend, the aforesaid Robin Hogg, of St Albans, who took the superb shot in Aberdeen. Robin himself appears on the Ramsgate Tunnel Railway train and boarding a Blackpool standard tram on Queen's Promenade.

Dad passed down his 1925-vintage Kodak Brownie No 2 box camera to me when I was 10 and all my black and white photographs that appear here, from 1948 to 1961, were taken with this box camera with a fixed shutter speed of 1/25th of a second. I had to hold the camera on my tummy, the viewfinder, only 12mm by 9mm, was 1 foot away from my eyes, and I could hardly see what I had in the picture frame. I had only eight pictures on a roll film so I used them sparingly. I should like to have taken more pictures, but pocket money did not extend to many films until I left school and started work in 1956. Then in 1961 I began using a Braun Paxette 35mm camera with 36-picture colour transparency film, at first only for the more colourful scenes, while continuing to use the box camera with black and white film for subjects that were more 'noir'.

A Chinese philosopher once said that a picture tells a thousand words, but I say that a caption can tell us so much more about a picture, and can make a dull picture interesting. It is not until we read the extended captions that we realise the significance of many of these pictures and see features we might not otherwise have noticed.

I have credited in the Acknowledgments and References (bibliography and videography) my sources of information about both the past and the present, and in writing the captions I have had to steer a course of discretion between conflicting facts and dates in many cases. I have revisited many of these locations to describe the changes but it was impossible for me to revisit all the places illustrated here and I have tried to update the information in the other captions by telephone calls to sources credited in the Acknowledgements and by reference to the Internet. I believe the information I've given about changes of scene and transport services to be correct at the time of writing, but changes come so rapidly these days that it might be out of date by the time you read it.

It has been immensely enjoyable writing the captions to the photographs in this collection but it saddens me to summarise the scene changes at the end of many of these captions and to know that in most cases – with the exception of the Manx Electric Railway – things are not like that any more. After finding out what changes there have been since these pictures were taken, I often felt like adding to the end of a caption: 'Sic transit gloria Britanniae' ('Thus passeth the glory of Britain').

Part 1, South-east England: Kent, London and Sussex

Kent

FOLKESTONE These old fishing boats in the outer harbour in August 1958 are propped upright on the sandy bed at low tide with their nets festooned from the masts and over the gunwales to dry. Thomas Telford designed the 360-foot-long breakwater in the background, built in 1829 with large oval boulders laid aslant and no dressed masonary or mortar. Telford constructed other piers like this to allow the water to flow between the stones, thereby reducing the impact of waves against the structure

This photograph was taken from the railway viaduct that divides the outer harbour from the inner harbour. Folkestone was one of seven continental ferry ports from Harwich to Weymouth that were all started by railway companies. The South Eastern Railway bought Folkestone harbour in 1843 and built a viaduct and swing bridge leading to a station on a stone pier for the ferry to Boulogne (26 miles). The harbour and town echoed to the sound of gulls and the combined exhausts of three steam tank engines lifting the London boat trains up the 1 in 30 gradient of the harbour branch.

The opening of the nearby Channel railway tunnel in 1994 led to the closure of Folkestone ferry port in 2000, when the cross-Channel ferry services were concentrated on Dover. The inshore fishing fleet survives but the craft are different now.

RAMSGATE The Regency terraced houses of Nelson Crescent and the arcaded brick retaining wall of Royal Parade tower above a motor coaster in Ramsgate harbour on 24 May 1962. This is the inner basin with the harbour office (centre) on the road along the north quay. As the inner basin is now a marina for private motor launches and yachts, the declining coastwise trade is confined to the outer basin, which also harbours some foreign trawlers and larger pleasure cruisers.

Above: **RAMSGATE** harbour and waterfront are seen on 9 September 1955. This is the inner basin of the 50-acre harbour built in 1749-1850. The harbour turned Ramsgate from a fishing village to a prosperous port for coastal trade, mainly with Russia, and accommodated about 400 sailing vessels. The town became a seaside resort with Regency and Victorian boarding houses on the clifftops. Here we see William Watkins's 1946 steam tug *Cervia*, of London, when out-stationed at Ramsgate for sea towage and salvage work. The treacherous Goodwin Sands are off the east Kent coast. *Cervia* was sunk while assisting at Tilbury in 1954 and is seen here after a refit on the slipway at Ramsgate.

Cervia is still a feature of Ramsgate harbour today. She retired from towage in 1985 and under private ownership returned to the harbour for preservation and has been restored and opened to the public. Ramsgate was a continental ferry port with a hovercraft service in 1966-69.

Right: **RAMSGATE**'s last trawler, *Jack and Eric*, arrives home from the fishing grounds on 9 September 1955. Earlier that year the crew caught a 7-foot mine in the nets off North Foreland and, after a six-hour struggle to free it, had to cut the nets adrift. In 1956 the vessel migrated to the Newlyn fishing fleet in Cornwall. In the background the narrow four-storey Regency and Victorian boarding houses stand high along Prospect Terrace (right) and Nelson Crescent (left) atop the west cliff. These chalk cliffs are buttressed by terraced Victorian red-brick arcading supporting roads on two levels, both on slight reverse curves. The lower terrace lifts Royal Parade from the harbour quay to the clifftop; this is the main road west to Sandwich and Canterbury. The brick arches along the quay were used as stores and ships' chandleries.

Left: **DUMPTON** An electric train stands at the Hereson Road suburban terminus of the three-quarter-mile 2-foot-gauge Ramsgate Tunnel Railway, which used a former main-line railway tunnel to Ramsgate sands and fairground. Thanet Amusements opened the line in 1936, ten years after the Southern Railway diverted the former main line around the back of the town. Railway passengers could change at Dumpton Park station to the Tunnel Railway to take them to the seafront. The small bore into the side of the main tunnel can be seen in the background of this picture on 29 July 1962. As the narrow-gauge train waddled through the black cavern of the main tunnel it triggered animated illuminations like those at Blackpool as an extension of the seafront fairground.

Two trains, built by English Electric with overhead trolley pickup at 460 volts DC, worked the single line, passing on a halfway loop in the main tunnel. The line worked during the summer holiday season only and closed in 1939, when the main tunnel was used as an air raid shelter with new pedestrian side entrances from the streets. Summer service resumed in 1946 but the line closed in 1965 following a runaway accident on the 1 in-15 gradient of the small-bore tunnel.

Right: **DUMPTON** The driving trailer end of a two-car electric train is seen at Hereson Road station on the same day.

GL 6148

CLIFTONVILLE Ethelbert Road is one of the many streets of terraced Victorian boarding houses between the main shopping street and the seafront of this eastern clifftop suburb of Margate. We can see the modest 'vacancies' signs in the bay windows and strings of coloured 'fairy lights' strung across the street in this 1954 view south towards Northdown Road. The only motorcar in view is this 1933 Austin, facing north, and only two gas lanterns can be seen lighting this section of the street. These houses were built between 1857 and 1865, when this street was on the eastern boundary of the built-up area; they were united by continuous iron railings and balconies.

Today Ethelbert Road is one-way with continuous lines of parked cars along both sides of the street facing south; there are no boarding houses and no 'fairy lights'. With the decline in British seaside holidays, the houses have been converted to flats and bed-sitting rooms and there are long breaks in the continuous line of balconies seen in this picture, although most of those at this north end of the street have survived.

Many streets in Thanet are named after Jutish, Saxon and Danish kings, commemorating the island's place in early English history, and Ethelbert Road is named after Æthelberht I, the Jutish king of Kent from 560 to 616. In Cliftonville's street names we also meet Æthelstan, Edgar, Godwin, Harold and Sweyn.

MARGATE High, wide and handsome in the rich red and cream colours of the East Kent Road Car Company, this Park Royal-bodied Guy bus has stopped to change crews in The Parade, a square by the harbour, in the summer of 1954. Forty buses of this high-bridge design, similar to the London RTW, were the first 8-foot-wide buses for East Kent, in 1951. Most of them were stabled at Westwood depot, halfway between Ramsgate and Margate, to serve the isle of Thanet and routes to Dover and Canterbury. Routes 49 and 50, from Ramsgate to Birchington, closely followed the former tramway of the Isle of Thanet Electric Supply Company from Ramsgate to Westwood, which was taken over by East Kent in 1936, the tramways closing in 1937. This bus was on its way to Birchington but the route blind had slipped. No FFN370 appeared on the front cover of the East Kent timetables for a few years, pictured climbing Royal Parade by Ramsgate harbour. These buses eventually replaced older ones across the entire East Kent service area, which extended from Thanet to Hastings and from Dover to Faversham.

BIRCHINGTON-ON-SEA This railway station was typical of the very substantial small stations built by the London, Chatham & Dover Railway to serve villages along the north Kent coast line from Rochester to Ramsgate in 1858-63. Birchington was only a village at that time and this station, which opened in 1863, stood at the end of a country lane from the village square. The railway company renamed the station Birchington-on-Sea in 1878 to promote holiday travel as the village grew into the far western suburb of Margate that it is today. This view west from the road bridge was taken in 1954, before the third-rail electrification of the line from Gillingham to Ramsgate in 1959.

The goods shed on the left and the goods yard behind it closed in 1962. The shed has gone, the yard (like many a station goods yard) is now a car park, and the down passenger shelter (right) was replaced in 1985 by a small glass shelter like a bus stop. The break in the white line marking the platform edges indicates the porters' boardwalk across the tracks. Birchington is the last stop on the Isle of Thanet, and from here trains head west for a straight sprint across the bleak marshes, which were once the sea, to the Kent mainland. The next stop, Herne Bay, is 8 miles west.

BRIDGE This is the traffic-free A2 London-Dover trunk road 3 miles south-east of Canterbury one Sunday morning in 1958. High Street, Bridge, is on the Roman road we call Watling Street. The slight hump in the main street is the bridge where the road crosses the Little Stour river, hence the name of the village. The picture shows the characteristic vernacular architecture of the villages on the old A2 through Kent, with the woods of Bourne Park on the slope of Barham Downs in the background.

With the rise in motor traffic from the 1950s and the increased use of the port of Dover, the A2 was rebuilt between Dover and Faversham, bypassing Bridge and Canterbury.

CHILHAM The picturesque Kent vernacular architecture of the hilltop village of Chilham is complemented to some extent by the collection of cars parked in the village square on 5 August 1962. On the front row are a Hillman and Standard of 1938-39 and a 1950s Bedford van. In the second row we can see a late-1950s Austin estate car. In the background are the White Horse Inn and St Mary's parish church. Chilham was on the ancient Pilgrims' Way from Canterbury to Winchester. As the post-war motoring era advanced, the squares and market places of our old villages and towns became glorified car parks, which annulled the opportunity to take photographs.

CANTERBURY Mounted on a plinth outside the city wall on the old Dover road (Watling Street) stood the pioneer railway locomotive *Invicta*, which helped to put Canterbury on the railway map four months before Liverpool and Manchester. She was built in Robert Stephenson's works at Newcastle, next after *Rocket*, and shipped to Whitstable for the opening on 3 May 1830 of the 6-mile Canterbury & Whitstable Railway, built to bring Tyne coal to Canterbury. Such were the gradients over a spur of the North Downs that *Invicta* could only pull trains over the 2 miles between Whitstable and Bogshole, and the rest of the line was worked by ropes and stationary winding engines. *Invicta* retired in 1836 and the line was rope-hauled all the way till the South Eastern Railway took over and worked the line by locomotives throughout from 1846. *Invicta* survived in store to be mounted on display at Charing Cross station from 1900 to 1906, then here at Canterbury by the Riding Gate. Looking down from the city wall in August 1958, we see her in red paintwork with inclined pistons that drove four 4-foot coupled wheels. The driver stood on the narrow, left-hand running board and the fireman stood on the tender.

The engine was restored by the National Railway Museum for display in the Canterbury Heritage Museum in Stour Street from 1979. The Museum closed in 2017 and the *Invicta* was transferred to the Whitstable Community Musum and Gallery in June 2019.She is now in original condition with varnished horizontal wooden cladding on her boiler, black ironwork and an effigy of Edward Fletcher as driver. Fletcher came with her from Stephenson's works to be her engineer for her seven years in service; he later became locomotive superintendent and designer of the North Eastern Railway and died, aged 92, in 1899.

CANTERBURY High Street was the A2 Dover-London road through the city when photographed in 1957 from the former *Kent Messenger* newspaper office looking north-west towards the West Gate and London. To the right is Guildhall Street leading to Margate. The classical stone Guildhall that stood on the corner was bombed in 1942 and demolished in 1951 to be succeeded in 1956 by the K Shoe Shop (selling Kendal-made shoes), an unworthy successor to the Guildhall on this key site in the city centre. The East Kent bus, rebodied by Park Royal in 1949 on a 1938 Leyland chassis, is on city service 26 from Hales Place to the Hospital; it is about to pass a 1953 Commer van and is followed by a 1951 Commer van and a Humber car.

The A2 now bypasses Canterbury, and High Street is part of a city-centre pedestrian zone with restricted vehicular access.

CANTERBURY The Park Royal low-bridge body of 1949-50 looked different on a post-war Guy chassis (centre) from a pre-war Leyland chassis (left), but only because of the windscreens, radiators and mudguards, which gave the buses a wholly different character. In this fine line-up of classic East Kent buses in the spare bus rank at Canterbury garage in St Stephen's Road we see (from the left) a 1949 Park Royal body on a 1936 Leyland TD4, a 1950 Park Royal body on a contemporary Guy, and a 1945 utility Weymann-bodied high-bridge Guy. By the time this picture was taken in 1960 these buses were relegated to secondary duties.

CANTERBURY The A2 from London and the road from Whitstable entered the city by the West Gate, as did the pilgrims and royalty of old. Motor traffic going the other way passed on the left of the twin towers. Here a 1950 Park Royal low-bridge Guy bus arrives in Canterbury on East Kent route 4 from Swalecliffe and Whitstable in 1954. To negotiate the West Gate buses had to be of the low-bridge design. The standard British low-bridge bus had low headroom in the upper saloon with four-in-a-row seating and a sunken offside gangway that gave low headroom for passengers sitting on the offside of the lower saloon.

The West Gate, rebuilt in 1380, is the only remaining portal of the medieval city wall, which once had seven gates. It was also the city prison after the Norman castle until the early 19th century and has since been a museum. The largest surviving fortified gateway in Britain, it was nearly lost to posterity in the philistine mid-19th century when only the mayor's casting vote in the city council saved it from demolition to allow the elephant vans of a travelling menagerie to visit the city! The West Gate and St Peter's Street are on an island surrounded by two courses of the River Stour.

CANTERBURY Country buses coming through the West Gate immediately turned right into St Peter's Place and reversed into the city's small, off-street bus station. From its opening in 1922 its proper name was St Peter's Road Car Station and it had a pleasant prospect, facing the gardens by the Great Stour river and St Peter's Church. This six-bay bus station was the hub of the system and the terminus of East Kent country services radiating from Canterbury to Folkestone, Dover, Deal, Ramsgate, Margate, Herne Bay, Whitstable, Faversham, Maidstone and Hastings as well as village bus services and some express coach services. Schedules had to be well coordinated to allow lay-over and loading time here, and some services terminated in Station Road West at busy periods. Here, at mid-morning in the summer of 1954, two 1950 Park Royal low-bridge Guy buses load for route 4 to Whitstable and Swalecliffe and route 6 to Herne Bay. One notice board says that routes 3 (Faversham), 4 and 6 will load in Station Road West between 3.30 and 6.00pm except Sundays. Another notice advertises the company's parcels service; it says: 'Send your parcels by service car' (East Kent called its buses 'cars'). There were at this time 72 parcels agents at shops, post offices, inns, garages and private houses along the bus routes in addition to the parcels offices at bus stations.

CANTERBURY In 1956 the bus station moved to a more spacious site in St George's Lane in the blitzed south end of the city centre, and here in August 1958 we see two of the 30 high-bridge Park Royal-bodied Guys delivered to East Kent in 1953. The traditional Guy radiator had been concealed in the streamlined bonnet, but there was still a Gardner engine inside and the Indian chief's head, which used to decorate Guy radiator caps pre-war, was back in place. These were East Kent's first buses with concealed radiators and platform doors. They are loading for route 17, the Elham valley route to Folkestone, and route 13 to Sandwich and Deal.

CANTERBURY The East Kent Road Car Company kept all its vehicles immaculate and shining. This chubby-looking 1938 Park Royal-bodied Leyland coach was the class of vehicle used on the London express services from Dover, Deal, Ramsgate and Herne Bay well into the 1950s. It was photographed in 1953 in Station Road West, the cul-de-sac approach to Canterbury West railway station, generally used for parking and loading East Kent coaches and loading buses during peak times. The company had its head office here before it was destroyed in the 1942 blitz. At the time these photographs were taken the head office was in a large country house at Harbledown, a mile west of the city.

Top right: **CANTERBURY** From the 1930s the railway companies began to replace horses with these 'mechanical horses', which were three-wheel, petrol-engined tractors pulling articulated trailers for 'town cartage' of goods, parcels and passengers' luggage in advance to and from the railway stations, although many railway horse-vans survived into the 1950s. Here is a 1947 Scammell with a two-wheel trailer van being loaded at Canterbury West station in April 1953. The tractor unit was a quaint-looking motor tricycle with only one headlamp, a bulb horn and a crank handle, having no starter motor. The single front wheel could turn 180 degrees in confined spaces and the two-wheel trailers were interchangeable and could be supported by a folding stand at the front end for loading while the tractor was out with another van. These vehicles were the forerunners of articulated trunk road haulage in the second half of the 20th century.

Right: **CANTERBURY** Two East Kent buses pass St Edmund's School on St Thomas's Hill in 1957. A 1950 Park Royal low-bridge Guy is descending towards the city on route 4 from Swalecliffe and Whitstable, followed by a 1945 utility Park Royal-bodied Guy on city service 27 from Rough Common to Thanington.

Left: **MAYPOLE** A wartime utility bus, a 1945 high-bridge Weymann-bodied Guy, stops at the Prince of Wales Hotel, Maypole, on East Kent's scenic, indirect bus route 7 from Herne Bay to Canterbury via Broomfield in 1953. This route followed the Roman road from Canterbury (Durovernum Cantiacorum) to Reculver (Regulbium). Guy Motors of Wolverhampton was the main supplier of bus chassis during the Second World War (the only others were Daimler and Bristol). The rugged cast-iron Guy chassis with its reliable Gardner engine won favour with bus operators and orders for more continued after the war, but the cheap utility bodywork was flimsy and furnished with wooden slatted seats; these were replaced by upholstered seats from pre-war buses after the war, and many a wartime Guy chassis was rebodied in the late 1940s for a new lease of life.

Today the Stagecoach East Kent Bus Company has perpetuated the traditional East Kent numbering of the main routes. The No 7 still serves this rural fringe and has been diverted to serve Beltinge, Hillborough, Hoath and Broadoak as well.

Right: **RECULVER** The road and the local bus route terminate at Reculver, on the corner of the sea and the Wanstum marshes at the east end of the 3-mile line of cliffs from Herne Bay. This low-bridge bus, with a 1949 Park Royal body on a 1938 Leyland chassis, was on one of Herne Bay's three town services, the 39 to Hampton Pier Avenue. The driver and conductress in their summer uniforms take the sea air during the terminal lay-over in the forecourt of the King Ethelbert Inn below the 12th-century twin Norman towers of the ruined 7th-century church. The inn is named after King Æthelberht, the first king of Kent (560-616), the first Christian English king and the first to write the laws in English, not Latin. He gave his palace at Canterbury to Augustine and his Christian missionaries in 597, and built a new palace at Reculver. From this remote corner of the country he ruled not only Kent but was the dominant figure in the confederacy of English kingdoms south of the Humber.

RECULVER This 1932-vintage Leyland Bison lorry and the bulldozer behind it are working for Willment Brothers, civil engineering contractors of Southwark, on the construction of a new sea wall along the coast from Birchington to Reculver in August 1953, after the North Sea flooded the Wantsum marshes and insulated the Isle of Thanet once again on 31 January that year. A fleet of these old lorries tipped successive loads of clay and hardcore, which was then bulldozed to form the embankment for the concrete sea wall to replace the 300-year-old clay bank that was badly breached by the storm surge. The picture was taken at the Reculver end of the works.

RECULVER Another old timer working on the sea wall construction at Reculver a year after the 1953 flood was this 1924 steam roller of the Demolition & Construction Company in January 1954. It was built by the Rochester firm of Aveling & Porter, which pioneered road rollers for America and exported them all over the world, being renowned for good design and workmanship. The firm also built steam tractors, ploughing engines, crane engines, lorries and railway shunters, but road rollers were two-thirds of its production and lasted in use on our roads well into the 1960s to compact newly laid tarmacadam. They were superseded by diesel rollers.

Behind the roller is part of the 9-foot-thick outer wall (once 15 feet tall) of the 8-acre Roman fort of Regulbium, built about AD 287 as one of the nine Roman 'forts of the Saxon shore' (Litus Saxonicum), to guard the north end of the shipping channel that insulated Thanet. Now only the southern half of the fort walls remain following coastal erosion that destroyed the ancient British, Jutish and medieval town of Reculver before Trinity House built a sea wall in 1810 to protect the twin towers of the ruined church as a landmark for shipping.

Right: **BROOMFIELD** Retired motorbuses, tramcars and railway carriages appeared around the edges of our fields as temporary homes for families made homeless by the air raids of the Second World War and by the North Sea floods in 1953. Many of these vehicles later became motor caravans for gypsies. This old London General single-deck bus was an AEC Renown built in 1931 and inherited by London Transport in 1933. It was photographed at Broomfield near Herne Bay in 1958. London General built its own coachwork for these buses at Chiswick Works and ran 200 of this three-axle LT (long type) class on outer-suburban services. They were retired from service in 1948-53.

Below: **HUNTERS FORSTAL** *Ada,* the East Kent Road Car Company's tree-lopper in the 1950s, was a bus with an interesting history. She was built in 1934 with a Weymann body on a Daimler chassis with a Coventry registration as a demonstration bus. She was bought by the Thanet Electric Supply Company as one of a small fleet of motorbuses on feeder services to the company's electric tramways linking Ramsgate, Broadstairs and Margate. The East Kent company bought the Thanet services in 1936 and closed the tramways in 1937. Under her new owners, *Ada,* so named from her registration, worked services from Westwood garage in Thanet, then from Herne Bay garage. During the war she was used as a mobile staff canteen at Dover. She returned to Herne Bay after the war and was employed on workmen's services to Chislet and Tilmanstone collieries in the east Kent coalfield. In 1951 she was cut down to an open-topper to prune overhanging trees along all East Kent bus routes. She was photographed in Mill Lane near Herne Bay in the late 1950s lopping trees for a projected bus route diversion that never materialised. There are no tree-lopping buses following privatisation of bus services in 1986; county councils are now expected to do this work.

Below: **HERNE BAY** In this 1954 view of William Street in the central shopping area we see some of the motorcars of the period parked at the kerb: on the left, a 1935 Lanchester and a 1949 Ford 8 and, on the right, a Standard Vanguard, an Austin A40 and a Ford Popular, all of 1949. Herne Bay Urban District Council painted its gas lamps silver. The view is from High Street towards Neptune Jetty on the seafront with Mortimer Street crossing midway. Today this is a one-way street with parking bays, a narrow roadway, trees, speed ramps and pedestrian priority. Most of the shops have changed hands and there are no sunblinds.

Above: **HERNE BAY** The East Kent Road Car Company bought 40 of these handsome Park Royal low-bridge Guy Arabs in 1950. This one has paused for its portrait at the top of Mickleburgh Hill on Herne Bay town service 43 from Clifftown Gardens to Beltinge in August 1953, when there were still open fields on the east side of the road from St Bartholomew's Church to Blacksole Bridge. The 43 was East Kent's oldest town service, starting in 1924 from the Clock Tower to West Cliff and extending east in 1929 to Blacksole Bridge and later to Beltinge. The Park Royal body on these buses was the same as on the Leyland bus we saw at Reculver, but the deeper windscreen and the radiator and flared mudguards of the Guy chassis gave the bus a different character.

HERNE BAY Here we see the emergency push-pull train of pre-Grouping stock that worked the main line from Faversham to Herne Bay after the sea washed out 4 miles of the line across the marshes between Herne Bay and Birchington in 1953. The ex-LSWR 'M4' 0-4-4T engine was sandwiched between four coaches with remote control driving cabs at each end and was photographed in Herne Bay station. This service ran from 2 March to 20 May and the main line to Thanet reopened on 21 May. Herne Bay and Whitstable had been cut off by rail for the first month after the flood on 1 February because of a washout on Seasalter Level west of Whitstable. The Canterbury and Whitstable branch line, which closed on 1 December 1952, reopened from 6 to 28 February to carry coal for Whitstable and Herne Bay, distributed from Whitstable harbour railhead by local coal merchants with lorries.

HERNE BAY This was East Kent's standard single-deck bus of the pre- and post-war period. The body design dates from the 1936 batch of 26 Dennis-bodied Dennis Lancets, and this bus is one of the 60 Park Royal-bodied Dennis Lancets delivered in 1947-49. It is seen at the Herne Bay pier terminus of route 38 to Whitstable and Faversham in 1956. The driver is in his white summer coat and cap.

HERNE BAY driver Idris Jones sports his white summer uniform beside an East Kent 1938 Park Royal-bodied Leyland coach parked on the excursion rank on Central Parade opposite the pier in 1953.

MEDWAY QUEEN

Left: **HERNE BAY** The paddle steamer *Medway Queen* of Rochester plied between the two longest piers in Britain on her two round trips between Southend and Herne Bay as part of her daily summer excursion from Strood, calling at Chatham and Sheerness on the way out and back. Here she is approaching Herne Bay pier on 6 June 1962, when a day return ticket from Strood to Herne Bay via Southend cost 11 shillings and allowed 4½ hours ashore here while she made another round trip to Southend.

Medway Queen was built by the Ailsa Shipbuilding & Engineering Company at Troon in 1924, 180 feet long and 316 gross tons, for the New Medway Steam Packet Company of Rochester, which was formed in 1919 as successor to the Medway Steam Packet Company of 1837. In 1936 it became a subsidiary of the General Steam Navigation Company of London, which had initiated steamer services to Herne Bay back in 1832. *Medway Queen* was refitted as a minesweeper on the Dover Patrol during the war and was one of the 'little ships' of the Dunkirk evacuation in 1940, when she brought home more than 7,000 troops to Dover and Ramsgate on seven successive night trips and shot down two enemy aircraft. After the war she plied from the Medway and Southend to Herne Bay daily except Friday, then from 1957 to Herne Bay or Clacton. Sheerness pier closed in 1954 and Chatham pier in 1957. Her final run was from Herne Bay to Southend and Strood on 8 September 1963.

She retired to a millpond by the river Medina in the isle of Wight as a floating restaurant and clubhouse in a marina but her structural condition deteriorated and she became derelict. In 1984 her hulk was towed on a barge back to Chatham for restoration by the Medway Queen Preservation Society but she continued to deteriorate as she was half submerged every high tide. Her hull was dismantled and, with £1.8 million from the National Lottery and £250,000 from the MQPS, David Abel Shipbuilders at Bristol built a new, riveted hull to the ship's 1924 specifications and restored her original engines and superstructure. She is now back on the Medway as a static museum at Gillingham pier. When fully fitted out and with a new boiler, it is hoped that she will ply on public excursions on the Medway again.

Above: **HERNE BAY** Amidships of the PS *Medway Queen* off Herne Bay pier on the same day can be seen the port paddle box and the house flag of the New Medway Steam Packet Company with the white horse of Kent on the funnel.

Above: **HERNE BAY** *Medway Queen* leaves Herne Bay pier for Southend, with the isle of Sheppey on the horizon, on 6 June 1962.

Left: **HERNE BAY** This view forward on the upper deck of *Medway Queen* was taken when leaving Herne Bay for Southend in 1953. The passengers are well dressed for a grey British summer's day at sea. The Isle of Sheppey lies on the port bow and the Essex coast on the starboard bow. The russet sails of Thames barges, which still traded between the creeks and harbours of the estuary, could usually be seen on the horizon. Passengers could descend to the warm saloons below deck and watch the thrashing steel piston rods and cranks in the engine room as they turned the great side wheels and drove the ship through the water or manoeuvred it into a pier.

Right: **HAMPTON** pier, at the west end of Herne Bay, is a short, concrete jetty, from which we can see, extending beyond it at low tide, the mussel-encrusted ruins of the original Hampton oyster pier and its tramway, standing 300 yards out to sea. The original pier was built in 1864-65 of rock, concrete and rubble, clad in timber, for the Herne Bay, Hampton & Reculver Oyster Fishery Company. In this photograph, taken from the surviving concrete pier in 1958, we can see among the ruins of the old pier the rails of the former Hampton Oyster Tramway, which linked the pier to an exchange siding alongside the Kent coast main line at Studd Hill to transport the oysters to Billingsgate fish market in London. The tramway ran along the line of what is now Hampton Pier Avenue. The company also built a row of 12 houses for the employees on land to the west. The solid construction of the pier, as distinct from one elevated on piles, impeded the natural flow of the tide and led to a scour that washed away the coast immediately to the west at Studd Hill, including the company houses, which were abandoned and demolished by 1912. The cost of building the pier, the tramway and the houses, combined with rivalry from Whitstable and Colchester oystermen and a series of severe winters, led to the failure of the Hampton oyster company. The tramway was lifted in 1883 and the company was wound up in 1884. Sources do not state the gauge or motive power of the tramway, but an old photograph shows that it was spiked to longitudinal timber sleepers. The tramway was probably of 3-foot gauge and worked by horses.

Below left: **WHITSTABLE** On a rough, grey day in 1953 the steam coaster *Boya*, of Dundee, is at the grain wharf by the granary on the west pier of Whitstable harbour. The rig of a Thames spritsail barge can be seen in silhouette on the extreme right at the east pier. In the foreground is a row of old ship's lifeboats used as fishing boats. This was the first railway-owned harbour in the world, built in 1830 to convey Tyne coal to Canterbury. The rails and the first locomotive, *Invicta* (see page 27), also came by sea from the Tyne. The railway tracks extended around all three sides of the harbour, ballasted in locomotive ash and coal dust covering the sleepers, with waggon turntables leading to the west pier. Passenger services on the 6-mile single line from Canterbury closed in 1930 but goods traffic continued. The Whitstable branch closed in November 1952, but reopened after the sea flooded the main coast line at Seasalter in 1953, and coal trains ran from Canterbury to this harbour again from 6 to 28 February to supply the stricken coastal communities. Trade declined in the 1950s because the south quay and the east pier were in danger of collapse. Whitstable Urban District Council bought the harbour from British Railways in 1958, rebuilt it in concrete and steel in 1958-59, and extended the west pier seaward in the 1960s. The harbour was inherited by Canterbury City Council with local government reorganisation in 1974 and it still trades in oysters, fish and roadstone.

CONYER A house barge colony of retired old Thames sailing barges is seen in Conyer Creek between Faversham and Sittingbourne on 12 September 1963. This creek was once a flourishing little barge port with a brickworks and a barge-building yard. The barges used to bring refuse from London for use in the Kent brickfields and returned loaded with bricks for London. Eastwood's Bricks, with its works at Conyer and elsewhere in north Kent, had a fleet of 45 barges in the trade. Nearest the camera is *Perseverence*, of 1889, which carried haystacks from Kent farms up to London for horses, and manure back to Kent farms. In her heyday she once sailed down the English Channel to Portland and back to fetch a load of stone in weather that kept all the larger sea-going schooner-rigged barges sheltering in Dover harbour. Next in line here is the coastwise barge *Gold Belt* (formerly *Orion*) of 1892, which traded from Faversham Creek. Both these barges were registered at Rochester. They lived out their twilight days here, and in other creeks around the Thames estuary, converted below decks to comfortable homes.

Conyer Creek was the location of the 1955 British comedy film *Raising a Riot*, with Kenneth More commanding an original sailing barge. The creek has since been transformed to a smart yacht marina.

SITTINGBOURNE From 1877 Edward Lloyd's newsprint paper mill at Sittingbourne grew up with a half-mile horse-drawn railway to barges on Milton Creek off The Swale channel that insulates Sheppey. As the creek silted up the barges were replaced by a 3¼-mile, 2ft 6in-gauge railway to a new dock on The Swale to bring in the wood pulp, china clay and coal and take out the giant rolls of newsprint. In 1924 a new mill was built halfway along the line at Kemsley, nearer the dock. At that time it was one of the largest paper mills in Europe. One of the new engines built that year to handle this extra traffic was this Kerr, Stuart 0-4-2 saddle-tank *Melior.* There were 14 steam engines on the roster, all fitted with spark arresters for shunting inside paper mills and hauling paper rolls; *Melior* has the type known in America as a 'balloon stack'. She is pictured outside the two-road engine shed by the wharf at Sittingbourne on 12 September 1963. This engine survives today on the Sittingbourne & Kemsley Light Railway.

SITTINGBOURNE The town's paper mill, which became part of the Bowaters group in 1948, ran timetabled passenger trains of home-made coaches to take workers between Sittingbourne, Kemsley Mill and Ridham Dock. This rake was built in 1957 on bogie pulp-truck frames with longitudinal seating inside. The locomotive, *Monarch*, a Bagnall 0-4-4-0 of 1953, was the last new engine built for the railway; it was a four-coupled articulated locomotive based on a type used on South African sugar estates. The train is crossing the viaduct over Milton Creek on 12 September 1963; the creek is visibly silted up and polluted with china clay. This concrete viaduct was three-quarters of a mile long and curved tightly to the right, then left, then right, and spanned five streets, a stream and a disused dock before descending to ground level.

Bowaters' railway was one of the last narrow-gauge industrial steam railways in Britain when it was closed on 4 October 1969, and replaced by lorries. However, Bowaters management was proud of its railway and granted the Locomotive Club of Great Britain a lease of 2 miles of the line between Sittingbourne and Kemsley. *Melior* and other engines were retained for service on what is now the Sittingbourne & Kemsley Light Railway. In 2008 new, foreign buyers closed Sittingbourne Mill, sold Kemsley Mill and gave the SKLR notice to quit by 2009. After negotiations with the backing of Swale District Council the railway reopened in 2012. *Monarch* is now on the Welshpool & Llanfair Light Railway.

GRAVESEND The Tilbury ferry *Rose* loads at Town Pier, and lines of William Watkins's tugs (left) and Sun tugs (beyond) wait for inbound ships coming up London River. The Gravesend-Tilbury ferry dates from the Middle Ages and was worked by Gravesend Corporation from 1694. The corporation built the Town Pier (right) in 1834, and in 1854 enclosed the full 157ft length and 40ft width of the pier with a classical wooden superstructure on tubular iron columns which is as it remains today (with modifications). The ferry passed to the London, Tilbury & Southend Railway in 1880 and the pier in 1895. Ownership passed on to the London Midland & Scottish Railway in 1923 and British Railways in 1948. The service was used mainly by Tilbury dockers from Gravesend and railway passengers from Tilbury. This view was taken from the vehicular ferry landing stage at West Street, Gravesend, in 1954. The passenger ferry *Rose*, dating from 1901, was 124 feet long and licensed to carry 600 passengers. She was the oldest of the 'dear old ladies' on the Tilbury ferry in the 1950s, together with the passenger ferries *Catherine* of 1903 and *Edith* of 1911 and the vehicular ferries *Tessa* of 1924 and *Mimie* of 1927. Diesel vessels took over the passenger service in 1961 and the three older steamers were scrapped. The under-river tunnel from Dartford to Purfleet opened in 1963 and that spelled the end of the vehicular ferry in 1964, when the last two steamers retired.

The railway gave up the ferry service in 1979 but a small diesel passenger ferry still plies half-hourly during the working day, operated by the Lower Thames & Medway Passenger Boat Company, subsidised by Kent County Council and Thurrock Borough Council.

County of London

WOOLWICH ferry *Will Crooks* cuts an anachronistic profile with its tall, upright, black smokestacks as it plies across London River from North Woolwich, in the background, in April 1953. On the left is a steam tug of William Cory & Son (later Cory Ship Towage), which handled barges on the river. The Woolwich ferry was already in existence when it was first recorded changing hands in 1308. London County Council started the free ferry service here in 1889 when it abolished bridge tolls up-river. *Will Crooks* (1929) was one of four identical, double-ended, side-loading paddle steamers, 166ft 5in long, together with *John Benn* (1929), *Gordon* (1923) and *Squires* (1922). These four black and tan vessels carried passengers on the main deck and vehicles on the top deck. The paddles were powered by separate engines for greater manoeuvrability in this busy shipping lane. This ferry steamer was named in memory of Will Crooks (1852-1921), a pioneer trade unionist from Poplar and a Member of Parliament, London County Council and the Fabian Society. The ferry service was busy day and night, linking the South and North Circular Roads. To speed up loading and cater for larger lorries, new end-loading diesel ferries took over the service in 1963; these were also capable of side-loading while new end-loading terminals were constructed in 1964-66. Woolwich free ferry passed to the new Greater London Council in 1966.

When in 1986 the GLC was abolished the ferry passed to Greenwich Borough Council, and since 2008 has been owned and funded by Transport for London and privately operated under franchise contracts. There is also a foot tunnel under the river, opened in 1912, directly below the ferry passage, and an extension of the modern Docklands Light Railway from King George V Dock station in North Woolwich to Woolwich Arsenal station.

ROTHERHITHE London's own railway system, the 'Underground', is seen at Rotherhithe station on the Metropolitan (East London) Line on 19 June 1968. London Transport's oldest stock was relegated to this 4-mile branch from New Cross to Shoreditch. This train is headed and tailed by two ex-District Railway, clerestory-roofed traction cars of 1927, sandwiching two LT flared-side trailer cars of 1938. In the background is the mouth of the oldest under-river tunnel in the world, built by Marc and Isambard Brunel, completed in 1843 and opened for the East London Railway in 1869. The line was electrified in 1913 on the four-rail system for through-running District and Metropolitan trains. LT took over in 1933 but after the 1941 blitz the East London Line was a detached branch line with passengers changing at Whitechapel. Both the 1927 and 1938 stock in this picture was scrapped in 1971, but examples are kept in the LT Museum store in Acton depot.

This short line has a long and complicated history. It was originally a cross-river link between six railway systems north and south of the river for through passenger and freight trains and carried immense tonnage of military armaments in both world wars. The line closed from 2006 to 2010 for a complete upgrade with new connections north and south of the river, and today forms the eastern segment of London's orbital 'Overground' third-rail electric system with through passenger services to Highbury & Islington, West Croydon, Crystal Palace and Clapham Junction. The stations have been modernised with escalators, white wall panels and strip lighting, but the sky light at Rotherhithe station has been reduced by two-thirds.

STEPNEY London Transport's bus route 82 from Rotherhithe tunnel entrance circumnavigated Surrey Docks then dived through the road tunnel under the river and terminated here in Bekesbourne Street, under the railway bridges at Stepney East station. This RTL class Leyland of 1949 is pictured at the Stepney terminus on 15 February 1958, with another bus behind it and a 1956 Ford Consul car parked opposite. The RT class was LT's first standard bus design to fit the Rotherhithe and Blackwall tunnels without adaptation. The first bus left here at 5.37am and ran every 7½ to 10 minutes, calling at Surrey Docks and Rotherhithe stations, till the last bus arrived here at 11.48pm. Route 82 was withdrawn in the 1960s and there was no bus through the tunnel until services in dockland were revised in the 1980s. Today Rotherhithe tunnel is for cars only.

Above the bridge stood the wooden signal cabin and brick sub-station for the electric railway that passes on the far side on a tight curve towards West Ham on the line from Fenchurch Street to Tilbury and Southend. The nearer bridge carried an abandoned section of the line to Blackwall and the East India Docks, and the manual signal cabin, which once served both lines, was removed in 1961. The former Blackwall platforms were rebuilt for the opening of the Docklands Light Railway in 1987, when Stepney East station was renamed Limehouse; the former Limehouse station, on the Blackwall line, was on Three Colt Road by Limehouse Town Hall.

The signal cabin and bus stop have gone, but otherwise Bekesbourne Street and the Railway Tavern on the far corner still look much the same today, although this is now a one-way street for northbound traffic. The three-storey shops and flats on Commercial Road in the background have been replaced by two-storey terraced houses in classic London 19th-century style and light-brown brick with a parapet hiding a low-pitched roof, plain but well-proportioned.

WAPPING
WAPPING STATION
TICKETS & TRAINS

WAPPING is on an island between London River and London Docks and was heavily bombed in the 1940-41 air raids. Here we see Wapping High Street and railway station from the corner of Wapping Lane on 15 February 1958. There were no shops in this High Street; it was lined with condemned houses, empty taverns and tooth-gap bombed sites and walled in by war-ravaged warehouses fronting riverside wharves, with footbridges for porters to trundle loads between the upper floors of warehouses on opposite sides of the street. The warehouses in the background were still partly in use in the 1950s, and a 1950 Bedford lorry is being loaded by a wall hoist. The wooden shed on the right was the entrance and booking office to the London Transport underground railway station after the earlier station building, which was also timber but in a classical style, was bombed in 1940. Wapping station was at the north end of the tunnel under the river from Rotherhithe on the Metropolitan (East London) Line and the octagonal ventilation shaft is seen to the right of the shed.

Wapping has now lost all its shipping and warehousing and the footbridges that spanned the High Street. The station entrance has since been rebuilt twice and displays an 'Overground' sign. All the warehouses on the right-hand side of the street have been replaced by new offices and luxury flats. Many old brick warehouses in Wapping High Street, including some of those on the left and in the distance, have been restored and converted to offices and flats, and the rest of the street has been transformed with modern brick flats and foreign restaurants.

LONDON BRIDGE bus station was in the forecourt of London Bridge railway station in Bermondsey and is seen here on 3 September 1955 from the portico of the terminus of the former London, Brighton & South Coast Railway. We see three of the RT family of Park Royal-bodied buses that dominated the streets of London in the mid-20th century. All of standard London Transport design, 6,956 of them were built on AEC and Leyland chassis from 1939 to 1954 and they lasted in service till 1979. On the right of the picture is the former South Eastern & Chatham Railway station with terminal lines fronted by the projecting buildings and canopy and high-level through lines on the viaduct in the background, which continues west over Southwark to Cannon Street and Charing Cross. A BR standard 2-6-2 tank engine is crossing the viaduct beyond the white van. Both the Brighton and South Eastern lines were worked mainly by third-rail 'Southern Electric' trains and all coaching stock was green. A solitary gas lamp on an island lights the station forecourt and in the background we can see the towering riverside cranes on Hay's Wharf. The first railway in London ran from London Bridge to Deptford in 1836 and on to Greenwich in 1838, all on viaduct over 878 extant brick arches.

The Italianate brick and timber station buildings of 1851 were knocked down in the 1970s and the station and forecourt have been rebuilt and remodelled two or three times since this photograph was taken. Stark glass skyscrapers have replaced all the buildings on the left and also dominate the skyline of the City of London in the background.

CANNON STREET railway terminus in the City of London, with clouds of steam, is viewed across the river from Bankside, Southwark, on 15 February 1958. The 1864 trainshed roof with its 190-foot span had its glazing removed as an air raid precaution in 1939 and the steel structure was removed later in the year that this photograph was taken. The twin hydraulic towers have been retained as a riverside feature; they were built to work the station lifts but no longer function. Cannon Street was the city terminus of the South Eastern Railway, opened in 1866 as a spur off the 1864 extension from London Bridge to Charing Cross with a triangular junction on viaducts that form a roof over the fruit and vegetable stalls of Borough Market in Southwark. At first all trains between London Bridge and Charing Cross were diverted via Cannon Street, where they reversed to continue, but soon trains were either terminating at Cannon Street or running direct to and from Charing Cross. Cannon Street itself was originally Candlewick Street, a street of candle-makers.

Right: **LONDON** Dumb barges, or lighters, which have been rowed or towed up-river, are berthed on the hard at the wharves and warehouses on the north bank between Southwark Bridge and Blackfriars Bridge in this 1961 photograph, with the dome of St Paul's Cathedral in the background. The picture was taken at low tide, showing the hard standings of shingle, retained by low, timber revetments, to save the flat-bottomed barges being stuck in the river mud. These steel river barges were used to bring bulk imports from ships berthed down-river of the road bridges. All these old warehouses have since been replaced by new blocks of offices and luxury flats of similar dimensions but allowing a better view of the cathedral. *George Greenwood*

UPPER POOL, LONDON The motor coaster *Bosphorus* unloads at New Fresh Wharf, just below London Bridge, in 1961. This was the nearest wharf to the centre of the City of London for seagoing ships. New Fresh Wharf incorporated the former Fresh Fish Wharf used by Billingsgate fish market and London Bridge Wharf for passenger excursion steamers to the Kent and Essex coasts before they moved station to Tower Pier in 1935. After the 1939-45 war, there was a regular cargo/passenger service from this wharf to the Canary Islands, and this 10-storey warehouse was built in 1953 with five travelling cranes and two conveyors on the 585-foot-long quay. The third London Bridge, astern of the *Bosphorus*, was there from 1831 to 1971.

New Fresh Wharf closed in 1970, shipping had left the Pool of London by 1972 and the modern warehouse was demolished in 1973. The adjacent Adelaide House still stands; it was London's first steel-framed building and the tallest in the city when it was built in 1921-24. Archaeologists found the remains of a Roman wharf, also used by the Saxons, on the warehouse site before a new office block, St Magnus House, was built there in 1978. *George Greenwood*

BLACKFRIARS The arms of the London, Chatham & Dover Railway in cast iron surmount the Southwark abutment of Blackfriars railway bridge over the river, built on stonework from the old Westminster Bridge (1749-1861). The date 1864 is cast on the scroll across the crowned 'V' for Queen Victoria. This lattice-girder bridge carried four tracks of the LCDR over the river into the city with through platforms at St Paul's and Ludgate Hill to a city terminus at Holborn Viaduct, while another line descended from Ludgate Hill through Snow Hill Tunnel to link up with the Metropolitan Railway at Farringdon Street. This gave the LCDR through passenger services to Moorgate Street, King's Cross and Barnet, while from the north side the Great Northern and Midland railways ran through to Victoria via Loughborough Junction. The link also gave through access south of the river for coal, freight, parcels and excursion trains from the Great Northern, Midland, London & North Western and Great Western companies and later British Railways until closure of the Ludgate Hill-Farringdon Street link in 1969. This crossing was doubled with an adjacent second railway bridge on the down-river side leading to a new terminus at St Paul's, renamed Blackfriars in 1937. The photograph was taken from Blackfriars Road bridge in March 1959.

The smoking chimney (extreme right) was on Bankside Power Station (1953-1980) now the Tate Modern Gallery. The other chimney was on the London Hydraulic Power Company's Falcon Wharf Pumping Station (1883-1935). This railway bridge was dismantled in 1984-85 but all 12 cast iron piers remain standing in the river as well as these abutments on the south bank and the cast iron arms of the LCDR have been painted in full hraldic colours.

WESTMINSTER This classic Tilling open-staircase ST bus, dating from 1930, was being operated by London Transport on a circular sightseeing service when pictured in Horseguards Avenue on 23 September 1972. Thomas Tilling designed and built these buses on AEC petrol-engined chassis at the company's works in Peckham and Hove and operated them in London and Brighton. In 1933 Tilling's London operations were amalgamated with London General and local independent operators into the new London Passenger Transport Board, which classified these buses ST (short type) and operated them on services from Bromley, Catford and Croydon garages. In 1938 Tilling renamed its Brighton subsidiary the Brighton, Hove & District Omnibus Company. Both London and Brighton STs were hired out to cities up country in the early 1940s to cover wartime shortages and this bus saw service with the Birmingham & Midlnd Motor Omnibus Company, returning to London Transport and was converted to a mobile staff canteen in 1946. The STs remained in service in Brighton and Hove till 1947 and in London till1951. LT restored this bus in 1971 for this circular tour of London and Westminster.

Distinctive features were a deep domed roof, three windows across the bowed front of the upper saloon, curved spandrels supporting the rounded canopy over the projecting driver's cab, destination boxes front and back, and an arched, open doorway at the top of the outside staircase into the upper saloon. This bus, No ST922 is owned by the London Bus Preservation Trust and stabled in the London Bus Museum at Brooklands near Weybridge, Surrey, running on rallies and excursions. It now carries the original 'Thomas Tilling' legend on the side panels instead of 'London Transport'.

KING'S CROSS Steam, sunlight and shadow enhance the appearance of British Railways' Class 'A1' 'Pacific' (4-6-2) locomotive No 60131 *Osprey*, built by the London & North Eastern Railway at Darlington in 1947-48 and seen here at King's Cross awaiting the right-away with the 'Queen of Scots' service one day in the spring of 1959. *Osprey* was stabled in turn at King's Cross, Grantham, Barnsley and Newcastle and from 1954 to 1959 regularly headed the up and down 'Queen of Scots' Pullman train between King's Cross and Glasgow Queen Street calling at Leeds, Harrogate, Newcastle and Edinburgh. Her other named trains included the 'Tees-Tyne Pullman', 'Yorkshire Pullman', 'The Norseman', 'Flying Scotsman', 'Bradford Flyer', 'West Riding' and the 'White Rose'. She also pulled the Royal train, specials, parcels, pigeons and freight and was scrapped at Sheffield in 1965.

Not much sunlight ever filtered through the pall of smoke that hung over King's Cross station in steam days. Smoke pothered out of the mouths of the steeply graded tunnels surrounding the station to the north, west and east. From a standing start in the terminus, trains toiled up the 1 in 105/110 gradient through Gasworks Tunnel and Copenhagen Tunnel on the main line to the north. The connections with the Metropolitan Railway for suburban passengers and goods lay through much steeper, tightly curved, single-bore tunnels opening on each side of the 16-platform station.

EUSTON The megalithic Doric propylæum was the triumphal entrance to Britain's first trunk railway, the London & Birmingham, opened in 1837. It stood 70 feet high and 44 feet deep and took four years to build, from 1836 to 1840, using huge blocks of Yorkshire granite, some of them up to 18 tons apiece. Though often called 'the Euston arch' or the 'Doric portico', it was a propylæum in architectural terms as it was the entrance to an enclosure, the station forecourt, not the portico to the station building, and it was not arched. The London & Birmingham Railway became the stem of the London & North Western Railway in 1846, the London Midland & Scottish Railway in 1923 and the London Midland Region of British Railways in 1948, and Euston station, in the borough of St Pancras, was always the headquarters. The propylæum was designed by Philip Hardwick, who also remodelled the station building in 1846-49, but the façade of the station we see in this March 1959 view had been modified in 1933-36. In the foreground are a 1948 Austin taxicab (right) and a 1935 Morris car (left).

In 1962 the old station and the propylæum were demolished for the wholesale reconstruction of the terminus, completed in 1968. Survivors of the old Euston station are the twin stone lodges, or pavilions, on Euston Road, built in 1869 as an inquiry office and a parcels office, their rusticated quoins inscribed with the names of all the towns served by the ramifications of the LNWR. Hardwick's original L&B terminus at Birmingham Curzon Street, a complementary Ionic stone building housing the station offices, also survives.

CHILD'S HILL After years of design work and trials with four prototypes in 1954-58, London Transport's first production Routemaster buses went into service in 1959. While the RTs replaced the trams, the RMs were to replace the trolleybuses. At a time when bus design favoured platform doors, Londoners preferred the RM's open rear platform. A total of 2,876 Routemasters, with Park Royal, Weymann or Eastern bodies on AEC or Leyland chassis, were delivered from 1958 to 1968. They were painted red in central London and dark green in the country area. This one, RM1960, was built in 1964 and photographed on Finchley Road, Child's Hill, near Hendon, Middlesex, on route 13 from Golders Green to Aldwych in May 1972.

Many were sold second-hand for further service with provincial operators and for private preservation, while London Transport reconditioned many of its remaining fleet with new engines for extended service. The last regular services of Routemasters in London ran in 2005, but one heritage Routemaster service still runs today through the cities of London and Westminster on a short working of route 15 from the Tower to Trafalgare Square. There is said to be a total of 1,280 Routemasters extant in tourist services and museums in Britain and abroad.

HASTINGS Fishing boats are drawn up on the beach below the East Cliff on 7 September 1963 because the old harbour has been wrecked by storms and only the ruins of a stone pier remain. There are 3 miles of these Wealden sandstone cliffs at Hastings along a coastline that otherwise consists of chalk cliffs and marshes. Above the fishermen's quarter here the cliff is scaled by a steep funicular railway. Hastings has two cliff railways, on the East Cliff and the West Cliff. This one, known as the East Hill Lift, opened in 1902 and climbs 265 feet to a viewpoint overlooking the whole town. It is worked by two cable cars on inclined trucks on 5-foot-gauge double tracks. The cars were counter-balanced with water tanks underneath at the time of this photograph, but the railway was converted in 1973-76 to electric cable haulage.

The West Hill Lift, 500 feet, runs most of its way in tunnel to the castle and caves. There are still 13 working cliff railways at English seaside resorts, including three at Bournemouth and three at Scarborough, together with two inland funiculars at Bridgnorth in Shropshire and Shipley Glen in Yorkshire.

EASTBOURNE With the town, pier and South Downs in the background, this scaled-down, 2-foot-gauge miniature tramway ran for three-quarters of a mile alongside the beach, through the edge of Prince's Park and across the shingle spit The Crumbles at the north-east end of the seafront from 1954 to 1969. The conductor collects the fares as car 7 of 1958 bowls alongside the shore between Royal Parade terminus and Prince's Park on 8 September 1963. Eastbourne was the pioneer municipal bus operator in 1903 and never had tramways until this line opened in 1954 to operate in the summer holiday seasons. This enterprise was promoted by the late Claude Lane of the Lancaster Electrical Company, New Barnet, Hertfordshire, which built battery-electric milk floats. Mr Lane created a portable miniature tramway originally for garden parties. He ran a 15-inch-gauge tramway at St Leonard's, Sussex, in 1951, and at Rhyl from 1952 to 1956 in tandem with this 2-foot-gauge line at Eastbourne from 1954. In 1969 it was ousted by Eastbourne Corporation to make way for a new road and the tramway migrated to Seaton, Devon, to reopen in 1970 as a 2ft 9in line along the roadbed of the former Seaton railway branch line, where it flourishes today.

EASTBOURNE Passengers board a 2-foot-gauge tramcar at Royal Parade terminus for the run through Prince's Park to The Crumbles on 28 September 1958. The line voltage was 60, stepped up later to 72 volts DC, generated from the company's large brick workshop halfway along the line. Eastbourne Tramway was owned and operated by Modern Electric Tramways of New Barnet, Hertfordshire.

EASTBOURNE On its return from The Crumbles on 28 September 1958, car 7 of 1958 runs alongside the car shed, where we see sister car 6 of 1954, newly rebuilt to a larger scale in the company workshops, and, in the shadows, a 15-inch-gauge scale replica of a streamlined Darwen car, No 238. The six cars in the fleet were inspired by those on the Llandudno & Colwyn Bay Electric Railway, closed in 1956, cars 6 and 7 being designed on the outline of the ex-Bournemouth open-toppers and car 238 being one of the ex-Darwen cars at Llandudno. Cars 6 and 7 had cross-bench seating on the lower deck for ease of access, with small saloons at each end on car 7 and reversible single seats each side of the gangway on the open top deck. Both cars had Dick, Kerr power controllers, two from Southampton on car 6 and two from Llandudno on car 7. They have since been re-gauged to 2ft 9in to run on the Seaton & District Electric Tramway.

EASTBOURNE The smart Corporation paint scheme enhances the handsome appearance of this 1950 AEC bus, with East Lancashire and Bruce coachwork, at Langney terminus of route 1 on 10 September 1963. Bruce Coach Works at Cardiff worked closely with East Lancashire Coachbuilders at Blackburn and applied the panelling of this batch of buses on East Lancashire frames. Eastbourne Corporation was the first municipal bus operator in Britain in 1903; 50 years later, in 1953 the Commercial Motor listed 97 municipal bus fleets in Britain, Man and Northern Ireland. Following the 1985 Transport Act for privatisation of bus services, today there are now only 11 municipal bus operators in Britain, and Eastbourne is not one of them; it sold out to Stagecoach in 2009.

EASTBOURNE An open-top Southdown bus heads west along Grand Parade towards the top of Beachy Head on 8 September 1963. Open-top buses were introduced when seaside resorts became popular again after the Second World War. Southdown Motor Services had many of these wartime Guy buses rebodied by Park Royal as open-toppers in 1949-59 on seaside services along the Sussex coast. Grand Parade is the central section of the seafront at Eastbourne, with the Burlington Hotel (left), the carpet gardens, the pier entrance (right) and more hotels on Marine Parade in the background. The Burlington Hotel opened in 1860, occupying the central section of this handsome terrace of former private houses built in 1851-55 to a Regency style of 30 years earlier. The modern pier tollhouse of 1951 in this picture was replaced in 1991 by a decorative neo-Victorian-style building with a clock cupola, more in keeping with the other buildings on the pier dating from 1870.

NEWHAVEN The paddle steamer *Consul* of 1896 was based here for the 1963 summer season of coastal cruises to Hastings, Eastbourne and Brighton piers. She is seen berthed at the east quay alongside Newhaven Harbour railway station on 10 September, 1963. She is in the colours of the South Coast & Continental Steamers, her sixth owners, who bought her early in 1963 from Cosens, of Weymouth, who had withdrawn her from service, consigned for scrap. She had an unsuccessful season on the Sussex coast because of mechanical failures but she had a successful week's charter to New Belle Steamers on trips from London (Tower Pier) to Thames estuary resorts for one week at the end of the season. In 1964 South Coast & Continental Steamers boldly moved *Consul* to 'Weymouth for what transpired to be her last season in service: on part of her old Cosens beat – in competition with her former owners! The final chapter in the story of this vessel, a review of her long career under seven owners and her part in two world wars can be seen in Part 2 of this book at Dartmouth on page 100.

NEWHAVEN harbour, on the River Ouse, is seen here looking inland to the South Downs on 10 September 1963. The view was taken from the swing bridge on the road from Eastbourne to Brighton. The London, Brighton & South Coast Railway developed the former fishing village of Newhaven as a cross-Channel ferry port on its Lewes-Seaford branch line, opened in 1864. The railway runs along the east bank and the town grew up on the west bank. The ferry berths were on the seaward side of the swing bridge. The Southern Railway inherited the port and ferry service in 1923. Newhaven was the main British military port for troops and equipment during the Second World War and the main port of embarkation for the D-Day landings in Normandy in 1944. Since then the docks have been filled in, the railway goods yard has closed, and the train ferry has been replaced by a road transport ferry run by a succession of private operators. Now owned by the British Ports Authority, Newhaven still also handles freight but these days it is mainly bulk cargo such as aggregates, biomass fuels, scrap metal and stone.

BRIGHTON An electric car arrives at the Black Rock terminus of Volk's Railway at Brighton on 8 September 1958. This station was built in Art Deco style to match the adjacent 1930s lido, but has since been rebuilt in a neo-Regency style to match the terraced houses of Kemp Town on the cliff top.

BRIGHTON Corporation trolleybuses and motorbuses stand around the Old Steine bus terminus at the south end of the town centre gardens (right) by the seafront and the Palace Pier (off right) in 1958. The terminus was designated 'Aquarium' on the destination blinds, as on Volk's Railway. All three trolleybuses and the two motorbuses in this photograph are Weymann-bodied AECs dating from 1939, the year when trolleybuses replaced the trams, operating from the same terminus. This was the last year of full trolleybus operation in Brighton; the routes covered 14½ miles but the eight services were replaced by motorbuses between 1959 and 1961. Brighton Corporation, and the Brighton, Hove & District Omnibus Company, had a joint working agreement for an integrated system. Their buses wore a matching paint scheme, a cheery red and cream, and their trolleybuses had almost identical bodies by Weymann, but the company motorbuses were Eastern-bodied Bristols, not seen here.

BRIGHTON Volk's Railway is the oldest electric railway or tramway in the world and has been a feature of Brighton seafront since 1883. The present line, built in 1884-1901, runs along the beach beside Madeira Drive below the East Cliff for just over a mile from the Aquarium terminus near the pier to Black Rock at the east end of the seafront. The 2ft 8½in-gauge ballasted sleeper track is electrified at 110 volts DC, fed by an off-centre third rail. This picture was taken on 8 September 1963 on the approach to the Aquarium terminus, supported on a steel trestle. The seven crossbench electric cars were built by the founder, Magnus Volk, in the workshops and date from 1892 to 1926.

BRIGHTON The Brighton, Hove & District buses here at Brighton clock tower on 10 September 1963 are the company's standard Eastern-bodied Bristol Ks, built between 1951 and 1957. The one on route 5 heads down North Street towards the Old Steine, while a 19 from the railway station waits at the signal in Queen's Road to turn right into Western Road for Hove, and a Southdown bus is on the other side of the clock tower. The latter was built in 1897 to mark Queen Victoria's 60th Jubilee and is one of the most elaborate in Britain, with its ornate cupola and finials, its classical pediments and columns framing mosaic portraits of the Royal Family and flanked by sedentary female statues representing industry, virtue, etc.

HOVE Classic cars in a classical square. A chain of Regency terraces, squares and crescents extends from Kemp Town in the east to Hove in the west. This is Brunswick Square, Hove, on 8 September 1963. All this late-Georgian or Regency development, from the 1790s to the 1830s, is a legacy of the town planning of the joint landowner Thomas Kemp (of Kemp Town) and his local architects Charles Busby and Amon Wilds. Brunswick Square was built in 1825-30 and became the centrepiece of a new town in the rural parish of Hove, which was then only a village around Hove Street. The Town Commissioners of Brighton had no authority here, so the Brunswick Square Act of 1830 established the Brunswick Square Commissioners to regulate municipal affairs in the growing new town west of Brighton, and they became the Hove Commissioners in 1873 and Hove Corporation in 1898. The wide streets are a legacy of Georgian and Regency town planning, allowing ample space for carriages in the 19th century and parked cars in the 20th. Ahead of the 1948 Bentley on the left is a Rover 75 of 1945-48. Other cars in view are Morrises, Fords, Austins and Standards of the 1950s.

HOVE A pre-war Southern Electric six-car train of 2-BIL stock (1935-38) pauses at Hove station on its way from Portsmouth Harbour to Brighton on 7 April 1970. This was the end of the green era on the BR Southern Region and the former Southern Railway as the last four cars have been repainted in BR's new standard blue paintwork. The modest yellow dash panel on the lead car was the precursor of the all-yellow cab fronts on the blue stock as a visible warning to anyone on the track ahead, and the black triangle meant that the unit could only be coupled to sets that were similarly marked.

Part 2, South and South-west England: Wessex to Cornwall

Hampshire

NEWPORT is the capital of the Isle of Wight and this is St James's Square, with its monument to Queen Victoria, in September 1957. As in many country towns in those days the square or market place doubled as the bus station. Here the buses are Eastern-bodied Bristols of the Southern Vectis Omnibus Company in green and cream. The Bristol Lodekka on the right was built in 1953, one of the first production models of the new generation of low-floor, low-bridge buses with an off-centre drive shaft under the seats, a dropped-centre rear axle, full-height saloons and 2+2 seating upstairs, giving a height of 13ft 5in. This arrangement superseded the low headroom and four-in-a-row seating upstairs of previous generations of low-bridge buses, such as the late-1940s Bristol K in the background. Vectis was the Roman name for Wight and the prefix 'Southern' commemorates the Southern Railway's half share in the bus company. Newport now has a bus station and St James's Square is a through road with no bus stops.

BOURNEMOUTH In the Corporation's yellow paintwork with maroon bands, this 1943 wartime utility Weymann-bodied Guy bus was converted to an open-topper in 1952 and is seen loading at the pier terminus in September 1957, for the exhilarating run east on route 12 along the clifftops via Boscombe Chine and Southbourne to the wilds of Hengistbury Head. The driver (right) takes a break during the lay-over and behind the bus are the overhead trolleybus wires and the public baths. This bus was later cut down further to an open-top single-decker.

BOURNEMOUTH This Corporation motorbus with a full-width cab over the engine is a 1939 Weymann-bodied Leyland that was built with a petrol engine and later converted to diesel. Like most other Bournemouth motorbuses and trolleybuses it was designed for improved passenger flow with front exit folding doors, front and rear staircases and the usual open rear loading platform. It was seen, complete with starting handle, at The Triangle off-peak parking area for buses on the west side of the town centre in September 1957. The left-hand road of this spare bus rank was used by trolleybuses.

BOURNEMOUTH Two Alexander-bodied Leyland Atlanteans of 1970, fleet numbers 250 and 251, meet in The Square on 27 July 1972. No 250 (left), on route 1 to Boscombe and Christchurch, gives way to No 251, emerging from Bourne Avenue destined for West Howe.

The trees are in the Pleasure Gardens flanking The Bourne stream that runs through the town centre into the sea by the pier. Seven roads converged on The Square, but this is now a pedestrian zone separating two through, reflex-angled loop roads: Exeter Road-Gervis Place and Avenue Road-Bourne Avenue. The other three roads are closed to motor traffic.

BOURNEMOUTH A Corporation 1971 Alexander-bodied Leyland Atlantean bus descends Gervis Place and pulls over to the offside lane to circumnavigate The Square and double back up Old Christchurch Road (left) on route 1 to Boscombe, Iford and Christchurch, also on 27 July 1972. To me the bowed front of the Alexander body echoed the bowed projection of the Dolcis building.

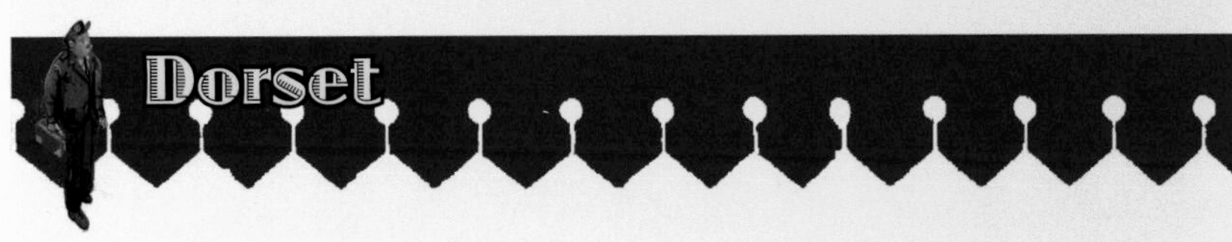

Below: **SWANAGE** The sunny south coast had more pleasure steamers than any other part of England because of its climate and the many seaside resorts and harbours. Embarking passengers at Swanage pier in Dorset is the PS *Monarch* on its way from Bournemouth to Weymouth in September 1957. Built in 1924 as the Southern Railway's PS *Shanklin*, she was sold to Cosens & Company of Weymouth in 1951, renamed *Monarch* and, based at Bournemouth, survived on this service till 1961, when she was scrapped. The last regular excursion steamer of that era, Cosens's PS *Embassy*, called here in 1966, following which the pier, dating from 1896, decayed for nearly 30 years and closed. Now it is owned by Swanage Pier Trust, which renewed the piles and decking, recast the Victorian railings, shelter and lamp posts in the original moulds and reopened the pier in 1998. It is 214 yards long and used for promenading, angling, diving and coastal cruising in small motor vessels. Now Britain's only surviving sea-going paddle steamer, *Waverley*, of Glasgow, has been calling at Swanage since 2009 as part of its annual summer visit to the south coast and the Thames estuary to resume the paddle steamer tradition.

Above: **SWANAGE** Next to the steamer pier in September 1957 stand the ruins of the old pier, built in 1859-60 for shipping out Purbeck limestone and marble, brought by narrow-gauge railway from the quarries. Ships also traded in coal, fish and timber and from 1871 excursion steamers tied up here on day trips to Bournemouth and Weymouth. After the construction of the new pier, the old pier was still used as a coaling stage for the steamships but by the time of this photograph it was in ruins. Sixty years later a crescent-shaped line of scanty wooden piles and a few cross-ties still mark the site of the old pier, and the narrow-gauge railway can still be traced atop the sea wall.

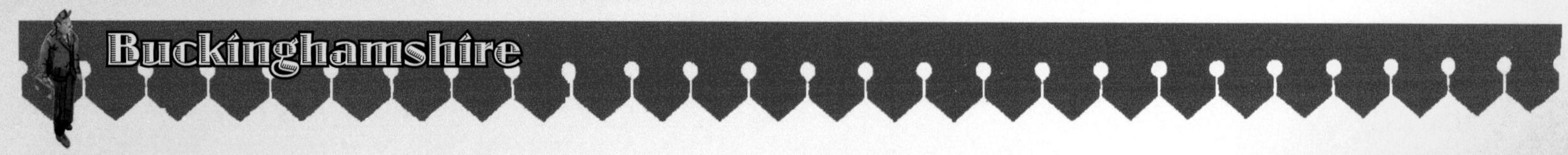

CHEDDINGTON At speed on the LNWR/LMSR main line through the Buckinghamshire countryside, photographed from an overtaking passenger train near Cheddington on 6 July 1962, *Scots Guardsman*, an ex-LMS 'Royal Scot' Class 4-6-0, heads a southbound parcels train to Euston. The locomotive was built in 1927 by the North British Locomotive Company and starred in the GPO documentary film *Night Mail* in 1936. The 'Royal Scots' were rebuilt in 1943-55 with tapered boilers, double chimneys and blastpipes and curved smoke deflectors to become the most powerful 4-6-0s on BR and more handsome than the original, chubby 'Royal Scots' of 1927. *Scots Guardsman* was the last to be rebuilt by the LMSR in 1947. The engine was stabled at Willesden (1A) and migrated north as the line was electrified from Euston to Crewe. It is now preserved in working order in its original LMS post-war livery and number 6115, owned by West Coast Railways of Carnforth.

APPLETON In this traditional country bus terminus scene in Berkshire in 1950, the driver, conductor and my old school friend Harry Green stand with their backs to the warm radiator during the terminal lay-over at Millway Lane, Appleton, with the route blind turned ready for the return journey to Oxford. City of Oxford Motor Services ran buses far out into the surrounding country and neighbouring counties. This bus, D129, was a 1939 low-bridge Park Royal-bodied AEC in the company's rich red, dark brown and cream colour scheme. The Appleton turn was a short working of the much longer route 67 through Berkshire to Faringdon.

Below: **BOTLEY** A mile and a half west of Oxford city centre, route 5 crossed the Berkshire/Oxfordshire boundary on a bridge over a branch of the River Isis. Oxford low-bridge bus G6 was one of six petrol-engined AECs of 1931-32 rebodied by East Lancashire Coachbuilders in 1944 with upholstered seats and none of the austerity of wartime bodies. It is pictured at the Black Horse stop on its way from Cumnor Hill Foot to Old Headington on 13 September 1949. These petrol-engined buses were quiet except for the 'pop-bang' explosions from the exhaust pipes as they slowed to a stop. East Lancashire Coachbuilders only started building buses in 1938 and, as one of the chosen few suppliers of bus bodies during the war, had enough parts to continue building new buses and rebuild old and blitz-damaged vehicles throughout the war without resorting to austerity bodywork.

Above: **BOTLEY** In 1944 Willowbrook rebodied two 1931 petrol-engined AECs in this box-like wartime austerity form as 53-seat low-bridge buses for further Oxford service. This one, D151, rests after reversing into Hurst Rise Road at Cumnor Hill Foot terminus in Botley on a warm autumn evening for the return journey to Old Headington on 7 October 1949.

OXFORD Salter Brothers built its own steam launches in its boatyards here at Oxford as well as vessels for other operators and for export. There is a smell of fresh water, steam vapour and cylinder oil as passengers board a launch berthed at the floating landing stage on the River Isis below Folly Bridge for a trip downriver. Christ Church Meadows are on the opposite bank. This was the traditional design of Salter's steamers: a flush foredeck with a canvas canopy and an aft saloon with an open deck above. At the time of this photograph in 1953 Salters had a fleet of 11 steamers built between 1897 and 1931, three steamers dieselised in 1945-47, and three original diesel launches built in 1930-47. The longest trip was a two-day scheduled service down the Thames & Isis Navigation from Oxford to Kingston (Surrey) with an overnight stop on the way. Passengers could make day return trips between stages and many of these passengers would be going to Abingdon (Berkshire) and back on the steamer.

Salter's Steamers, as they are known today, are still owned and operated by the Salter family and run day return trips downriver from Oxford to Abingdon and between five other steamboat stations as far as Staines. The through service to Kingston ended in the 1970s but the voyage can still be made in short stages from Oxford to Staines with six changes of vessel and would take five days. The present fleet of 12 vessels includes seven motorised steamers, the oldest dating back to 1901.

82
TO OXFORD
LWL 305

OXFORD Stopping opposite Magdalen College this 1946 Park Royal-bodied AEC bus is entering the city on the long country route 82 from Aylesbury in 1949. Magdalen College was founded in 1458 and the tower, seen here, was built between 1492 and 1509. These City of Oxford buses, in their rich red, dark brown and cream, provided a nice foil to the grey and honey coloured stonework of the university city.

Right: **OXFORD** The subtle curve of High Street presents an ever-changing townscape panorama of stonework from the Gothic to the classical, the great sycamore tree nicely breaking up the line of building at the apex of the bend. This 1949 scene shows the two types of buses new to City of Oxford Motor Services in 1948. There were 19 of the high-bridge Weymann-bodied AECs, like that on the right on route 3 from St Margaret's Road to Rose Hill estate, and 14 Northern coachbuilt AECs like the one at the stop by University College (left) on route 6 from Headington quarry to North Hinksey turn. University College was founded in 1249 and rebuilt in 1643-77. On the right are All Souls' College, completed in 1443, and the 188-foot steeple of the 14th-century University Church of St Mary. In the background are Brasenose College and the steeple of All Saints' Church.

Above: **OXFORD** Bicycles and buses are the main forms of transport in Oxford: bicycles for the college students and buses for the residents. There are eight cyclists and three pre-war Oxford buses in this 1949 view of the city centre crossroads at Carfax, looking into High Street with the steeples of All Saints' and St Mary's churches in the background. It is a hot summer's day with all windows open, including the windscreens of the buses. All three buses here are Park Royal-bodied AECs of 1937-38. On the nearside of the first bus is a new 1949 Morris Minor car, built at Cowley, an eastern suburb of Oxford.

Above: **OXFORD** renewed its bus fleet in 1949 with 23 of these high-bridge Weymann-bodied AECs, which were a sleeker version of the 1939 Weymann AECs we see on on the left of page 81. This one was photographed when new at the top of High Street with Carfax church tower on the extreme right and Queen Street beyond. It is on route 2 from Summertown to Barton Estate West beyond Headington.

Below: **OXFORD** The country bus services terminated in Gloucester Green bus station, the former cattle market. This 1935 low-bridge Weymann-bodied AEC, K71, was one of the first batch of oil-engined buses for Oxford. Low-bridge buses went west under the GWR station bridge, like this 54 to Witney. The photograph was taken on 4 December 1949.

OXFORD This 1937 Weymann-bodied AEC single-decker for country services has a luggage rack on the roof reached by recessed steps up the back of the bus. It is parked on the spare bus rank outside the company's inquiry and parcels office at Gloucester Green bus station on 4 December 1949. The bus station was created for the growing country network on the site of the old cattle market in 1934, when the market moved to St Ebbe's beside the railway sidings. The bus office here on the left was the former Central School for Boys, built in 1899-1901. The architect was Leonard Stokes, an eminent and prolific London architect noted for church schools, telephone exchanges and villas. Its collegiate architecture befits the bus station of an old university city. The station was used for country buses and for coaches on express services and tours.

After the 1986 privatisation and deregulation of bus operations, Oxford buses became part of the Go Ahead Group and most of their country services went to Stagecoach, Thames Travel and ten other new companies. The country services now operate from street terminals on the edge of the pedestrianised city centre. Less than half the old bus station is still a coach station, but the old school and bus office survives as a listed building, now used as a restaurant.

OXFORD After a short working of route 44 (Oxford-Chipping Norton-Long Compton), K121, one of 17 high-bridge Park Royal-bodied AECs built for Oxford in 1937-38, is parked on the spare bus rank at Gloucester Green in 1949. This was the high-bridge version of the low-bridge K71, seen earlier. This style of bodywork, with the straight, raked-back front above the radiator and the straight, upright back, was a standard style of double-deck body in Britain in the period 1935-46, built mainly by Metropolitan-Cammell, Park Royal, Weymann and Willowbrook. Route 44 timetables connected at Long Compton with Stratford Blue Motors' service to Stratford-upon-Avon and by 1951 this was a through, joint service.

Above: **OXFORD** Just arrived on route 13 from Abingdon, D142, a 1939 Weymann-bodied AEC, is unloading its passengers outside the fire station in Gloucester Green on 13 September 1949. This was the high-bridge version of the low-bridge D129 we saw earlier at Appleton. Oxford had 29 high-bridge buses of this design from both Park Royal and Weymann in 1939-40. Compare this 1939 design with the 1949 Weymann bus we saw at Carfax.

Right: **OXFORD** had only two of these boxy-looking low-bridge buses that had been rebodied by Willowbrook in 1944 on AEC petrol-engined chassis dating from 1931. This is D160 loading in Gloucester Green for route 74 to Great Milton and Little Milton in Berkshire on 13 September 1949. The other was D151, which we met at Cumnor Hill Foot terminus, Botley. Willowbrook replaced the original 48-seat bodies with 53-seaters, an important consideration in the 1940s when most people travelled by public transport..

OXFORD Among the service operators to Oxford bus station was the Bristol Tramways & Carriage Company, and this Bristol-built Bristol bus is seen arriving in Gloucester Green bus station in 1953 at the end of the 42-mile route from Cheltenham. The Cheltenham-Oxford service was begun by Great Western Railway buses in 1928 because there were no direct trains; it was taken over by the Bristol bus company in 1932 when the railways had given up bus operations for shares in the large territorial bus companies. The Cheltenham run was not a joint service with Oxford, but Bristol and Oxford buses did run a joint service between Swindon and Oxford.

OXFORD was also on the Liverpool-London express coach route operated by Crosville Motor Services of Chester. Convoys of up to eight of these pre-war Harrington-bodied Leyland Tiger coaches, built in 1936-38, ran the service until the early 1950s and loaded on the street along the west side of Gloucester Green bus station. This oil-engined KA class, photographed in 1950, was Crosville's largest batch of pre-war single-deckers, this example dating from 1938. Behind it is one of Crosville's new Duple-bodied Bedford OBs of 1949. The pre-war Harrington 32-seat saloons were furnished to a standard of luxury and comfort not known since. Crosville started the London express service in 1927 and took the scenic route in that pre-motorway era. The route from London served Beaconsfield, High Wycombe, Oxford, Woodstock, Stratford-upon-Avon, Warwick, Kenilworth, Newport, Whitchurch, Chester and Birkenhead, then went through the Mersey Tunnel to Liverpool. The route skirted Birmingham, stopping at Erdington tram terminus; passengers for Birmingham finished their journey into the city by tramcar until 1953, then by bus. At the time of this picture the Liverpool-London express coach service ran twice daily; with the overall speed limit of 30mph for buses and coaches in those days the daylight service took 10 hours and the night service 9 hours.

Express coaches are now run by new companies with faster and more frequent services using motorways and today's service bypasses all the intermediate towns that were formerly served. The Liverpool-London run calls only at Stoke-on-Trent or Milton Keynes and averages 5½ hours.

Right: **OXFORD** Contrasting styles of classic coaches, both built in 1948, are seen in the coach park at Gloucester Green bus station visiting Oxford on tour in 1953. The traditional front-engined, half-cab Southdown coach (left) is a 32-seat Beadle-bodied Leyland, while the full-fronted BMMO coach (right) is a 30-seat Duple-bodied BMMO with a centre door and under-floor engine. The Birmingham & Midland Motor Omnibus Company built its own chassis and engines from 1924 to 1970 and specified the body designs. From 1946 the company standardised on full-fronted single-deck buses and coaches with under-floor engines and reached this acme of coach design with this class C1 coach in 1948. Both coaches looked smart with the main house colour on the panelling and dark colours on the roof, windows and mudguards, the Southdown coach being in two-tone green with cream bands and the BMMO in red and black. Southdown coaches carried the fleet name on the side panels in cursive script while these BMMO coaches carried the company monogram in a roundel on the sides. Both types of coach worked express services in the late 1940s and early '50s and continued on excursions and tours into the early 1960s.

OXFORD REWLEY ROAD Oxford had two railway stations, side by side, at the west end of Park End Street, half a mile west of Carfax. Their buildings were weatherboarded and lit by gas. The LMSR station, on the corner of Rewley Road, was the terminus of the former LNWR branch, 31 miles long, from Bletchley, Buckinghamshire. This portico and trainshed were built on a frame of prefabricated cast-iron sections, bolted together, by Fox, Henderson Ltd, the company that built the Crystal Palace the same way for the Great Exhibition in Hyde Park, London, in 1851, the year that this railway and station opened. The Buckinghamshire Railway Company built the line but it was leased and operated by the LNWR, which took over ownership in 1878. The railway was inherited by the LMSR in 1923 and by BR in 1948. This photograph was taken in 1950, and the following year, just as the station reached its centenary, it was closed. The site is now occupied by a plain, cubic building housing a university school of business.

The plain and cross-braced frieze on the right-hand side of the portico was inserted after a lorry collided with the column. The side formerly matched the more ornate structure on the front and left-hand side of the portico with based columns and arching spandrels supporting a frieze with roundels. The portico and trainshed were subsequently removed to store and have been resurrected at the Buckinghamshire Railway Centre at Quainton Road station near Aylesbury, where the portico has been restored compete with matching new ironwork on the right-hand side.

OXFORD REWLEY ROAD The train in the platform was the only through train of the day from Oxford to Cambridge and this service was the last direct public transport link between the two university cities. The engine crew sit in the afternoon sunshine with their ex-LNER 'D16' Class 4-4-0 locomotive from Cambridge shed awaiting the 2.42pm departure for Bletchley, Bedford and Cambridge. This was the one round trip of the day from Cambridge. The only other trains from here were six to Bletchley including one on to Bedford, worked by ex-LMSR engines from Bletchley shed, as this was formerly an LNWR branch line.

This photograph was taken in 1950, a year before passenger services were switched to Oxford General station via Oxford North Junction. In this picture a school friend, Roger Lowman, is standing by the first carriage. In the background we see the LNWR and GWR signal cabins and the GWR engine shed. The goods yards on both sides of this passenger platform were always busy with shunting until they, too, closed in 1984 with the demise of loose-coupled freight. The Oxford-Bletchley passenger service ended in 1967, but in 2016 it was reopened to Bicester and linked up with the ex-GWR/GCR for through service between Oxford, High Wycombe and London Marylebone. The Bletchley-Bedford section is still open and there is a long-term plan to reopen this ex-LNWR through route between Oxford, Bletchley, Bedford and Cambridge to serve new housing and industries along the way.

OXFORD GENERAL

Alongside the ex-LMSR terminus and goods yards, divided only by the station approach road, was Oxford General station on the busy ex-Great Western main line from Didcot to Banbury, and this provided a scene of constant animation in contrast to its sleepy next-door neighbour. The four tracks between the main up and down platforms were busy with freight on the centre tracks and passenger trains calling at the platforms on their way to Paddington, Swindon, Swansea, Hereford, Wolverhampton and Birkenhead, inter-regional trains to Margate, Bournemouth and York, and local branch-line trains to Princes Risborough, Woodstock and Fairford. Thus Oxford General saw a fascinating mixture of GWR, SR, LNER and pre-Grouping locomotives and carriages. The station buildings, dating from 1852, were weatherboarded like stations in the Wild West and the canopies dated from 1893, when they replaced the former overall roof. The old, wooden, gaslit station lasted till 1970-72, when it was rebuilt in the austere idiom of the time; it has since been rebuilt once more.

This view north from the down platform in 1953 features an interesting range of GWR platform furniture: the water column, brazier, gas lamps, the wooden signal posts with their ball-and-spike finials and the screen on the post with slides showing when the road was clear from the main or bay platforms. Beyond, from left to right, we can see the soot-black, wooden GWR engine shed, the brick LMSR engine shed, the GWR Oxford Station North signal cabin, and the tower of St Barnabas Church. The church tower is the only structure in this photograph to survive today.

SHIPTON-ON-CHERWELL Halt was the only intermediate stop on the 3½-mile branch line from Kidlington to Woodstock. The line was built by the Woodstock Railway Company in 1890 but worked from the start by the GWR, which bought the Woodstock company in 1897 and added Shipton-on-Cherwell Halt in 1929. The original low-level platform was rebuilt to standard height in 1933. The terminus in Woodstock was by the main gate to Blenheim Palace, home of the Dukes of Marlborough, and was named Blenheim & Woodstock. This photograph was taken shortly after the line closed in 1954, which is why the platform is bereft of its nameboard and the oil burners in the two lanterns. This quaint little one-carriage platform, built of railway sleepers, with a small shelter and two oil lanterns, was typical of the many halts on the Great Western for local train services on both main lines and branch lines.

BANBURY MERTON STREET station was the terminus of two branch lines off the LNWR/LMSR main line at Bletchley (21 miles) and Blisworth (20 miles), converging at Cockley Brake Junction. The line from Bletchley diverted from the Oxford branch at Verney Junction. The original survey for the London & Birmingham Railway (later the LNWR main line) went via Tring, Aylesbury, Buckingham and Banbury, but the Duke of Buckingham opposed it, so the route was diverted via Leighton Buzzard, Bletchley and Blisworth. A rival to the LBR, the GWR proposed a route from London via Tring, Aylesbury, Bicester and Banbury to Evesham, Worcester and Wolverhampton, so when the branch from Bletchley opened in 1850 the terminus at Banbury was built of wood as a temporary station prior to an extension of the line into the Midlands – but the GWR checked that move. Thus the 'temporary' wooden terminus remained to the end, with its weatherboarded building and its low-level, wooden island platform that was common in the mid-19th century.

In 1950 this station saw only four trains a day to Bletchley and two to Blisworth. The Banbury-Blisworth service closed in 1951. The iron framework was all that remained of the trainshed roof in this 1954 photograph, the timber cladding having been removed for safety. The low-level platform was equipped with a portable set of three steps to help passengers on and off the trains. As at Oxford, the sleepy Banbury branch terminus was right alongside the busy GWR through main-line station, and the goods yard was extensive. The old station was spruced up in 1956 when the steam trains were replaced by a more frequent service of seven trains a day with two single-unit, double-ended, Derby lightweight diesel railcars and two new halts on the way to Buckingham. The new cars cut costs by one-third and revenue increased fourfold, but not enough for the accountants; most stations were too remotely situated. The Bletchley-Banbury line closed to passengers in 1960 and to goods in 1964. The station was then used as a British Road Services depot but road haulage was later denationalised and today this is the site of Banbury's Royal Mail delivery office.

Above: **BANBURY** town centre is seen from Bridge Street in 1957, showing the Town Hall in the fork between High Street (left) and the Market Place (right). The motorcar parked on the right is a 1955 Standard. Buses took their terminal lay-over standing casually around the upward-sloping edges of the main street. Oxfordshire projected into the southern limit of the Midland bus service area and three Midland buses in overall red (trading as Midland Red) are parked left of the passenger shelters and another stands in front of the Town Hall, while a Black & White express coach loads passengers under the trees en route from Kettering to Cheltenham. Oxford buses also terminated on the left.

Today this space is no longer used as a bus station and the scene has a different aspect with an expanse of pedestrian paving, restricted motor access to a roundabout in front of the Town Hall and several new buildings, and the area is shaded by mature trees. Fairs and markets have been held here since the 12th century. The stone Town Hall, looking like a Gothic church, is Banbury's fourth, opened in 1854.

Above: right **BANBURY** This portrait of an Oxford bus at its terminal lay-over in High Street on 14 September 1963 shows off the rich, warm, red and dark brown colour scheme of the Oxford buses that, at their peak in about 1950, was seen in an area extending up to 80 miles across the country from Bedford to Swindon and from Reading to Stratford-upon-Avon. This bus is a 1956 Weymann-bodied AEC on route 99 from Bicester. On closer inspection the dark brown roof and windows were actually a dark shade of maroon and the cream bands under the windows were tinged light green (not the green bands of later reproductions of this paint scheme). This was an artistic blend of colours, which was lost after nationalisation in 1969, when the buses were repainted 'poppy' red and off-white.

Left: **BRISTOL** Shipping in the port of Bristol seemed to be integrated into the townscape and the impounded Floating Harbour snaked through the old city centre on a loop and a creek of the narrow River Avon. The Bristol sand dredger *Harry Brown*, built on the Floating Harbour in 1962, was berthed in Bathurst Basin off the main River Avon in this picture of the Bathurst Hotel on 19 June 1971. The Regency-style hotel gracefully curves around the corner from Wapping Road into Bathurst Parade. *Harry Brown* was the last vessel to leave the old port of Bristol when it closed to commercial shipping in 1992, moving downriver to a new berth at Avonmouth docks.

Above: **CHELTENHAM** The Black & White Motorways' coach station in St Margaret's Road opened in 1931 and became a central hub and interchange point in the nationwide coach service network from 1934 till 1984. After nationalisation in 1969 the Black & White identity still prevailed in this line-up of coaches on 20 June 1971, destined (from the left) for Derby, Liverpool, Paignton, Wolverhampton and Wellingborough. The coach station closed in 1985, by which time the motorway coach network had established a new coach hub in Birmingham. This station was demolished in 1990.

CHELTENHAM Many smaller British tramway systems closed in the hard financial times between the wars, when infrastructure and rolling stock were due for renewal and it was cheaper and easier to replace tramways with motorbuses. Relics of tramway infrastructure survived long into the second half of the century, when car sheds were used as workshops and traction poles as lamp posts, and the wall fixtures for the overhead span wires are still to be seen on the buildings in narrow streets, where they were used instead of traction poles. Here in St George's Road, Cheltenham, on 9 May 1971, is a traction pole that suspended the overhead wires of the Cheltenham & District Light Railways, which ran from 1901 to 1930. In the background is Royal Well Terrace, built in 1837-40.

Cheltenham had 10 miles of 3ft 6in-gauge tramways with two cross-town lines, from Charlton Kings to Lansdown and from Leckhampton to Cleeve Hill. St George's Road was on the line to Lansdown Castle, which served the town's three railway stations at that time: St James, Malvern Road and Lansdown. The line to Cleeve Hill was a long, rural, roadside sleeper track with a final gradient of 1 in 9 up to the village. This traction pole, not being used as a lamp post, has since disappeared, but Cheltenham Borough Council has saved four other tramway poles in succession along Prestbury Road on the line to Cleeve Hill. Complete with ornate bases, scroll brackets and finials, like this one, they have been 'locally indexed' as an integral part of a conservation area.

SEATON & District Electric Tramway was laid along the trackbed of the former Seaton railway branch line, which closed in 1966. This half-scale tramway migrated here from Eastbourne in 1969-70 when its three-quarter-mile line there was threatened by a new road scheme. In 36 round trips with two lorries and a trailer they brought nine tramcars, track and points, 160 traction poles, overhead wire, workshop machinery, generators, dynamos, batteries and many tons of stores. By 1971 the first 2 miles of 2ft 9in-gauge track had been laid from Seaton to Colyford and the cars were re-gauged (from Eastbourne's 2 feet) and running with a battery trailer until the overhead line was erected. Car 8, of 1968, was the first car in service and is seen here pushing its trailer through the Axe valley from Seaton to Colyford in June 1971. The village of Axmouth is in the distance on the left and Seaton is silhouetted on the right horizon.

SEATON Car 12 was built at Eastbourne in 1966 as a single-deck winter service car and is seen here at Seaton terminus on the old station site on 27 July 1972, when work car 02 in the background was starting to erect the overhead line equipment. Car 12 has since been rebuilt at Seaton as an open-top double-decker in the style of a London 'Feltham' car in red and cream. Car 02, dating from 1952, was rebuilt in 1968 and has changed its guise twice since. The overhead line was electrified in 1973 at 120 volts DC and the track was extended at the Seaton end to Harbour Road car park and an extra mile north from Colyford through the hills to Colyton's extant railway station, making a total run of 3 miles. On the right is the estuary of the River Axe, with marshes that form a nature reserve. The growing number of passenger cars (13 at the last count) run all the year round: a public service for holidaymakers from April to October and special cars in the off-season for birdwatchers, who can use the tramcar itself as a hide.

Right: **SALCOMBE** A 1959 Western National, Eastern-bodied Bristol Lodekka loads at Salcombe bus garage for route 105 to Kingsbridge in 1963. The Western National Omnibus Company had its headquarters at Exeter, crossroads of the Southern and Western National Omnibus Companies and the Southern and Western Regions of British Railways. The two bus companies served the namesake territories of the former Southern Railway and Great Western Railway, which had part ownership of their local country bus companies from 1930. This is why the Southern National buses ran south-east and north-west of Exeter and the Western National buses ran north-east and south-west of the city. *George Greenwood*

Left: **BARNSTAPLE** This curving, single-track steel bridge across the River Taw linked the railway from Exeter to Barnstaple Junction (for Torrington) on the south bank with Barnstaple Town station on the north bank and the extension to Ilfracombe. Rumbling across the bridge with a southbound train on 16 May 1960 is 'M7' Class 0-4-4T locomotive No 30247, designed and built by the LSWR. Dating from 1897, these engines were still common everywhere on the former LSWR system in SR and BR Southern Region days. Through express trains ran over this bridge between Waterloo and Ilfracombe via Exeter, including portions of the 'Atlantic Coast Express' and the 'Devon Belle'. The line to Ilfracombe closed in 1970, the Taw bridge was demolished in 1978 and the railway from Exeter now terminates at what was Barnstaple Junction station. Most of the buildings in the background of this picture have gone and new blocks of flats have been built on the river bank.

WHT 312

Left: **EXETER** This was the site of the old port of Exeter on the River Exe: the quay, the limestone and red sandstone warehouses of 1835, the 18th-century transit shed and the Custom House of 1681 in the background. This was a location for the BBC television series *The Onedin Line* in 1971-80, representing 19th-century Liverpool. At the time of this photograph, taken on 23 September 1969, the quay and transit shed were a parking place for vehicles, and here we see a 1956 Morris Minor car (a design launched in 1948) and a British Road Services lorry trailer. The warehouses were then part of the Exeter Maritime Museum, housing boats and the ticket office. Visitors crossed the river by ferry to the main part of the museum at the head of the Exeter Canal. The warehouses here have since been converted to flats and a night club above ground-floor shops and a restaurant. The transit shed is still there and the Custom House is now used for the City Archives. The open space here is now cluttered with rows of chain-linked iron bollards.

EXETER The 86-foot-long steam tug *St Canute* of Fowey lords over the collection of vessels, mostly boats, at the Exeter Maritime Museum on 17 June 1971. This was the first maritime museum in Britain with full-sized vessels, opening in 1969. The collection was housed in the basin and warehouses at the head of the Exeter Ship Canal, built and developed in stages between 1564 and 1599. It was 5 miles long with two pound locks, and carried ships of up to 150 tons into Exeter. The tug was built in Denmark at Frederikshavn in 1931 as the *Sct Knud* for the Odense harbour commissioners. In 1960 it was bought second-hand by Fowey harbour commissioners in Cornwall to assist china clay ships up and down the river. Here it was renamed *St Canute*, the anglicised version of the name of King Knud (1080-86) and patron saint of Denmark. The tug was retired from Fowey to the maritime museum when the latter opened in 1969. All the signs and lettering in the wheelhouse and engine room were still in Danish. The museum closed in 1997 for lack of visitors. Most of the collection is now in the World of Boats at Eyemouth, Berwickshire, and the tug was bought for preservation at Stocka in Sweden and renamed *Stockirk*. The canal -head warehouses are now used as an antiques store and an art gallery.

EXETER Traditional-style, half-cab, 7ft 6in-wide buses with open, back platforms were still being built in 1960, the date of this City of Exeter, Massey-bodied Guy at St David's railway station on 17 June, 1971. A local tradition was the use of route letters instead of numbers.

NEWTON POPPLEFORD station on the former LSWR/SR branch line from Sidmouth Junction to Exmouth was in the evening of its life when photographed on 31 August 1965. This was one of several stations in the south-west with a siding for camping coaches, which the railways hired out to holidaymakers. In the 1951 timetable there were 11 daily branch-line services and through carriages between Waterloo and Exmouth that hooked on and off the main-line trains at Sidmouth Junction on summer Saturdays. The cast-iron lamp posts along the platform were twisted like barley sugar; this style was also seen on other Southern Railway stations. The line closed in 1967.

EXMOUTH This Hillman Minx car, new that year, was parked on the Esplanade at Exmouth in August 1948. Parked behind it is a 1947 Morris M. Both cars were in the standard black of the time and substantially the same as the 1940 models, but the Morris now had a horizontal grille with a central stem and the Hillman had the headlamps moulded into the front mudguards for the first time, the gear lever was mounted on the steering column, and the chrome flashes each side of the radiator, previously vertical, were now horizontal, like late-1930s American cars. This was the smartest design of any of the popular cars in 1948. Hillman was part of the Rootes Group, together with Humber and Sunbeam Talbot, all built at Coventry, while Morris cars were made at Cowley, Oxford. The following year Hillman, Morris and most other popular British cars turned to small, colourful versions of flashy American cars with the mudguards moulded into a streamlined bonnet and wide, grinning, horizontal grilles, and that became the norm of British car design through the 1950s and '60s, which we see in some of the street scenes of that period; however British cars of the 1930s and '40s in black were still a common sight till well into the 1960s. These two new cars were probably visitors to Exmouth on holiday; the Hillman was registered at Grimsby and the Morris in Hampshire. In the background is the Ionic colonnade of the stone-faced open-air swimming pool and the ragstone wall of Gunfield Gardens. The pool has gone the way of all open-air swimming pools in Britain; in 2010 it was replaced by a bowling alley and restaurant.

EXMOUTH is a seaside resort, but at the west end of the seafront, on the corner of the Exe estuary, the harbour was still busy with commerce and three coasters were unloading cargoes when this picture was taken on 1 September 1965. In the foreground the Dutch coaster *Auriga-G* of Groningen is unloading timber at the east quay and through the rigging and slings we see the coal hoist unloading Yorkshire coal from the British coaster *Burtonia* of Goole direct into railway wagons on a siding on the north quay. At the same time, though not in the picture, another Dutch coaster, *Nautic*, also of Groningen, was unloading paper pulp on the south quay. In the background are holiday chalets on the west quay.

Commerce has given way to leisure here as in many other parts of Britain in the last 50 years. The coastal trade has left Exmouth and the harbour is now a marina for pleasure craft, entirely surrounded by three-, four- and five-storey flats with pitched roofs.

EXMOUTH The Exmouth-Starcross ferry is one of the oldest in south-west England, having been established in the 8th century by the Bishop of Sherborne to connect his lands on both sides of the River Exe. He set up a stone cross at the landing steps on the other side of the river, hence the name Starcross ('stair-cross'). Exeter Corporation bought the ferry in 1267 and leased it to private operators. In 1845 the Corporation sold it to the South Devon Railway, which built a wooden pier from the down platform of Starcross station in 1846; the SDR became part of the Great Western Railway in 1876. From the opening of Exmouth harbour in 1865 the ferries plied from stairs in the harbour entrance, as in this picture. The ferry passed in 1869 to the Exe Bight Oyster Fishery & Pier Company, then in the 1880s to a Finnish sailor named Gronberg, in 1891 to the Exmouth & Great Western Ferry Company, and in 1898 to the Devon Dock, Pier & Steamship Company, owners of the PS *Duke of Devonshire*, which we shall see later at Dartmouth. In its heyday in the 1930s there were two vessels in service and 16 round trips a day on this 20-minute passage, timed to meet trains stopping at Starcross, then named Starcross for Exmouth. In this way the GWR could compete with the LSWR/SR's Exeter-Exmouth branch for passengers to and from points west. The Devon Dock, Pier & Steamship Company still owned and operated Starcross ferry at the time of this photograph in 1948, when the MV *Exonia* was only a year old. She was 55 feet long with accommodation for 172 passengers, the most commodious vessel ever to ply this passage. With internal cone propellers, she could draw less than 2 feet of water to berth at Starcross at low spring tides. She was withdrawn in 1973 and sold to Torquay.

Today the ferry is operated by Exe-to-Sea Cruises from April to October only. It has a landing stage at the same place in the harbour entrance and all the structures on the left of this picture have been replaced. *George Greenwood*

BETWEEN TEIGNMOUTH AND DAWLISH The 20-mile stretch of the Great Western Railway between Exeter and Newton Abbot is probably the most scenic and spectacular railway in Britain, running by the wide estuaries of the rivers Exe and Teign with panoramic views to the wooded hills beyond, interspersed by this run along the foot of the cliffs beside the sea punctuated by tunnels through the red sandstone bluffs between the bays. This was the passengers' view from a Plymouth to Manchester train by the Parson & Clerk rocks between Teignmouth and Dawlish on 4 October 1962, headed by ex-GWR No 5934 *Kneller Hall* piloting a BR 'Warship' Class diesel locomotive.

NEWTON ABBOT *King George V*, first in the lineage of the Great Western Railway 'King' Class 4-6-0 locomotives in 1927, heads a down passenger express at Newton Abbot station on 4 October 1962, two months before retirement for preservation. The brass bell on the buffer beam was a gift from the Baltimore & Ohio Railroad when the locomotive took part in the American company's centenary celebrations in 1927. The 'Kings' were Britain's most powerful locomotives in their time with a tractive effort of 40,000lb but their weight limited them no further than Plymouth, Bristol and Wolverhampton. BR allowed them to venture further to Shrewsbury and Cardiff and refitted them with double chimneys. *King George V* is now in the Museum of the Great Western Railway at Swindon.

TORQUAY was the head office of the Devon General Omnibus & Touring Company, although Exeter was the centre of the wide route fan around the county. The touring arm of the company, Grey Cars, offered day tours to beauty spots in Somerset, Devon and Cornwall. Devon General was one of the first companies to adopt the new Leyland Atlantean with Metropolitan-Cammell bodywork in 1958, and one of those is seen here in Torquay town centre on 12 July 1966.

Above: **DARTMOUTH** The veteran south coast paddle steamer *Consul*, of 1898, which we saw at Newhaven in Part 1 of this travelogue, ended its life in old home waters, restored to its original name, *Duke of Devonshire*, and the house colours of its first owners, the Devon Steamship Company, for its final role as an accommodation ship for sailing holidays at Dartmouth from 1965 to 1968. The *Duke* is seen here from the Kingswear shore with Dartmouth Naval College in the background on 2 July 1966. The Devon Steamship Company (renamed in 1898 the Devon Dock, Pier & Steamship Company) ran excursions from Torquay and Exmouth as far as Weymouth and Plymouth, serving Lyme, Teignmouth, Brixham and Dartmouth on the way. During the First World War the *Duke* was requisitioned for minesweeping in the Mediterranean, then returned to south Devon service in 1921. In 1933 it was sold to P. & A. Campbell, but only laid up at Exmouth and sold on to Cork Harbour Commissioners as a tender and excursion steamer. Alexander Taylor purchased it and brought it back to Devon for excursions from Torquay in 1936-1937.. In 1938 it was sold to Cosens & Company of Weymouth and renamed *Consul* for cruises to Lulworth Cove, Swanage and Bournemouth. In the Second World War *Consul* was on contraband patrol for the Royal Navy, based at Weymouth. It was converted to oil firing in a post war refit and resumed excursions to Bournemouth with special duties in the Solent and Spithead. Cosens withdrew *Consul* in 1962 and it was bought by South Coast & Continental Steamers for Sussex excursions in 1963 and was back on its former Weymouth to Lulworth run for its last season in 1964 - but still under the SC&C flag in competition with its former owners, and running evening cruises from Weymouth as far as Yarmouth (IOW). Finaly *Consul* passed to her seventh owner, Sail-a-Boat Holidays at Dartmouth, in 1965. At age 70, the last surviving Victorian paddle steamer in British waters, it went to the breakers in 1968.

Above right: **DARTMOUTH** is seen again across the River Dart over the foredeck of the ferry *Adrian Gilbert* at Kingswear landing stage. Dartmouth's GWR station, which can be seen on the river bank opposite (left of the stanchion), was actually a steamboat station with a floating landing stage for a ferry to take passengers to the railhead here at Kingswear, and sold tickets for the combined ferry and railway journey. The passenger ferry was started by the South Devon Railway in 1864 and inherited by the GWR in 1876; it is popularly associated with the 520-passenger screw steamer *Mew*, which operated the service from 1908 till 1954. At the time of this photograph, 8 September 1965, the passage was worked by the 150-passenger motor vessels *Adrian Gilbert* and *Humphrey Gilbert* (two Devon maritime explorers), built by Blackmore at Bideford in 1956 and continued in service at Dartmouth till 1976. British Railways sold the ferry rights in 1972 to Dartmouth Borough Council and the service is now run by the Dartmouth Steam Railway & Riverboat Company. *Adrian Gilbert* was sold for further service on the Gravesend-Tilbury ferry, then on the Falmouth-St Mawes passage. The Dartmouth company also operates the former River Dart paddle steamer *Kingswear Castle* of 1924 on its old run upriver to Totnes. *Kingswear Castle* was restored by the Paddle Steamer Preservation Society at Chatham and returned to the Dart in 2012.

Below: **KINGSWEAR** In this closer view of the ferry landings at Dartmouth in August 1955, the floating landing stage for the railway ferry, with an arched roof and a long, covered passenger bridge, is seen on the left of the Royal Dart Hotel, while the vehicular ferry slipway is on the right at the foot of the main street.

Above: **KINGSWEAR** and its two ferries from Dartmouth are also seen on 8 September 1965. The two ferry landings were on the left and right of the Royal Dart Hotel, the balconied Regency house on the river front. The railway ferry, *Adrian Gilbert* (left), is approaching the floating stage with its arched canopy, and the railway trainshed and coach sidings can be seen beyond it. On the right the vehicular ferry, a raft with a small diesel tug lashed alongside, is approaching a stone slipway; this is the lower ferry, which dates from 1365. Early ferries were rowing boats for passengers and a raft for horses propelled by long oars. Steam power came in 1867. The car ferry is now owned and operated by South Hams District Council.

Left: **KINGSWEAR** Long lines of railway carriages in BR crimson, against the wooded hills on 8 September 1965, are a sign of the time when Kingswear was a busy terminus for local and long-distance trains before BR curtailed its operations at Paignton in 1967. There were 19 arrivals and departures a day in the 1952 timetable. The regular branch-line trains connected at Newton Abbot with the Paddington-Penzance main line, and through trains to Kingswear included the 'Torbay Express' from Paddington, the 'Cornishman' from Wolverhampton, the 'Devonian' from Bradford and unnamed through trains from Sheffield and Liverpool. The journey from Bradford took 10 hours 18 minutes on weekdays and 11 hours 16 minutes on Saturdays. The schooner *Olivia* of Jersey (left) and the fishing ketch *Boy Eric* of Lowestoft are double-berthed at the wharf, which was closed to freight in 1964; branch-line freight ended in 1965. The carriage sidings and former goods yard between the station and the wharf are now a car park and boat store.

Right: **KINGSWEAR** Inside the terminus of the former GWR branch from Newton Abbot, a Class 103 diesel multiple unit awaits departure for Paignton on 2 July 1966. The line opened in 1864 as a branch of the 7-foot broad-gauge South Devon Railway, later the GWR, and was converted to standard gauge in 1892. BR closed the last 6 miles of the branch from Paignton to Kingswear in 1967, but the Dart Valley Railway took over the next day and kept the section open. The trails of white steam alongside the river estuary against the backdrop of wooded hills is still one of the sights of Dartmouth today, if only from Easter to October. The railway is a commercial operation, not relying on volunteer labour.

Left: **BRITANNIA HALT** One mile up the branch from Kingswear terminus was this quaint wooden halt with a platform less than one carriage long, a canopy covering the whole platform and two gas lanterns under the canopy. It was accessible only by steps from the road leading down to the slipway to the Higher Ferry, a 'floating bridge' crossing the river on a cable. The location is Noss, but the halt was named after the Britannia Royal Naval College on the other side of the ferry passage at Dartmouth, and was a request stop for the naval cadets. In this 1955 picture we see the guard's van at the end of an up goods train running along the east bank of the river. The halt fell out of use and in 1988 the railway company demolished it as the structure had begun to lean dangerously backwards over the river.

Below: **PAR** The down 'Cornish Riviera Express' stops at Par, junction for Newquay, in the summer of 1949. The train left Paddington at 10.30am, first stop Plymouth, next stop Par at 4.02pm, then Truro, Gwinear Road and St Erth, arriving in Penzance at 5.25pm. It is headed by GWR 4-6-0 locomotive No 5098 *Clifford Castle*, built at Swindon in 1936 and scrapped in 1962. Par signal cabin (left) on the south end of the up platform, was built in about 1879 and extended in 1893. The cabin is now a listed building and still operates the points and signals for the main line and the Newquay branch with an electronic panel supplementing the lever frame. The covered footbridge has been replaced by a modern one without a roof.

Above: **NEWQUAY** A Southern National bus loads at the Western National bus station in Newquay for the journey to Ilfracombe in August 1949. Such long and arduous journeys through the hilly and sparsely populated south-western peninsula were a feature of Southern and Western National operations, with both single-deckers and double-deckers, to link the towns not directly connected by railway. The Southern and Western National Omnibus Companies served the respective areas of the Southern and Western Regions of British Railways (ex-SR and GWR) – Ilfracombe was on the Southern and Newquay on the Western. This bus has been re-bodied with post-war Eastern coachwork on a 1929 Leyland chassis, registered in Norfolk. The bus station office (right) displays panels advertising day coach excursions. Today Newquay bus station is in Manor Road and this location in East Street at the corner of Trebarwith Crescent is now unrecognisable. The smart dress of the period, as worn by the young couple here, would be conspicuous in Newquay today.

NEWQUAY Seaside coach parks provided an interesting array of second-hand, vintage coaches in the post-war period due to the dire shortage of vehicles caused by wartime requisition of coaches for troop transport and restrictions on new construction. These two old coaches, on a day excursion to Newquay in August 1949, were operated by G. Julian of Grampound Road, a village between St Austell and Truro. Both were second-hand vehicles: the 1929 AEC (left) from Nottingham, and the 1930 Dennis (right) first owned by the Royal Military Academy at Sandhurst, Berkshire. Although the bus on the left is the elder of the two, it looks as if the chassis, which dates it, was re-bodied in the mid-1930s. These two vehicles represent the transition in single-deck bus and coach design from what was designated 'normal control' (right), with the driver behind the engine under a protruding bonnet, to 'forward control' (left) with the driver in a half-width cab beside and above the engine. The buses are parked in a yard off Crantock Street behind the Methodist church on Wesley Hill. In non-conformist Cornwall there were three Methodist churches in Newquay at that time. Today this church is an 'open learning centre' and coaches no longer park here as the yard is on the junction with a new street, Manor Road, built along part of the disused railway to the harbour.

NEWQUAY This is the harbour in August 1949, with the town ranged along the clifftops above the sandy bays in the background. Towan Blystra was the old name of the village that grew up here by the original harbour; the name Newquay was adopted when the harbour was rebuilt in 1586. The present harbour was built in 1849 with railway sidings along the two piers in this picture for the export of china clay from the hinterland. The harbour branch, technically a long siding, extended from the site of the present passenger terminus with 1 in 4 and 1 in 6 cable inclines through a tunnel down to the harbour, where the sidings were shunted by horses. This was a busy harbour in the 19th century with pilchard fishing, while ketches and schooners brought coal for mine pumps and loaded Cornish china clay, copper, iron and lead ores.

Today's Newquay is a modern town as no building antedates 1876, the year when the Cornwall Minerals Railway offset its losses with passenger trains along the line from Par. In 1896 the GWR took over the line and promoted Newquay as a seaside resort. The last china clay schooner left the harbour in 1921, as that traffic had moved to deep-water berths at Par and Fowey. The harbour branch closed with the last fish train in 1926. The 1930s and 1950s saw the heyday of the holiday trade with many new hotels. Much of the route of the harbour siding is now used as a public footpath. There is still a good fishing fleet here though the harbour is used largely by pleasure craft. *George Greenwood*

Right: **POLPERRO** Pilchard fishing boats lie in the rocky outer harbour at Polperro, 3 miles west of Looe on the south coast of Cornwall, on 1 August 1960. The 'FY' port of registry, Fowey, is 5 miles west. The post-war fleet of about 40 fishing boats has declined to about 13 boats today, and the inner harbour is used mainly by pleasure craft. Boats no longer berth in the outer harbour since the construction in 1978 of a hydraulic floodgate across the entrance of the inner harbour to protect boats from storm damage and the houses from flooding; boats are imprisoned in the harbour on windy days, when the gate remains shut. Pilchards have declined in numbers and are no longer the staple fish catch of Polperro. The catch is now mixed: bass, crabs, lemon sole, mackerel, monkfish, pilchard, pollock, rays and turbot. There is a cold store on the inner harbour and fish is sold to markets at Looe and Plymouth and to continental buyers.

Left: **ST IVES** The harbour and old town are viewed from the rocks at Pedn Olva on 27 September 1962. This ancient fishing port was the principal pilchard fishery station in Cornwall in the 19th century, and copper and tin ores and roadstone were also shipped out. The harbour is sheltered by the stone pier (right) built in 1766-70 by the famous civil engineer John Smeaton and extended in 1888-90. The harbour light was erected in 1832. As the fishing and mineral industries declined, artists and holidaymakers came to sustain the town's prosperity, drawn by the clear light, the firm, clean sands and the quaint granite streets, alleys, courtyards and cottages of the old town on its narrow northern promontory. The town, originally Porth Ia, takes its name from St Ia, a 5th-century Irish woman Christian missionary, who settled here.

PENZANCE is seen from the harbour on 3 October 1962. This is the furthest west town and railhead in England, and in the foreground is the berth for the ferry to the Isles of Scilly. In the harbour are two F.T. Everard coasters, and on the skyline in the background are St Mary's parish church (left) and the white dome of the old Market House (extreme right), converted to the Trustee Savings Bank. The only freighter from Penzance today is the one to the Isles of Scilly and the harbour is crowded with pleasure craft and fishing boats.

PENZANCE-SCILLY ISLES The deserted deck is viewed from the bow of the Isles of Scilly Steamship Company's MV *Scillonian* on the 36-mile passage from Penzance to Hugh Town, the capital of the Scilly Isles, in a force 7 wind on 29 September 1962. The *Scillonian* was built by John Thornycroft & Co at Southampton in 1955. This service carries passengers and cargo but all the other passengers on this trip had gone below because of the sea conditions. Land's End can be seen on the horizon left of the bridge. The turbulent sea off Land's End is caused by the confluence of sea currents.

NEW GRIMSBY This harbour in a bay on the west coast of the isle of Tresco is the main landing place for the island and its famous sub-tropical gardens. It is seen here from an inter-island ferry boat from Hugh Town arriving on 2 October 1962. The stone pier is equipped with a crane, a wharfinger is preparing to catch the ropes and tie up, and a few passengers await the return trip to Hugh Town. The old port for Tresco was Old Grimsby in a bay on the east coast of the island. There was one, circular road on Tresco, linking New Grimsby, the Abbey Gardens, Old Grimsby and Dolphin Town; it was a narrow, rough, stony track used only by tractors and trailers.

HUGH TOWN Scillies inter-island ferrymen Guthrie Pender (left), skipper of the motor launch *Southern Queen*, and Lloyd Hicks (right), skipper of the motor launch *Swordfish*, wait on the pier to meet the passengers from Penzance for the outer isles on 2 October 1962. Hugh Town, the capital of the islands, is on the main island, St Mary's, and the ferries connect it with the four other inhabited islands of Tresco, St Martin's, Bryher and St Agnes. Hugh Town pier was built in 1750.

Norfolk

POPPY LINE There I was in the middle of a field, about to take a photograph of the poppies among the barley in this view between Sheringham and Weybourne, when a train emerged out of the landscape. I had no idea there was a railway nearby. The train was a two-car, green, BR Derby lightweight diesel multiple unit of 1955 on its way from Cromer to Melton Constable, the last remnant of the former Midland & Great Northern Joint Railway, in August 1961. This line closed in 1964 but was taken over by volunteers for preservation and reopened for service in 1975 as the North Norfolk Railway, running 5½ miles from Sheringham to Holt and branded 'The Poppy Line'. This north-east corner of Norfolk was called 'Poppyland' by Clement Scott, a Victorian columnist in *The Daily Telegraph*, and he made it a fashionable area to visit.

BURNHAM MARKET village green on the B1155 road from Docking to Holkham is seen first on 16 May 1962 – a placid scene with a modest BP petrol station on the left and a 1959 Austin A35 van parked on the right. At that time Burnham Market was the terminus of the ex-GER west Norfolk freight branch from Heacham, which closed in 1964.

The equivalent view on 30 August 2013 shows the rise in motorcar ownership in the second half of the 20th century. There was hardly a car to be seen in the first picture, in contrast to the second, where there is hardly a parking space to be found (the space behind the red car had just been vacated before the photograph was taken). Today North Street (left), Front Street (right) and the B1155 road through the green are overwhelmed with parked cars that disfigure this attractive village. Otherwise the scene has been enhanced by maturing trees, the cottages are unchanged or restored, and the overhead wire poles have gone (except the one on the extreme right, now without crossbars). Many of the homes around the green have been converted to estate agencies, restaurants and shops selling expensive clothes, gifts, arts and crafts as the village has become a Mecca for holiday cottages and retirement homes for wealthy people, mainly from London and the Home Counties. Most picturesque old towns and villages of England are now not worth a picture because they are spoiled by motorcars.

CAMBRIDGE On 18 May 1958 Drummer Street bus station is in a glade of mature trees with the station offices and waiting room under a steep pitched roof on an island platform in the middle of the road. Three bus companies are represented here: the Eastern Counties Omnibus Company, of Norwich (first on the right), Premier Travel, of Cambridge (second right), and the United Counties Omnibus Company, of Northampton (left). The two 'omnibus companies' were in the Tilling/BTC group that was nationalised from 1948 and their buses were post-war Eastern-bodied Bristols, the Eastern Counties in red and cream and the United Counties in green and cream. Premier was an independent company and this second-hand, ex-Southdown wartime utility Weymann-bodied Guy is in Premier's blue and cream.

Cambridge bus station is still here with trees on the right, but occupies a smaller site. The island buildings have gone, the number of loading bays has been reduced and the buses line up side-by-side in a row to a front-loading platform on the right with an overall canopy, and have to reverse out into the path of buses entering the station. None of the bus companies represented in this photograph is to be found here today as they have all been sold to new companies.

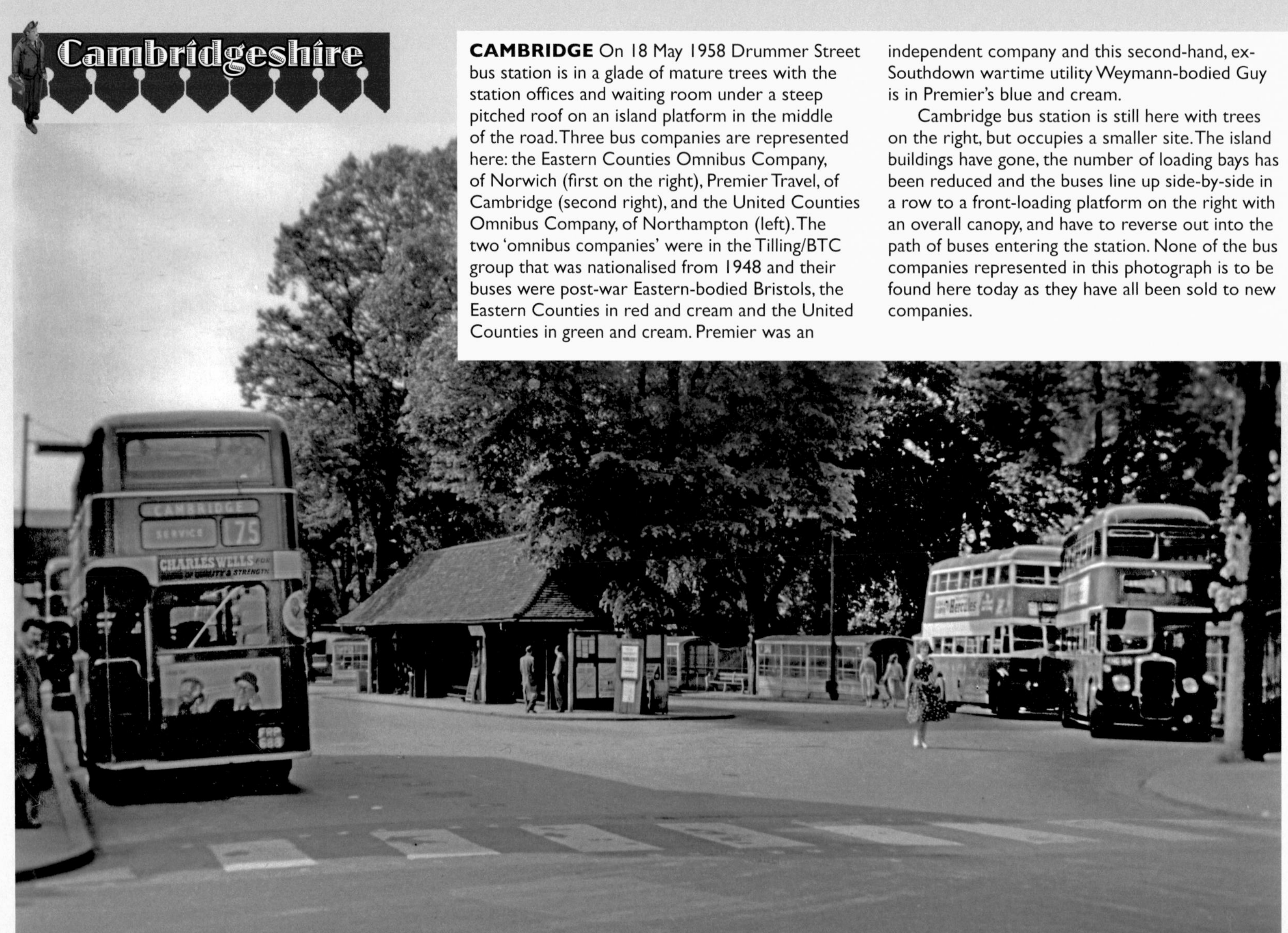

BOSTON Railways across the flat fens of west Norfolk, north Cambridgeshire and south Lincolnshire feature little in the way of cuttings, embankments, bridges or viaducts, and most highway crossings are on the level with the railway and were paved with timber until late in the second half of the 20th century. This is Maud Foster, the crossing of the Skegness-Nottingham line and Frithville Road on the northern outskirts of Boston, on 15 June 1970, featuring a Great Northern Railway signal cabin, heavy timber crossing gates, timber paving, the Italianate GN railwayman's house, a GN semaphore signal on a latticed steel post and a row of telegraph poles carrying the railway's internal telephone lines. The timber signal cabin, mounted on a brick locking room, had a 12-lever frame controlling this and two nearby level crossings. The cabin, cottage and signal in this picture all dated from 1877.

Sections of line across Lincolnshire were singled in 1981, and this section is single from Sibsey to Hubbert's Bridge, except through Boston station. Maud Foster signal cabin was removed in 1985 as this and other crossings along the line are now protected by colour-light signals and barriers automated by mechanical treadles or electric currents triggered by approaching trains. This crossing has been repaved in asphalt with steel panels flanking the rails. The cottage was still there at the time of writing and the line was still controlled by traditional mechanical signalling and semaphore signals, but due for complete modernisation.

HUBBERT'S BRIDGE

Left: **HUBBERT'S BRIDGE** was a quaint, wooden halt, with derelict oil lanterns, alongside the South Forty Foot Drain in Holland Fen on the line between Boston and Sleaford, also pictured here on 15 June 1970. The line and the halt are still open today for trains between Nottingham, Grantham and Skegness but the track converges from double to single immediately east of the platforms and the halt has been rebuilt with platforms paved in asphalt, a steel and glass shelter, tall electric lamp posts, and small metal nameplates. The brick goods shed on the left has gone and the stockade of old railway sleepers that fenced the former coal yard from the down platform has been replaced by a timber post-and-wire fence.

Right: **GRIMSBY** British Railways ran these large single-deck tramcars on the Grimsby & Immingham Electric Railway to carry workers to Immingham Dock, which was developed by the Great Central Railway in 1906-12. The railway was opened by the GCR to Immingham (town) in 1912 and Immingham Dock in 1913. These original GCR cars, built between 1911 and 1915, were still in service when the line closed in 1961. They were built by the Brush Electrical Engineering Company at Loughborough, 53ft 2in long with 72 seats. Car No 3 in front was built in 1911. With the growth of industries along the way from 1948, the service was supplemented by ex-Newcastle and ex-Gateshead single-deck bogie tramcars in 1948 and 1951 respectively. The cars ran right around the clock on a basic half-hourly service with extra cars at peak times, when a total of 19 cars were in service, including six of these big GCR cars in convoy for the change of shift at Immingham Dock.

The line was single on bullhead rail on sleepers with passing loops and a 500-volt overhead wire, and ran alongside a steam freight line on a 5-mile straight across the flat, semi-industrial fenland between the two towns. In addition, there was 1¼ miles of double street track in Grimsby and half a mile of single track on street in Immingham, where cars reversed for the 1-mile extension of 1913 on roadside reservation to the dock. The line passed to the LNER in 1923 and to BR in 1948; the former company's carriage liveries gave way to BR multiple unit green with the 'lion and wheel' emblem on the sides. Owing to the peak-time congestion of tramcars, the street section in Grimsby closed in 1956 and the Grimsby terminus was cut back to Cleveland Bridge (over the railway to Alexandra Dock), where this picture was taken on 18 July 1958. Buses replaced the closed section, but many workers obviously came here by bicycle. Fares on the remaining 6½ miles to Immingham Dock were 1 shilling single and 1s 6d return. The off-peak and night service was replaced by buses in 1959 on the zigzag 11-mile road route. The electric railway closed with the opening of a direct motor road to Immingham Dock in 1961.

IMMINGHAM Eight cars stand at Immingham Dock terminus of the Grimsby & Immingham Electric Railway on the same day. The two cars at the end of the line are ex-Gateshead & District bogie cars built in 1927 and sold to BR in 1951 when Gateshead tramways closed. They would take up service after the first six ex-GCR cars have cleared the dockers at the next change of shift. The GCR, Newcastle and Gateshead cars on this line were the only clerestory-roofed stock still run by BR at that time. Thanks to BR's purchase and life extension of the ex-Gateshead single-deckers, two of them from this line are now preserved at the National Tramway Museum, Crich, and at the North of England Open Air Museum, Beamish, back in County Durham.

BROCKLESBY station, on the main line from Sheffield to Grimsby and Cleethorpes, is a good example of architectural stations found on great country estates. It was built on the 50,000-acre estate of Brocklesby Hall, seat of the Earl of Yarborough, Charles Anderson-Pelham, a philanthropist, model landlord and chairman of the Great Grimsby & Sheffield Junction Railway (later the Great Central). He hoped the coming of the railway, in 1848, would improve the prosperity of his tenant farmers. The railway company had a good standard of station architecture, by Weightman and Hadfield of Sheffield, and the Earl insisted that this station was built of red brick with limestone dressings in the Jacobean style with Dutch gables and his own private waiting room. The station was 1½ miles from the hall and the village of the same name and passengers were scarce for this noble station. This picture was taken from the island platform looking west on 15 June 1970, one year after the withdrawal of station staff, and the platforms are in need of weeding. Four tracks ran through here because of the heavy freight traffic, but one track had been removed by the time of this picture. Brocklesby Junction signal cabin (right) was built by the GCR in 1914 and controlled the junction east of the station where the line divided to Grimsby and to Immingham Dock and New Holland. West of Brocklesby, beyond Barnetby, the line divided to Lincoln, Gainsborough and Scunthorpe. The station closed in 1993 and the signal cabin was decommissioned in 2015 following resignalling. Both listed buildings, the station house is now a private residence and the signal cabin is owned by Network Rail.

NEW HOLLAND PIER

NEW HOLLAND PIER This windswept wooden railway terminus on a quarter-mile-long pier on the Lincolnshire bank of the Humber was the landing place for the ferry passage to Hull from 1848 till 1981, when the suspension road bridge upriver replaced the ferry. Trains from Grimsby connected with the railway-owned ferry. The coal trucks on the centre road of this three-track layout were for coaling the ferry steamers. The coal was trans-shipped from the trucks on the pier by small, pneumatic-tyred, four-wheel 'tubs', towed by small electric tractors up and down the bridge to the landing stage and manhandled on deck to the stokehold hatch. Motorists using the ferry had to drive along left-hand (west) platform and turn right behind the bufferstops to access the suspension bridge down to the landing stage – on a gradient of 1 in 9 at low tide.

There were other ferries across the Humber from Roman times, but New Holland ferry, which began in 1803, was the sole Humber crossing by 1930. New Holland was named after a creek used by smugglers of Dutch gin. The Great Grimsby & Sheffield Junction Railway took over the ferry in 1846, then built the pier and opened the railway from Grimsby in 1848. For a few months of 1848 New Holland and Hull were on the East Coast railway route from London to Scotland via Peterborough, Grimsby, Selby and York, passengers and mails crossing the ferry, till a continuous and more direct railway link was completed further inland. The railway ferry passed in turn to the GCR, LNER and BR.

The pier is now owned by New Holland Bulk Services, exporting wheat, barley and rape seed and importing animal feed, aggregates and stone. The wooden platforms, station buildings and signal cabin are still there, but the space between the platforms is covered by conveyors and pipelines to the pier head.

NEW HOLLAND PIER This was the way we crossed the Humber from Lincolnshire to Yorkshire on foot and by car before the suspension road bridge opened in 1981. BR still ran coal-fired paddle steamers on this passage until 1978, superseded by a diesel-electric paddler. It was a 20-minute passage from here to Hull on the Yorkshire bank, seen on the distant horizon. The PS *Tattersall Castle*, seen berthed on 16 June 1970, was built in William Gray's yard at West Hartlepool in 1934 for the LNER, like her sister ship on this passage, *Wingfield Castle*. These side-loading car ferries replaced older vessels that had to load and unload vehicles by crane. The passenger accommodation was forward of the bridge and the vehicle deck was aft. The third vessel on this passage was the identical PS *Lincoln Castle*, built by A. & J. Inglis at Glasgow in 1941. Two were in service while one was kept spare. In 1948 the *Tattersall Castle* was the first paddle steamer in the world to be equipped with radar, to cope with Humber fogs. She retired from service in 1973 and *Wingfield Castle* in 1974, when BR drafted its 1947 diesel-electric paddler *Farringford* from the Solent to maintain the two-ship service. Humber ferries were always paddlers because of the shallow draughts required for this wide river with its many sandbanks. The *Lincoln Castle* was the last coal-fired paddle steamer in British waters when it retired from service in 1978, leaving the *Farringford* to soldier on alone till the ferry closed in 1981. The *Tattersall Castle*, much altered, is berthed as a floating restaurant at Victoria Embankment, Westminster.

HUMBER FERRY We are now crossing the Humber on the foredeck of the 1934 PS *Wingfield Castle* from New Holland to Hull on the same day. The radar scanner can be seen on the extreme right. The wind was singing in the rigging and the paddle wheels threshed the water with a regular rhythm while the heartbeat of the pistons could be felt underfoot. Sister ship *Tattersall Castle* is passing on the left on passage to New Holland.

WATFORD GAP Part of a line-up of Standerwick and Scout 'Gay Hostess' double-deck coaches is seen at Watford Gap service station on motorway express service from London to north-west England on 12 September 1965. This was the first year of the integrated motorway express services operated by Ribble Motor Services of Preston through its two subsidiary express coach companies, W. C. Standerwick of Blackpool and Scout Motor Services of Preston, which had been taken over by Ribble in 1932 and 1961 respectively and still operated under their separate names. These are all Metropolitan Cammell-bodied Leyland Atlanteans of 1960-61, fitted out by Weymann with luxury seating, serveries and toilets. There were 34 seats upstairs and 16 downstairs, and smartly dressed hostesses served food and drinks. The first four coaches in the line are destined for Colne, Blackburn, Blackpool and Blackpool; others in the line were going to Skipton, Preston and Keswick.

LEICESTER Lorries on the A6 trunk road through the city mix with local traffic and tramcars in this photograph taken outside the railway station (right) on London Road in 1948. Passengers stand on the steps of the conductor's platform, ready to alight, as inbound tramcar 135 on route 1, Belgrave to Western Park, approaches the stop for the station, followed by a 1947 Vauxhall car. An oncoming tramcar is climbing the slope from Granby Street. London Road station was rebuilt by the Midland Railway in 1892 with this long, west-facing, arcaded portico in orange-brown terracotta with separate levels and arches for arrivals and departures by cab. At this time Leicester had four railway stations – Belgrave Road, Central, London Road and West Bridge – but this is now the city's only one.

The portico and booking hall survive as listed buildings but the platforms were completely rebuilt in the 1970s and '80s. The new inner ring road now passes through this location with a three-way junction in front of the station, and the handsome buildings beyond the station have been demolished. The white buildings on the corner of Granby Street in the background still stand but two incongruous skyscrapers, one in profiled concrete, the other with blue panels, now form the backdrop to this view.
George Greenwood

WARWICK Church Street leads from the central crossroads to St Mary's parish church with its 174-foot tower; the arch under the tower leads into Northgate Street. On 6 July 1958 a Midland bus stops on its way to Leamington. The Birmingham & Midland Motor Omnibus Company (BMMO) designed and built most of its own buses in its central workshops at Edgbaston from 1924 to 1970. Its post-war single-deckers were of the underfloor-engine design with full-width fronts and front entrances, like this 1950 model S10 with a BMMO chassis and engine and an 8-foot-wide, 44-seat Brush body to BMMO design. The buses, painted overall red, carried the fleet name 'Midland' on the side panels and the company was branded 'Midland Red' on stop flags, timetables and publicity. The company operated more than 1,000 local and limited-stop services from 28 depots throughout Warwickshire, Leicestershire, Worcestershire, Herefordshire, Shropshire and south Staffordshire as well as parts of neighbouring counties.

BIRMINGHAM Three Corporation buses in dark blue and cream emerge from Colmore Row to join Congreve Street in Victoria Square on 16 May 1959, with the Council House (right) and the Town Hall (left) as a noble backdrop. These were Birmingham's distinctive standard buses of the period with identical bodies by Crossley, Metropolitan Cammell and Saunders Roe on Crossley, Daimler and Guy chassis; they were in service from 1950 to 1977. Bus stop flags in Birmingham were circular, both for the Corporation and the Midland, the latter having a 'circle and bar' sign based on a bus wheel and tyre with the company name across the bar. Two Midland buses can just be seen in Congreve Street loading outside the Art Gallery, marked by the 160-foot clock tower known as 'Big Brum'.

The Council House, built in 1874-79, housed the city council chamber, committee rooms and offices. The grand, classical Town Hall with its Corinthian colonnades on a massive, rock-faced, arcaded base was built in 1832-37 for public assemblies and concerts. The architect was Joseph Hansom, who invented the Patent Safety Cab, the revolutionary, two-wheel, two-passenger 'Hansom cab', in 1834. This was held to be more stable than other horse-drawn carriages because of its fine balance with the axle below the passenger seat and the driver standing behind and above. By 1896 there were 7,586 Hansom cabs in London alone; they were the Victorian forerunners of the motor taxicab. The tall Victorian Gothic building behind the Town Hall is the Liberal Club of 1885, demolished in 1965 to be replaced by an incongruously modern extension of the central library, built in 1973.

The whole of this scene is now a pedestrian zone and Congreve Street, which brought the main road from Dudley into the city, has been wiped off the map and blocked by grey, grim, concrete extensions of the library and the municipal buildings. the expanding Midland Metro now runs a tramline through the south side of Victoria Square past the Town Hall.

WEDNESBURY Buses from West Bromwich (right) and Walsall (yonder) meet at this strategic junction of the Black Country, the White Horse, on 7 July 1958. Here the A41 trunk road from London to Birkenhead, which is also the main road from Birmingham to Wolverhampton, forks left from Bridge Street into Holyhead Road, and Lower High Street forks (right) into Wednesbury town centre. The West Bromwich Corporation bus is a 1951 Weymann-bodied Daimler in two-tone blue and cream. This was the terminus of route 75 from Birmingham through West Bromwich, run jointly with Birmingham Corporation; it was formerly operated solely by Birmingham trams with the same route number. Beyond is the connecting Walsall Corporation bus in overall blue. At one time this three-way junction was the terminal meeting place of tramways from Birmingham, Walsall and Bilston and a triangular junction was laid to link the three lines. South Staffordshire Tramways' pioneer electric line from Bloxwich via Walsall terminated here in 1893 and the company later operated a 'Black Country Through Car' from Bilston to Birmingham via White Horse junction from 1912 to 1924. Then the three lines were cut back here to terminal stubs and from 1930 to 1939 Birmingham's were the only trams operated from the White Horse.

The White Horse Hotel (the white building seen over the roof of the West Bromwich bus), which gave its name to this junction, was demolished in the 1990s and the entire scene is unrecognisable today because of 'improvements' to the A41. St John's Church, built in 1846, was demolished in 1985. Left of it, Lloyd's Bank, near the apex of the junction, was demolished and rebuilt soon after this photograph was taken, but even the new bank has now closed. In the left foreground is a nice example of a blue police-public telephone post, but that has gone too.

OLD HILL station was a typically humble little stop in the south Staffordshire Black Country on the former Great Western Railway from Smethwick Junction to Stourbridge Junction. When this picture was taken on 3 March 1962 trains stopped here on a half-hourly service between Birmingham Snow Hill and Stourbridge Junction and passengers changed here for the branch to Dudley. This line was also the route of semi-fast trains from Snow Hill to Worcester and Hereford. Here was a soot-stained, wooden booking office, waiting room and canopy on the up platform for Birmingham (left), the signal cabin sat on the down platform, and down passengers waited in an open-fronted, wooden shelter (extreme right). The two platforms were slightly offset as tracks diverged at this end of the station for the Dudley branch (off left) and at the far end for the Halesowen branch (off right). The large running-in board on the left reads: 'Old Hill Change here for Halesowen, Windmill End branch and Dudley'. The Halesowen branch closed to general passenger service in 1927 but the line went on beyond Halesowen to Longbridge and workmen's trains continued to use the branch to the Austin motor works there till 1958 and goods trains till 1964. The Great Western water tank stood at the up end of the down platform, handy for engines off the Halesowen branch. The Dudley branch closed to passengers in 1964 and to goods a few years later. Trains still stop at Old Hill today but the old wooden station was badly damaged by fire in 1967 and rebuilt in 1968 looking like a Portakabin dressed in pale grey brick with a felted concrete top and plastic weatherboarding above the windows and doors.

The signal cabin closed in 1973 following resignalling. Old Hill now has a half-hourly service of diesel multiple units on an extended run up through Snow Hill to Shirley or Stratford and down to Stourbridge or Worcester.

WOLVERHAMPTON British Waterways' narrow boats *Severn Dolphin* and *Mendip* are double-berthed on the Birmingham Canal at Broad Street bridge on 25 June 1960. Trolleybus wires turn the corner into Railway Street (left). *Severn Dolphin* of Worcester (left) was inherited from the Severn & Canal Carrying Company on nationalisation in 1948 and was carrying coal from Brownhills to the Royal Worcester porcelain factory from 1959 to 1961. *Mendip* of Northwich (right), new to British Waterways in 1949, made two round trips a week with chocolate crumb from Cadbury's Knighton factory on the Shropshire Union Canal to Cadbury's Bournville factory on the Worcester & Birmingham Canal. These two boats displayed British Waterways' corporate colour scheme of yellow and blue, disliked by boatmen used to the traditional company colours. Here at Broad Street British Waterways had a depot for trans-shipment to local road haulage, a fitting shop for servicing boat engines and a washroom for crews. *Mendip* was retired in 1961 and is now restored as a working boat of the 1880s at the National Waterways Museum, Ellesmere Port.

WOLVERHAMPTON LOW LEVEL STATION The classical Italianate façade of the former GWR station is seen on 25 June 1960, with a Wolverhampton Corporation bus parked on the forecourt. The station was built in 1854-55 and was a main stage on the routes from Paddington to Birkenhead and Aberystwyth. It closed to passengers in 1970 together with Birmingham Snow Hill two years after Paddington-Shrewsbury trains were diverted via Birmingham New Street and Wolverhampton High Level. Low Level station was retained as a railway parcels depot until that closed in 1981.

The listed main building seen here on the down side was bought by Wolverhampton Corporation and renovated with the intention of using it as a transport museum. However, this project foundered as the building was transferred to the Black Country Development Corporation, which did nothing with it during its term of office. By the time the development corporation was dissolved, Wolverhampton Corporation no longer had the funds to develop a transport museum. The building, with its magnificent, classical entrance hall, is now Wolverhampton Grand Station, an events centre for banquets, conferences and weddings. The rest of the station has been demolished and redeveloped with blocks of flats and a hotel.

WOLVERHAMPTON LOW LEVEL STATION was the most northerly station on the original Great Western broad gauge. The first GWR standard-gauge train ran from Paddington to Birkenhead in 1861, and Wolverhampton Low Level remained the relay point to change engines. Viewed from the leading coach of a Birkenhead train at the north-west end of the station on 8 May 1960, No 4903 *Aston Hall* (right) is moving forward to take over from No 6000 *King George V* at the head of the train and take it on to Chester; a big 'King' had to hand over to a 'Castle' or a 'Hall' because of the limited axle load on bridges beyond Wolverhampton, and the 'Kings' were stabled here. A pannier tank engine stands in the shadow of Wednesfield Road bridge as a Wolverhampton Corporation bus crosses overhead. Although this picture was taken 12 years into the British Railways era, all three locomotives are of GWR pedigree, as are the water column, semaphore signals and signal cabin seen through the left portal of the bridge.

WOLVERHAMPTON HIGH LEVEL STATION The handsome, Italianate façade is viewed from Railway Drive on 25 June 1960 with its Romanesque arcading and windows and the arms of the Shrewsbury & Birmingham Railway in the pediment. The SBR withdrew its alliance with the LNWR before opening and teamed up with the GWR at the adjacent Low Level station. High Level was opened by the LNWR in 1852 on the route from Birmingham New Street to Stafford. In this picture, taken in the days of BR Midland Region, a billboard advertises cheap Sunday trips to Manchester for 11s 8d return and a sign on the canopy valance directs passengers to the left through a subway to the parallel Low Level station, although that station had its own road approach from Corn Hill. In the 1950s there were six lines radiating from Wolverhampton; now there are only three. During the electrification of the main line in 1964-67 BR demolished and rebuilt this station to make it look modern but, in that philistine decade, it resulted in the mean, austere, cubic composition of prefabricated concrete panels and windowless, pale grey brick walls that we have today. Its stark ugliness is ineffectively screened by a small grove of trees. Network Rail has earmarked this station to be rebuilt in the near future.

CHURCH STRETTON railway station, at 613 feet, is the highest point on the main line from Hereford to Shrewsbury. It was characteristic of Great Western main-line stations with its spacious platforms, wide canopies, ample architectural buildings, covered wooden footbridge, gas lamps, rock gardens and (though not seen in this view) large, legible station nameboards with white cast-iron capital letters on black boards in white frames on the platform ends where the trains run in. The station was relocated and rebuilt here in 1914, and its opening stimulated the town to develop as a small, secluded inland resort with hotels, shops and villas on the foothills of the Long Mynd in this beautiful valley where a Roman road passed between two great ranges of wooded hills. In this picture we are looking south along the line towards Craven Arms and Ludlow in June 1960. The station became an unstaffed halt in 1967 and the buildings were demolished and replaced by two stone shelters with sawtooth valances on the canopies and an open footbridge.

IRONBRIDGE This general view of the town centre on 19 June 1960 shows part of Iron Bridge & Broseley railway station in the foreground with the level crossing, footbridge and station offices on the Severn valley line of the former GWR from Worcester to Shrewsbury. We see the road from the station crossing the famous iron bridge, built in 1779, over the River Severn. This was the first iron bridge in the world and gave its name to the town. The bridge closed to motor traffic in 1934. Over the bridge we see the arcaded Market House in the Market Place (centre) and St Michael's parish church on the hillside. The railway closed in 1963 and the track north of Bridgnorth was dismantled but the line south of Bridgnorth to Kidderminster was reopened progressively from 1970 to 1984 for restoration as the Severn Valley Railway. Iron Bridge & Broseley station nameboard was saved by the author and is now in the Coalbrookdale ironworks museum, where the iron bridge was built. This district was the cradle of the Industrial Revolution based on coal and iron found in these hills. At the time of this photograph Ironbridge was a quaint, sleepy, run-down, industrial town, with ironbound kerbs in the streets, ornamental ironwork on street lamps and buildings and fishermen in coracles on the river. Today Ironbridge has a heritage trail leading tourists to five museums on original industrial sites but there are no longer coracles on the river.

NOTTINGHAM MIDLAND station frontage on Carrington Street was photographed on 20 March 1960. The Midland Railway rebuilt the station in 1900-04 with this west-facing Edwardian baroque portico and clock tower in orange-brown terracotta trimmed with red sandstone on the crest of the road bridge spanning the railway tracks. The bridge was rebuilt and widened at the same time. Like Leicester London Road station, the long façade is a screen with Romanesque arches giving access to a covered forecourt for cabs and carriages under a glass roof. The grand booking hall behind has yellow ochre sandstone walls with pilasters, Romanesque arches and portholes on a dado of dark green glazed tiles and is lit by a barrelled skylight. Electric overhead wires indicate that this was a city of trolleybuses with a line branching down Station Street (left). Nottingham's large trolleybus network closed in 1965-66. A green Corporation AEC motorbus rolls by towards the city centre.

BUXTON Among the properly dressed promenaders in The Crescent on 22 April 1962 we see a Silver Cross pram and a 1957 model of the 1949-style Ford Anglia car, both in black. Dark grey stonework, iron and glass colonnades and landscaped parkland are characteristic features of this hilly spa town. At just over 1,000 feet, Buxton is the highest town in England and, like Bath, has been a spa since Roman times. The building on the left is the north end of The Crescent, a Georgian leisure centre with assembly rooms and accommodation for visitors to St Ann's Well. Next is the Cavendish Arcade of shops built around a thermal bath of 1854. Buxton now has nine springs of warm, pale-blue mineral water that gush from 3,500 to 5,000 feet below ground in this limestone country.

ALTRINCHAM & BOWDON

These 1931-vintage, 1,500-volt DC electric multiple unit trains were still groaning along the 8-mile line from Manchester Oxford Road through Stretford to the more salubrious Cheshire suburbs of Sale and Altrincham south of the Mersey when this picture was taken at the Altrincham terminus on 9 April 1969. Meanwhile work was commencing on the half-mile between London Road South Junction and Oxford Road to re-electrify the whole line to 25,000 volts AC. This non-corridor compartment stock was built by the Metropolitan Cammell Carriage & Wagon Company, Birmingham, for a joint venture by the LNER and the LMSR to operate the first railway in Britain to be electrified at 1,500 volts DC, being the suburban section of the former Cheshire Lines Committee route from Manchester to Northwich and Chester. The CLC was a joint committee of the Great Northern, Midland and Great Central railways, thus from 1923 it was still a joint operation of the LNER and LMSR. The line's high-voltage AC era did not last long as the section reverted to a 750-volt DC light railway in 1992, the first leg of Manchester's new tramway system.

CHESTER One of Chester City Transport's seven new Massey-bodied Guy buses of 1961-62 stops in Eastgate Street in the evening sunlight and shadows of 16 August 1962 on route 5 to Saltney. These were Chester's first 8-foot-wide buses, 30 feet long with forward entrances. The bonnet and radiator was designed for a South African order and was known in Britain as the 'Johannesburg front'. Guys dominated the Corporation bus fleet after the war and Chester had the last Guy bus built for Britain, in 1969.

Eastgate Street was the main thoroughfare of the city before the inner ring road was built; it is now totally pedestrianised. Behind the bus is the large Grosvenor Hotel and the Georgian stone arch over the street with its Victorian clock turret, marking the site of the former fortified East Gate of the city. Georgian archways now carry the continuous circuit of city walls over the main streets north, south, east and west. On the right is one of the 'rows' of two-tiered shops with the first-floor row of shops fronting a covered walkway, integrated into the building, above the ground-floor shops, a feature found only on the main streets of this old city centre.

CHESTER GENERAL STATION Steam in the evening sunshine at the west end of the station on 11 August 1962, with locomotives left, right and centre and a group of trainspotters on the end of the platform. A GWR 'Manor' Class 4-6-0 idles in the bay platform (left), and an LMSR Fowler 4MT tank engine has two vans in tow in the shadow of Hoole Road bridge. Chester No 5 signal cabin stands beyond the bridge and in the background is the profile of a locomotive on the turntable within the triangle of tracks between Chester station and those left to Shrewsbury and Holyhead and right to Birkenhead.

ELLESMERE PORT station is seen looking east along the Hooton-Helsby line to the Mersey Iron Works (right), Burnell's steel mills (left), Stanlow oil refinery, Ince power station and the hills of the Delamere Forest. This line was part of the GWR and LNWR joint line from Birkenhead Docks to Manchester, opened in 1863, and this station was one of the original Jacobean-style buildings in red sandstone with curved Dutch gables and clusters of tall chimneys in red pressed Ruabon brick. Ellesmere Port No 3 signal cabin sits on the west end of the eastbound platform. The photograph was taken in September 1962 from the road bridge opened in 1961 to replace the busy town centre level crossing on the main street.

When the station opened in 1863 it was named Whitby Locks after the nearest village and the terminal locks on the railway-owned Shropshire Union Canal from Ellesmere, Shropshire – before the town of Ellesmere Port was built. Burnell's steel works shut down in 1962 and the Mersey Iron Works, founded by the Wolverhampton Corrugated Iron Company, carried on till closure in 1997. The Wolverhampton company migrated here in 1903, building houses for the workers and creating the suburb of Wolverham; it was the town's biggest single employer with 1,850 workers in 1939. The two iron and steel works together once employed 2,600 people.

ELLESMERE PORT Manchester Ship Canal railway tank engines stand outside the engine shed and workshop at West Junction on the Helsby-Hooton main line in September 1962. This repair shop serviced the seven MSC locomotives that worked a 20-mile network of industrial railways east and west of the town, using the BR main line in between. West Junction served the docks, ship canal wharves, the large cattle food and flour mills seen on the skyline, and North Road industrial estate, including Bowaters' pulp and paper mills and two oil companies. East Junction served the oil refineries and ship canal wharves at Stanlow. The ship canal railways at Ellesmere Port were isolated from the rest of the MSC railways, which ran alongside the canal from Manchester to Warrington, but the entire system has since closed together with the decline of industry and shipping and the growth of road haulage. The dockside granaries and mills in the background of this picture have all been demolished.

ELLESMERE PORT Here the Shropshire Union Canal locked down to the trans-shipment docks connecting with the River Mersey and, from 1894, the Manchester Ship Canal, cut along the south bank of the river estuary. In this picture, taken in September 1962, are two flights of locks, dating from 1795: broad locks in the centre for barges and narrow locks on the right for narrow boats being lowered and lifted between the upper and middle basins. The lock between the warehouses in the background took boats to the lower level, where goods were exchanged with Mersey barges and seagoing ships, either directly or by storage in the warehouses. The port facilities were much enlarged and aggrandised by the civil engineer Thomas Telford in 1830-44 with a large new trans-shipment dock on the middle level and a complex of massive stone warehouses serving both lower and middle levels. Some Black Country narrow boats ventured into the ship canal to berth at Stanlow oil refinery and they were the last regular cargo-carriers to use the Shropshire Union Canal, in 1955. The smokestack marks a hydraulic station that powered capstans, hoists and cranes and pumped water into the middle basin when it ran short.

Today all the giant trans-shipment warehouses of Telford's grand terminus have gone and the wharves of the middle and lower basins have been redeveloped with a hotel, flats and shops in a mock industrial style of architecture, as seen in the comparison view taken on 23 September 2003.

ROCK FERRY pier and landing stage were still open for use by Mersey tugmen calling ashore for supplies, by local yachtsmen and fishermen to store their dinghies, by anglers and by promenaders for 18 years after the ferry closed. The users were charged 1d in the tollhouse at the pier entrance. The tug berthed here at the landing stage is a 'Cock' tug of the Liverpool Screw Towing & Lighterage Company. The stage retained the old ferry fog bell tower and navigation light and one of the two arched-roof passenger shelters. The lean-to extension was added during the Second World War to convert the building for storage. The stage was 150 feet long and 45 feet wide, about the size of a Mersey ferry steamer of the period 1930-60.

Birkenhead Corporation ran a half-hourly ferry service from here to Liverpool until closure in 1939. The service extended to New Ferry until that pier was wrecked by a ship in 1922. The Eastham ferry company's double-ended paddle steamers also called at Rock Ferry on the way between Eastham and Liverpool till that service ended in 1929; they were the last paddle steam ferries on the Mersey. The pier and landing stage closed in 1957 and were removed.

ROCK FERRY This old ferry landing place on the Cheshire bank of the Mersey gives its name to a southern suburb of Birkenhead. The ferry passage from The Rock, in the parish of Bebington, to Liverpool dated from 1660. The red sandstone slipway (left) with its runway for horse waggons was built in 1820 and steam ferries plied from here from 1832. King George III stayed at the original Rock Hotel while hunting in Wirral, hence the Royal Rock Ferry Steam Packet Company was formed in 1836 to operate the ferry, to build a river wall and to develop the neighbourhood. The ferry service was acquired in 1896 by Birkenhead Corporation, which built the iron pier in 1899; it was 260 yards long with a suspended bridge down to the floating landing stage, from which this picture was taken in 1952. The slipway had to be shortened to accommodate the stage. The ferry service closed in 1939 but the pier remained open for tugmen, fishermen, yachtsmen and promenaders till 1957. It was then replaced by the south pier of Tranmere oil terminal in 1960. Ashore we see the Royal Rock Hotel, rebuilt in 1836, the single-storey Doric-style bath house for sailors, converted in 1896 to cottages, and the trees of Rock Park, a bosky residential estate of Italianate villas built in 1836-50 for Liverpool merchants and 'professional gentlemen' attracted here to rural Wirral by the introduction of steam ferries.

In the 1970s the hotel and Doric cottages were demolished and the cottages replaced by a block of flats; the river front is now a scene of utter dereliction, but the Royal Mersey Yacht Club and the Tranmere Sailing Club still have their headquarters here and use the slipway to row out to their yachts moored in the river.

ROCK FERRY station was on the GWR/LNWR main line from Chester to Birkenhead and these three tracks were the bay terminus of the Mersey Railway from Liverpool Central Low Level. The Mersey Railway was the first steam railway in Britain to be electrified, in 1903, and this was one of the original electric trains, pictured at Rock Ferry in 1954; they survived in service till 1956. The line from Liverpool ran in tunnel under the Mersey and Birkenhead, surfacing at Tranmere. It opened in 1886 with condensing steam locomotives, but the smoke in the 4 miles of tunnel with 1 in 27 and 1 in 30 gradients forced electrification. The American firm of British Westinghouse Electric did the job in 1901-03 with no interruption to the steam service! There was a power station in Birkenhead feeding 650 volts DC through a side conductor rail, the centre rail returning current to the power station. The head office, car sheds and workshops were at Birkenhead Central station. This original stock was built by G. F. Milnes, at Hadley, Shropshire, on Baldwin-Westinghouse Electric bogies in 1900-02. A branch ran to Birkenhead Park, where it met the Wirral Railway, and when the LMSR electrified the Wirral lines in 1938 with new metal stock, these wooden trains also ran from Liverpool through to New Brighton, Monday to Saturday, and to West Kirby on Sunday, but no new LMSR stock came to Rock Ferry. The Mersey Railway, however, remained independent till nationalisation in 1948, and its dark Indian red trains were repainted in 1950-54 to BR multiple unit green. The power station closed in 1959, when the railway switched to the national grid. Rock Ferry station had six platforms, four on the four-track main line and two on the Mersey Railway, spanned by a covered wooden footbridge with four wooden lift towers. The Liverpool-Rock Ferry electrification was extended under the name Merseyrail to Hooton in 1985, Chester in 1993 and Ellesmere Port in 1994 with new BR stock. Rock Ferry station has been reduced to two platforms, with open footbridge and ramps, on the double-track through electric line; there are no main-line services and no freights to or from the docks.

BIRKENHEAD A ship in dry dock (left) lies alongside Birkenhead Woodside railway station (right) in this photograph from August 1954. There was a row of six Grayson, Rollo & Clover Graving Docks along the Mersey bank south of Woodside station. When a ship was afloat on entering or leaving the nearest dock, its hull and superstructure towered high above trains entering and leaving the station. The ornate iron canopy covered the luggage and parcels loading bay on the south side of the station. The line-up of railway-owned vehicles drawn up under the canopy for loading comprise an Austin lorry, a Dennis van, two Karrier vans and another Austin lorry, all built in the 1940s. The clock tower of Birkenhead Town Hall dominates the skyline.

BIRKENHEAD WOODSIDE A Paddington train is drawn up in Platform 1 inside the northernmost passenger terminus of the legendary Great Western empire in May 1959. Paddington-Birkenhead through trains ran via Banbury, Birmingham, Shrewsbury and Chester from 1861 till 1967. The Chester-Birkenhead line terminated at Grange Lane in 1840 and was extended to Monks Ferry in 1842 and diverted to Woodside in 1878. The twin-arched trainshed spanned five platforms and a motor road for parcels and luggage vans between Platforms 1 and 2. The clock tower of Birkenhead Town Hall is framed in the fan screen of the arch in the centre of this picture. Trains also ran from here along the GWR route to Pwllheli and on joint services with the Southern Railway/Region via Birmingham to Bournemouth and Margate. The GWR/BR(W) shared this terminus with the LNWR/LMSR/BR(M) for stopping passenger services on the joint lines to Chester, Helsby and West Kirby via Hooton. The West Kirby service closed in 1956, that to Margate in 1959 and to Bournemouth in 1961. Woodside station closed in 1967 and the remaining local services terminated at Rock Ferry to connect with the Mersey Railway. The listed station building was demolished and replaced by office blocks and bus and car parks. Nikolaus Pevsner's architectural guide to Cheshire described Woodside station as 'one of the few really good main line termini outside London'.

BIRKENHEAD WOODSIDE The railway and bus terminus at Woodside ferry was the focal point of Birkenhead and faced Liverpool waterfront across the half-mile-wide River Mersey. A ferry has plied from Woodside on the road from Chester to Liverpool since about AD 1150. Stage coaches from Chester terminated here from 1762 and the GWR to Birkenhead (1840) was extended here in 1878. Woodside was a hamlet around the original ferry landing on the birch-wooded headland before the new town of Birkenhead was developed from a nucleus by the priory with the advent of steam ferries in 1820. Beside the trainshed in the first view, from August 1954, the green country buses of Crosville Motor Services, Chester, stand on the slope of Chester Street loading for Loggerheads, Chester and Heswall, while another leaves for Ellesmere Port. The first two buses are Eastern-bodied Bristol Ks, a 1948 low-bridge and a later model high-bridge. Crosville buses served Cheshire and north and mid-Wales. Down on the ferry approach are Birkenhead Corporation's blue buses. On the left is the Mersey Motor Works on the corner of Bridge Street and the black, gabled lairage of the Mersey Cattle Wharf, which imported Irish cattle. The long pedestrian crossing has no refuge island; these

'zebra' crossings were introduced nationally in 1954 after area trials from 1949.

The busy bus station is seen again on 10 August 1961. The single-decker on the right is a 1948 Bristol L6A for Meols. The Lodekkas behind, bound for Burton, Heswall and Ellesmere Port, were new in 1960. The twin-arched trainshed (right) was the northern terminus of the Great Western Railway from 1878 till 1967.

This scene has changed completely. The railway terminus has been replaced by two red-brick office blocks, the motor works site is a car park and the lairage site is a 'business park'. The Liverpool waterfront buildings are now dwarfed by a new skyline of black, white and khaki skyscrapers of concrete and glass.

BIRKENHEAD WOODSIDE
Stranger in town: Ribble Motor Services of Preston, which ran local and express services in Lancashire, Westmorland and Cumberland, also operated these double-deck, 50-seat, Leyland Atlantean coaches on the X25 service between Liverpool and Bristol, calling at Chester, Whitchurch, Bridgnorth, Cheltenham and Gloucester on the way. They ran through the Mersey Tunnel between Birkenhead and Liverpool. The Metropolitan-Cammell coachwork was fitted out by Weymann with reclining seats, a toilet and a servery for refreshments. The bus is pictured on Chester Street by Woodside station on 10 August 1961.

BIRKENHEAD WOODSIDE This 1939 Birkenhead Corporation, Massey-bodied Leyland TD5, at Woodside bus station in August 1954, was one of a batch of 40 that set the style for the buses Massey built for Birkenhead over the next 19 years (with the exception of the angular, wartime, utility design). This 1930s streamlining, with well-rounded roof domes and windows, the semi-circular ends of the lower saloon windows, the flared skirting of the lower side and back panels and the curved body flange to the front nearside mudguard, was seen on the streets of Birkenhead until 1975. Like all Birkenhead buses built from 1933 to 1939, this was built as a 'gearless' bus with a hydraulic torque converter for the ease of former tram drivers not used to changing year following the transition from trams to buses in the period 1925-37. The 1939 batch was converted to manual gear change by 1959. Parked on the left are a 1953 Austin A35 car, a 1932 Morris Minor two-seater sports coupé and a wartime Crosville bus. The North Circle route 90 embraced the two contrasting sides of Birkenhead: the slums and industry of dockland and the villadom west and south of the park.

BIRKENHEAD WOODSIDE The rounded and flared body style with stout window pillars inherited from the pre-war designs can be seen on this 1949 Massey-bodied, Gardner-engined Guy bus at Woodside in August 1954. Like all Birkenhead buses of the period it had blue leather seats, chrome handrails and Art Deco lampshades. Under the bonnet was a six-cylinder Gardner diesel engine with a deep-throated throb and gear whine. This was one of a batch of 15 Guy Arabs that served Birkenhead from 1949 to 1963. A total of 85 Daimlers and Guys with this style of bodywork (including 15 rebodied wartime Guys) operated in Birkenhead in the 1950s and '60s, the last nine, built in 1956, retiring from service in 1972. This bus, No 147, is pictured alongside Woodside railway station for the New Chester Road service to Bromborough (6 miles for 5d then). Birkenhead Corporation bus routes extended well beyond the borough boundary and the blue and cream livery was seen as far afield at Eastham, Clatterbridge, Heswall, Thurstaston, Moreton and New Brighton. A Wolseley 450, also of 1949, is facing us in the single-file car park (left) through the middle of the bus station for ferry commuters.

BIRKENHEAD WOODSIDE One of the 15 Massey-bodied Daimlers of 1950 for Birkenhead Corporation is pictured on the corner of Hamilton Street and Shore Road (left) at Woodside. It has just arrived on route 73 from Irby via Arrowe Park on 10 August 1961. These buses were in service till 1964. Birkenhead Corporation continued ordering new front-engine, rear-platform Guys and Leylands with half-width cabs and open radiators until they were no longer available. The last traditional Leyland PD2 batches in 1967 overlapped Birkenhead's first orders for rear-engine, front-entrance Daimler Fleetlines in 1964 and was followed by Leyland Atlanteans in 1968. Parked right of the bus is a 1948 Austin car of a design introduced in 1939.

BIRKENHEAD WOODSIDE From the foot of the floating road that was used for the vehicular ferry service from 1868 to 1941 we see the twin-screw passenger ferry steamer *Bidston* arriving at the floating landing stage on the ebb tide in 1954. This steamer was built by Cammell Laird at Lower Tranmere in 1933. On the right are the barrel-roofed bridge and wooden waiting shed and the tower housing the navigation light and fog bell. We can also see Liverpool Cathedral in the background, a mile and a half away across the river. The stage dated from 1861 and the covered accommodation from 1863. It was said to be the oldest floating structure in the world when it was towed away in 1985 and replaced by the present Woodside stage.

BIRKENHEAD WOODSIDE The ferry steamer *Hinderton* arrives on the flood tide at Woodside landing stage in 1950 on the three-quarter-mile passage from Liverpool. Through the smoky haze of industry and shipping we can see a cargo ship in mid-river and the massive granaries at Coburg Dock, Liverpool (left). *Hinderton,* 484 gross tons, was built in 1925 and set the standard design for Birkenhead Corporation ferries in service for the next 35 years, being the prototype for her three consorts, *Thurstaston*, *Claughton* and *Bidston,* each 487 gross tons, which followed in 1930-33. They were all twin-screw steamers built by Cammell, Laird & Company at Lower Tranmere, each 158 feet long, 43 feet in beam, licensed to carry 1,433 passengers, and coal-fired to the end. Birkenhead Corporation always gave its ferry steamers local place names, Hinderton being the old name for Lower Tranmere. Two steamers plied the passage every 10 minutes in the peak periods and every 15 minutes in the off-peak, and one steamer plied hourly through the night until the night service ended in 1956. *Hinderton* also plied excursions upriver to Eastham and downriver to the Bar lightship in 1942-48 and was occasionally on charter to Wallasey Corporation as a relief ferry on Seacombe and New Brighton services. She was retired from service in 1956 after two mid-river collisions weakened her hull plates, and was scrapped in 1958. Woodside ferry was municipalised from 1848 and traffic peaked in 1919-41 and again in 1948-50 with between 10 and 14 million passengers a year. From 1950 passengers slowly drifted to the railway and road tunnels.

BIRKENHEAD The last Birkenhead steam ferry on the Mersey was the TSS *Claughton*, built in 1930 and pictured here on passage from Woodside to Liverpool with her birthplace, Cammell Laird's shipyards at Lower Tranmere, in the background on 9 June 1961. *Claughton* retired from service at the end of that year after plying the passage for 31 years, and was scrapped in 1962. The evening sunlight picks out the pale green hull of the Shell tanker *Sepia* (42,000 tons gross) in the fitting-out basin at Laird's shipyard, which employed more than 10,000 men when it was busy. The *Sepia* was in service till 1983. Oil tankers were taking over from colliers about that time and in the left background we can see Tranmere oil terminal, which opened in 1960. Oil was piped to storage tanks onshore, thence to Stanlow refinery near Ellesmere Port.

BIRKENHEAD This picture of the Mersey Bar lightship *Planet* in Egerton Dock, Birkenhead, on 15 August 1962, after a refit and repaint, is an interesting record of her original appearance, in view of her recent saga. This floating lighthouse, with no engine, was anchored to the sandbar at the mouth of the Mersey shipping channel 12 miles north-west of New Brighton, and was known to mariners as 'the lantern on the front door of Liverpool'. She was manned, owned and maintained by the Mersey Docks & Harbour Board, and had to be towed by tug to and from her station, being replaced by a large automatic navigation buoy when brought into dock.

This 125-foot steel vessel was built by Philip & Son at Dartmouth in 1959 and was fitted with a 1,000W electric globe with 124,000 candlepower, a radio beacon, radio telephony and a powerful fog signal. She was stationed on the Mersey bar with a crew of seven from 1960 till 1972. Then she was sold to Trinity House, London, rebuilt and, as *LV23,* served on three stations in the Thames estuary till 1989. Apart from Trinity House, only the Mersey and Humber port authorities provided their own lightships until the 1970s and the bar station was one of four manned lightships in the Mersey approaches, all now replaced by large, automatic buoys.

This vessel was sold for scrap in 1991 but saved by some Liverpool businessmen and towed to Birkenhead docks with the intention of restoring her to her original appearance. Following her Trinity House rebuild she has a higher prow and her superstructure is entirely different from what we see in this picture. She was open to the public alongside Seacombe mills on East Float from 2002 to 2004. She has been resold twice since and, with the word BAR again emblazoned on her sides, she became a floating bar and café in Canning Dock, Liverpool, from 2011 to 2016. In arrears of dock dues, she was then towed away by the Canal & River Trust, which added the cost of towage and berthing in Sharpness dock near Gloucester to the bill. She has since been resold and was last reported in 2019 at Sharpness awaiting collection by the new owner.

BIRKENHEAD Corporation's first diesel ferry, the TSMV *Mountwood*, of 1960, is in a storm light on the Mersey under a grim cloud over Birkenhead and its shipyards on 26 September 1964. This vessel was not built in those shipyards of her ancestors but by Philip & Son at Dartmouth, with Crossley diesel engines, and she was slightly smaller than the steamers at 152 feet by 40 feet, 464 gross tons, and licensed for 1,200 passengers. For the first time there was a saloon on the upper foredeck, restricting the business commuters' traditional counter-clockwise, four-abreast march around the open promenade deck enjoyed on the steamers. Following the merger with Wallasey Ferries under the new Merseyside Passenger Transport Authority and the Mersey Ferries flag in 1969 and a refit in 1990 for cruising, including a fully covered bridge, this vessel has been in Mersey ferry service longer than any other and is still on the roster today, renamed *Royal Iris of the Mersey* after one of the famous old Wallasey steamers, *Royal Iris* (1906-31).

BIRKENHEAD This stern view of *Mountwood's* twin sister, *Woodchurch*, shows her screws churning the water as she swings out from Liverpool landing stage on a flood tide and heads for Woodside on 14 June 1964. In the background is the silhouette of Birkenhead dockland (left) and Wallasey Town Hall (right) on the Cheshire bank. *Woodchurch* was also built in 1960, following *Mountwood* off the stocks and into service. She was laid up for sale in Morpeth Dock, Birkenhead, from 1981 to 1983, but then overhauled for further ferry service. After a major refit in 1989, again with a fully covered bridge, *Woodchurch* is also still in ferry and cruise service, now renamed *Snowdrop* after another old Wallasey ferry. A third and similar diesel ferry, *Overchurch*, from Cammell Laird in 1962, later refitted and renamed after another old Wallasey steamer *Royal Daffodil,* was laid up in 2013 and languishes in dock. The decline in the number of passengers accelerated from 1986 with a new bus service through the Mersey Tunnel. Seacombe ferry now runs at peak times only and since 2010 there has been no Woodside ferry service as such – just an off-peak river cruise on a triangular run that calls at Woodside, Liverpool and Seacombe. The two remaining ships also carry on an old Wallasey ferries tradition of cruises along the Manchester Ship Canal.

BIRKENHEAD The Great Western's farthest north railhead was Morpeth Dock goods station and sidings, where 4-6-0 locomotive No 6959 *Peatling Hall*, from Old Oak Common shed in west London, is pictured raising steam for its return trip with the evening fast freight, 'The General', to Paddington on 15 August 1962. There were numerous named fast freights and unnamed slow freights between Morpeth Dock and points on the GWR system in the Midlands, London and south Wales. The GWR aspired to reach Liverpool but ended up within sight of the famous waterfront across the river with the Royal Liver Building prominent. Goods were shipped across the river in barges from a basin inside the goods shed to GWR warehouses in Liverpool docks and direct to and from ships in dock or anchored in the river. This goods station was rebuilt in 1929-30, the basin was filled in and the marshalling yard was enlarged to a capacity of 850 wagons, shunted by GWR pannier tank engines, and goods were carried across the river by GWR lorries and vans using Woodside vehicular ferry and later the Mersey road tunnel. The goods station and yard closed in 1972. The adjacent Wallasey Dock was filled in and the whole site is now a waiting area for cars and lorries going aboard a vehicular ferry to Belfast, which berths at a new landing stage on the river wall between Woodside and Seacombe.

BIRKENHEAD These two 0-4-0 saddle tank dockside shunting engines, *Glanmor* and *Jessie*, both built in 1907, are pictured on the weed-overgrown sidings at Duke Street Wharf in 1951. They were owned by Cudworth & Johnson of Wrexham and leased to Rea Ltd, ship and tug owners, master porters and stevedores in the export of coal and iron ore from the adjacent wharf. *Glanmor* (right) was built by Hawthorn, Leslie & Company at Newcastle and *Jessie* (left) by Peckett & Sons at Bristol. On the right is a steam coal crane and on the left we see the stern of a cargo-passenger liner at Henderson's Wharf on the far, Wallasey side of the West Float.

BIRKENHEAD Three steam tugs of J. H. Lamey Ltd, Liverpool, are berthed at the former LNWR's Cathcart Street goods station on the East Float, and the floating crane *Mammoth* loads a Clan liner in Vittoria Dock in this general view of dockland on 22 October 1962. *Mammoth*, owned by the Mersey Docks & Harbour Board, was Dutch-built in 1920 with twin smokestacks and a 200-foot jib that could lift up to 200 tons. Cathcart Street warehouse was first used as a hostel for emigrants awaiting passage by sailing 'clippers' from the wharf to the Australian gold rush in the 1850s. The 'Emigrants' Depot', as it was called, opened in 1852 to protect the emigrants from the predatory spivs on Liverpool waterfront. As the docks were extended, Birkenhead exported coal, iron, steel, engineering, pottery, chemicals and railway locomotives and carriages from the industrial hinterland and imported grain, livestock, meat, heavy oil, molasses, timber and iron ore. By 1969 these docks were handling 40 per cent of the tonnage in the port of Liverpool. Today Vittoria Dock is used by mothballed ships and we see very little activity in the other docks between Birkenhead and Wallasey as trade has followed the shift to containerisation in new and larger docks at Bootle and Seaforth on the mouth of the Mersey.

BIRKENHEAD A ship of the Head Line, owned by the Ulster Steamship Company, discharges grain at Joseph Rank's Ocean Flour Mills, built in 1912, on the West Float in August 1954. To the right are Vernon's mill of 1898 and its post-war concrete silo, which stand on the site of the former Canada Works of Thomas Brassey, the world's greatest railway contractor. To the left of Rank's mills is Gill Brook Basin, the site of William Laird's first shipbuilding yard (1828-56) before it moved to the Mersey bank at Tranmere. The picture is framed between a railway goods wagon (left) and the stern of the Ellerman cargo-passenger liner *City of Liverpool* of 1949 on the Wallasey side of the docks. All the mills in dockland between Birkenhead and Wallasey have disappeared and Merseyside's only grain terminal and mill is at the new Seaforth Dock at the river mouth.

SEACOMBE The Rea Towing Company's steam tug *Dongarth* of 1922 leads this procession of cargo-passenger liners through Alfred Dock into the East Float in August 1954. Its towlines are secured to the bow of Alfred Holt's Blue Funnel liner *Polydorus* of 1944. Berthed on the left is the Shaw, Savill & Albion passenger liner *Gothic*, which had been used as a Royal Yacht for Queen Elizabeth and Prince Philip from Jamaica to Australasia and Aden on their tour of the British Commonwealth in 1953-54. Alfred Dock is the vestibule dock to the 2½-mile line of docks between Birkenhead and Wallasey, and the drawbridge on Tower Road has been raised for the passage of the ships entering the docks from the river at high water. Tower Road was a causeway across the docks from Birkenhead to Seacombe, with three drawbridges and one swing bridge that opened for the passage of ships and held up road and rail traffic between the two towns; there was a fifth dock bridge on Spike Road. With the closure of Morpeth and Egerton Docks and the infilling of Wallasey Dock, this drawbridge at Alfred Dock is the only one left on Tower Road, but spectacles like this will never be seen again.

SEACOMBE The 0-4-0 saddle-tank engine *Cyclops* of 1895 takes water in William Lee's one-road engine shed off Birkenhead Road in 1954; W. J. Lee specialised in general repair work on any dockside locomotives. This engine was built by Hudswell, Clarke at Leeds and worked at Woolwich Arsenal before being bought second-hand and rebuilt by Cudworth & Johnson of Wrexham and leased to Joseph Perrin & Sons Ltd, one of the Birkenhead dockside haulage contractors, based at a shed on Shore Road, Birkenhead. *Cyclops* was used to shunt the Mersey Cattle Wharf at Woodside, the flour mills at Seacombe and other industrial premises in dockland. The pit-prop across the buffer beam was for shunting wagons on an adjacent track! For its size *Cyclops* could haul long trains along the streets and soldiered on with its melodious chime whistle echoing against the mills and warehouses till 1964, when it was scrapped. The double-track dock railway alongside Birkenhead Road served the coaling stage for the steam ferries at Seacombe.

SEACOMBE Back in the days when two vessels ran direct between Seacombe and Liverpool, the 1958 TSMV *Royal Daffodil II*, the last tonnage built for Wallasey Corporation Ferries, is seen leaving Seacombe for Liverpool on 26 September 1964 as tugs escort an Ellerman cargo-passenger liner into Alfred Dock to berth in the West Float. The *Daffodil* was built by James Lamont at Port Glasgow, 149 feet by 46 feet, 609 gross tons, and licensed to carry 1,950 passengers. She was sold to Greece in 1977, partly rebuilt to carry vehicles aft on a ferry service out of Piraeus and renamed *Ioulis Keas II*.

SEACOMBE Wallasey Corporation buses unload at the ferry terminus in Victoria Place in 1954. Ten bus routes converged on this ferry and the buses were timed to meet the steamers, running every 10 minutes in the peak period and every 15 minutes in the off-peak. Alighting passengers entered under the grand, classical, 1930s Portland stone colonnade and Romanesque arch and walked through the booking hall, with its varnished Art Deco wooden kiosks, and down the bridge to the floating landing stage and the waiting ferry steamer. The bus conductors have already turned their rear destination blinds for the return journeys: 1 to New Brighton via Seabank Road, 4 to Saughall Massie Hotel via Moreton Shore, and 2 to Harrison Drive via Liscard. The buses seen here (from left to right) are two Metropolitan Cammell/Leylands built in 1946 and 1951 and an 8-foot-wide Weymann-bodied Leyland of 1952.

SEACOMBE This picture illustrates the colour scheme of Wallasey Corporation buses and the style of lettering and fleet numerals. The legend 'Wallasey Corporation Motors' was in gold leaf, shaded dark blue with the borough coat of arms in the centre. There were no advertisements till declining revenue saw their advent in 1952. The Metropolitan-Cammell Carriage & Wagon Company, Birmingham, built this style of bus body for Wallasey Corporation from 1937 to 1951 on Leyland and AEC chassis, and this is one of the 1951 stock on Leyland PD2 chassis. Wallasey had a total of 118 buses with this style of Metropolitan-Cammell bodywork and 101 of them were in service when this last batch arrived. The 1951 stock remained in service till 1972-73. Interior features were beige leather seats, French-polished mahogany window frames and beading on the ceilings, and a mock clock dial on the rear bulkhead showing boarding passengers the time of the ferry connection to Liverpool. The photograph was taken at the loading colonnade in Victoria Place at Seacombe ferry in glorious evening sunshine on 15 August 1962, the clock showing 7.25pm. Route 17 was the 'trip round the island', the most circuitous of the five routes from Seacombe to New Brighton, running through Poulton and Wallasey, 5¼ miles against 2¼ miles by the direct route 1.

SEACOMBE After unloading at the ferry tollhouse, the buses line up in herringbone order, backing up to the loading colonnade on the south side of Victoria Place as the passengers stream off the ferry. At departure time, the inspector will blow his whistle, all the cab doors will slam in quick succession and the buses will leave together in convoy like elephants nose-to-tail to disperse to all parts of the borough. There were loading bays for 17 buses here, including short workings, on the ten routes that terminated at Seacombe ferry. This picture was taken in 1950 when nearly all the buses were Metropolitan-Cammell-bodied Leylands built in 1937-48. The ferry buildings and bus station were rebuilt in classical red brick and Portland stone in 1930-33 to the design of the borough surveyor, Lionel Wilkinson. Atop the clock tower on the ferry tollhouse is a radar scanner to navigate both Wallasey and Birkenhead ferries in fog. The buildings on the right housed the ferry offices and workshops, a two-storey garage for 200 cars for ferry patrons, the bus inspector's office, a waiting room, a teetotal refreshment room and a confectionery kiosk. *George Greenwood*

SEACOMBE In the mid-20th century Merseyside was the biggest flour milling centre in Europe and second in the world after Minneapolis in the North American prairies. Grain arrived by ship from North and South America, Australia, India and Europe. Here we see ships berthed at the giant granaries and mills on the Wallasey side of the East Float at Seacombe on 22 October 1962. From the left are the Belgian ship *Schelde* at Buchanan's mills, dating from 1893, two smoking J. H. Lamey tugs lying alongside the Irish ship *Irish Rowan* at Paul Brothers' Homepride Mills, a third Lamey tug by the old granary of 1868, and a third grain freighter at the colossal new concrete grain silo belonging to the Liverpool Grain Store & Transit Company. We can also see Alfred Dock drawbridge raised and part of another ship loading at Vittoria Wharf, Birkenhead, on the right.

SEACOMBE & EGREMONT railway terminus was sited at the top of Victoria Place by the ferry and bus terminus at Seacombe, but three-quarters of a mile from Egremont. It was one of four obscure LNER railheads on the west coast of Britain, the other three being Southport Lord Street, Silloth and Mallaig. When this picture was taken in 1952 this quiet and lowly station saw only eight passenger trains a day on a route through mid-Wirral to Connah's Quay and Wrexham Central. The last two coaches seen here are ex-Great Central, the nearest dating from 1904. There were also goods trains delivering Welsh coal to coalyards. The Seacombe branch was owned by the Wirral Railway, later part of the LMSR, which ended its Seacombe-West Kirby service in 1938, leaving the LNER to continue running the Seacombe-Wrexham service. The LNER did not own the lines to Seacombe and Southport but had running powers to work the trains, having access over the former Great Central and Cheshire Lines. The Seacombe branch closed to passengers in 1960 and to goods in 1963. Wrexham passenger trains were diverted from Bidston to New Brighton and the trackbed of the Seacombe branch was replaced by the dual-carriageway approach to the second Mersey road tunnel, which opened in 1971. Wrexham trains now terminate at Bidston for connections with the Mersey and Wirral line electric trains.

POULTON We meet the dock engine *Cyclops* again on Duke Street, as it runs light between shunting duties towards the drawbridge that divides the East and West Floats and carries one of the three roads across the docks from Birkenhead into Wallasey. Ambling in reverse, the engine is about to overtake a horse and cart. Double tracks ran along the middle of Duke Street from this junction with Dock Road, Poulton, to Corporation Road, Birkenhead, the bridge being the frontier between the two boroughs. Goods trains took their place in the normal order of road traffic on Duke Street, dwarfing private cars and filing closely past buses on the joint cross-docks routes 10, 11 and 12. Buses on these routes were also subject to delays by ships passing the open bridge and by long BR goods trains across Duke Street alongside Corporation Road. The electric drawbridge here replaced a hydraulic swing bridge in 1931. On the right is the dock master's office by the West Float.

SEACOMBE Dock Road passed through the canyon of mills by the East Float and here, in 1954, we see a horse-drawn waggon preceding a Birkenhead Corporation bus dropping a passenger at the corner of Oakdale Road. The bus is a 1948 Massey-bodied Leyland on the Birkenhead and Wallasey joint route 12 from Charing Cross to Seacombe Ferry via Park Station. A 1947 Bedford articulated lorry is parked on the left, laden with sacks of flour. Behind it are Paul Brothers' Homepride Mills and beyond are Buchanan's Flour Mills, connected by footbridges, with their animal food mills on the right. Most of these mills have been demolished but a listed granary of 1868 has been converted to flats.

WALLASEY The classic Wallasey bus in the typically wide, quiet, tree-lined streets of Wallasey. This is No 93, one of the 1946 stock of Metropolitan-Cammell-bodied Leyland PD1s, at its terminal lay-over in Grove Road at the junction with Hose Side Road (ahead) and Warren Drive (to the left). This was the terminus of route 6 from Seacombe ferry. Bus 93 was sold out of service in 1959 to a dealer at Walmer Bridge near Preston and exported to Sarajevo, Jugoslavia, in 1960 for further service.

Wallasey route 6 followed a devious, zigzag route through streets broad and narrow, threading through Wallasey, Liscard and Egremont to Seacombe. It went via Belvidere Road, Rullerton Road, Mill Lane, Westminster Road, Grosvenor Street, Martin's Lane, Serpentine Road, Trafalgar Road, Brighton Street and Demesne Street to the ferry, returning via Church Road instead of Demesne Street. On fine summer Saturday and Sunday afternoons from 1947 the route was extended from Grove Road via Sandcliffe Road to New Brighton seafront, then from 1950 the extension was via Harrison Drive to Wallasey Beach. With the decline in the fortunes of public transport route 6 closed in 1965.

LISCARD & POULTON George, the friendly booking clerk, porter and general factotum at this other station on the Seacombe branch, poses with his luggage trolley of racing pigeon baskets on the up platform. The eaves of the station roof were extended to form a scanty canopy over the platforms. The view is looking west to Breck Road bridge and Bidston Moss. The station and coal siding, off Mill Lane, Poulton, lay in a rock cutting, hewn through the red sandstone of the Wallasey plateau, which deepened as the line passed through Poulton towards Seacombe. Access to this island platform was by a covered, wooden footbridge off the ramp to the coalyard, and trains left this side for Wrexham. The line was popular among Wallaseyans for a day return to rural Wirral stations, to Caergwrle Castle & Wells or Cefn-y-Bedd in Wales (see Part 6) for a walk and a picnic. The station closed to passengers in 1960 and to goods in 1963. Then from 1966 the rock cutting was widened to take a four-lane dual carriageway from the M53 Wirral motorway to the second Mersey road tunnel, from Seacombe to Liverpool, opened in 1971.

NEW BRIGHTON The J. H. Lamey tug *Alfred Lamey*, built in 1908, is seen on the Mersey off New Brighton on a windy 19 September 1964. New Brighton, on the corner of the Mersey and the Irish Sea, was a thriving seaside resort and saw a post-war resurgence in 1948-65. Most of the features we see in the background, the Tower Building, the Tower fairground, the Tivoli Theatre, the ferry pier and the pleasure pier, have all disappeared, but the trees (left) and Perch Rock lighthouse (extreme right) still feature.

The Tower Building of 1898 stood at the base of a latticed steel tower like Blackpool's but slightly taller and octagonal in plan. It was the tallest structure in Britain when it was completed in 1900, but it closed in 1914 for the Kaiser war, when neglect made it unsafe, and was dismantled in 1919-21. The Tower Building that remained housed a theatre and ballroom among the largest in Britain but was gutted by fire and demolished in 1969. Today New Brighton has reverted to its origin as a pleasant residential town for Liverpool businessmen.

NEW BRIGHTON Wallasey had a foretaste of the future when the Corporation took delivery of the first production model of Britain's first rear-engine, front-entrance double-deck bus, the Leyland Atlantean, in 1958. Wallasey Atlantean No 1 appeared at that year's Commercial Motor Show at London's Earl's Court and entered service in Wallasey on 8 December. It seated 77 passengers compared with the usual 56 and was easily adapted to one-man operation that resulted from staff shortages and rising costs in the 1970s. Wallasey had 30 Atlanteans, delivered from 1958 to 1961. The plain, rectangular, Metropolitan-Cammell bodies looked neat and smart in Wallasey's yellowy-green and cream colours divided by black beading and with the traditional lettering and fleet numerals on the side panels, but this presentation was changed under new management from 1961. No 9 was new when pictured in Virginia Road bus station, New Brighton, on 11 May 1960, loading for route 1 to Seacombe via Seabank Road. The Mark 1 Atlanteans served Wallasey till 1979 but this is still the basic design of modern double-deckers on the road today.

GREASBY Coke-fired steam lorries dating from the 1920s and '30s were still at work in the mid-20th century, and Liverpool dockland was their last stronghold. The Sentinel Waggon Works of Shrewsbury went on building steam lorries until 1950 and maintained a service depot at Duke's Dock, Liverpool, until 1957. The last steam lorry there worked between the mills and the docks in 1962. This Sentinel steam tar sprayer, dating from 1929, pictured working on Frankby Road, Greasby, in September 1954, was the last steam road locomotive in commercial use in Britain, working until 1984. It was a Sentinel DG4P: a double-geared (two-speed) four-wheeler on pneumatic tyres. It had a vertical boiler and chimney at the front of the cab, the engine slung under the chassis and chain drive (with two giant bicycle-type chains) to the back axle. It was built as a flatbed lorry for a Birmingham brickworks and was sold in 1942 to a Chester mineral water company. In 1944 Robert Bridson & Son, contractors, of Neston, converted it to a tar sprayer with a tar boiler on the back platform, heated by steam from the boiler in the cab; a small steam pump, spray bar and hand lance were fitted at the back. It worked on Wirral roads till 1968 and moved on to Lloyd-Jones Brothers of Ruthin, spraying Denbighshire roads until 1984, when it was retired. It languished till 1997, when it was sold for preservation. It is now restored to full working order and runs on steam rallies.

WEST KIRBY Outside the railway terminus (right) on Grange Road in September 1954 are two Wolseley taxicabs of 1937-39, a girl riding a bicycle with a basket on the front, and a 1949 Morris Isis car, with its bowed radiator and double windscreen, rounding the bend from Meols Drive. A 1952 Hillman Minx car is parked on the left and a boy on a scooter pauses before crossing the road. The railway station was rebuilt in 1896 at the western terminus of the Wirral Railway from Birkenhead, electrified by the LMSR in 1938. Beyond the station, the Edwardian baroque Barclay's Bank in red sandstone, on the corner of Meols Drive and Dee Lane, terminates the view.

WEST KIRBY The Crescent was the shopping centre of town and on this day in September 1954 we see, parked on the left, a 1931 Morris 8 car and a 1948 Austin A40 van, while on the right is a 1953 Rover 75 car. Today the iron and glass colonnade and the canvas sun blinds have disappeared and the three storey building with the decorative timber framework that terminates the view has been replaced with a stark, modern block. The shopping centre has moved to a supermarket in Dee Lane.

Part 4, Lancashire: Widnes to Furness

OLDHAM This Oldham Corporation Roe-bodied Leyland Atlantean bus was new when photographed in High Street on 13 June 1965; these were Oldham's first rear-engined buses. On the right is a perfect example of a cabmen's hut, now a rare piece of street furniture. Parked alongside is a Humber Hawk Series IV saloon car. Oldham bus routes were lettered to avoid confusion with tramway route numbers, although this designation could be the letter O or the number 0. The last Oldham tram ran in 1946 but the buses retained route letters until they were numbered in 1968. Oldham buses ran not only local services but also to Middleton, Mossley, Stalybridge, Ashton, Rochdale and Manchester (Cannon Street and Piccadilly). In 1969, one year after changing to route numbers, a Transport Act resulted in Oldham Corporation buses losing their identity in an amalgamation into the new South East Lancashire & North East Cheshire Passenger Transport Authority, later the Greater Manchester PTA.

MANCHESTER OXFORD ROAD

This 1931-vintage LNER/LMSR joint stock is working the Manchester South Junction & Altrincham Railway route from a bay platform at Oxford Road station on 9 April 1969. The service had been cut back the half-mile from South Junction (an adjunct of London Road station) while a start was made on re-electrifying this pioneer 1,500-volt DC line to 25,000 volts AC. These original three-car sets of compartment stock were built by the Metropolitan Cammell Carriage & Wagon Company, Birmingham, and the stock was almost identical in appearance to the LMSR's electric multiple units on its Watford and Ormskirk lines. Oxford Road station was on an LNWR/LMSR line across the south side of the city centre from South Junction to Castlefield Junction, where it joined the main Cheshire Lines route out of Manchester Central station. The Altrincham end of the MSJAR is illustrated on Page 133 of this travelogue.

The short-lived high-voltage AC line was replaced in 1992 by a 750-volt light railway operated by articulated tramcars on a through route from Altrincham to Bury, using the former railway roadbed but diverting to street tracks across the city from Central to Victoria stations, becoming the first line of Manchester's new tramway system, Metrolink.

WIDNES Britain's grandest transporter bridge spanned the Manchester Ship Canal and the River Mersey at Widnes (in the background) from 1905 to 1961, when it was replaced by today's high-level road bridge. This span, with a suspended moving platform, or 'gondola', was cheaper than a high-level road bridge to allow the passage of ocean-going ships on the canal. The gondola was suspended from an overhead trolley, or 'traveller', on rails, which groaned along its slow, weird, aerial voyage from Widnes to Runcorn with its load of cars, lorries, motorcycles and foot passengers suspended above the wind-whipped waters of the tidal Mersey for the 3-minute transit of the 330-yard gulf between the two piers. The gondola is seen above the ship canal, with the river behind the dividing wall, as it comes in to land at Runcorn on 14 July 1958.

The transporter bridge replaced the 700-year-old Runcorn ferry, immortalised in music hall comic verse by Stanley Holloway. The new structure not only worked more easily, quickly and safely than a ferry but also circumvented the wall that had divided the ship canal from the river since 1894. On the left is the London & North Western Railway bridge, built in 1863-69, carrying the main line between Crewe and Liverpool 75 feet above the ship canal, the same height as the span, or 'boom', of the transporter bridge. Beside the railway bridge we can see the concrete piers for the new, high-level, steel, bowstring road bridge that replaced the transporter in 1961.

There was a smaller transporter bridge upriver at Warrington to Crosfield's soap works; the ruined towers remain. Two working transporter bridges in Britain survive at Middlesbrough on the Tees and at Newport on the Usk.

WIDNES The elegant structure of the 190-foot-tall steel towers of the transporter bridge loomed large over the twin towns and dominated Mersey Street, Widnes, as seen in this picture on 18 May 1959. Bridge traffic queued down the street on to the pier, seen beyond the control room gantry, to await the next passage to Runcorn (Cheshire), saving drivers a 15-mile detour inland via the nearest fixed bridge over the river at Warrington and the swing bridge over the canal at Stockton Heath. It also saved the cost and demolition inherent in building approach embankments and viaducts to a high-level bridge, but the 20-minute transporter service with a capacity of 12 cars per trip was insufficient for the growing volume of road traffic in the 1950s, which led to the construction of the high-level bridge and approaches in 1961. The new bridge is now carrying ten times more traffic than it was designed for, so a new steel suspension bridge built to motorway standard, up-river between Warrington and Widnes, opened in 2018.

WIDNES This was the amazing view of the transporter bridge that passengers had from the train between London and Liverpool as it crossed the high-level railway bridge over the narrows of the River Mersey between the sandstone bluffs of the Runcorn Gap at Runcorn and Widnes. This picture, taken from the public toll footpath along the parapet of the railway bridge, shows the transporter gondola approaching Widnes pier on 18 May 1959 while cars queue along the pier waiting to cross on the next passage. St Mary's church lords over its brood of terraced houses on the headland on the Lancashire bank, and the Mersey widens again upriver towards Warrington.

The transporter bridge was built in 1905 for the Widnes & Runcorn Bridge Company and was taken over in 1911 by Widnes Corporation. It was a fantasy of lattice steel construction like a giant Meccano model that the cartoonists W. Heath Robinson or Rowland Emett might have designed. The twin steel towers on opposite banks of the river supported a steel girder span with a traveller that ran on rails suspending the gondola, which was 55 feet by 24 feet. The bridge was designed and constructed by the Arrol Bridge & Roof Company, of Glasgow, which also built the Forth railway bridge, the second Tay railway bridge, station trainshed roofs and the Humber road bridge. The firm closed in 1986 with the rundown of heavy industry in Britain.

Right: **BOLTON TRINITY STREET** A three-car diesel multiple unit passes Bolton West signal cabin as it takes the curve into the station on its way from Southport to Manchester Victoria, Rochdale, Halifax, Bradford and Leeds on 6 June 1968. The long, long footbridge spans this triangular junction at the north end of the station, and the clock tower of Bolton Town Hall is in the background.

These DMUs were built in 1961 by the Birmingham Railway Carriage & Wagon Company for the Eastern and Midland Regions of BR. They mainly served the populous south of Lancashire and Yorkshire and became known as the Calder Valley units. They were powered by four Rolls Royce engines mustering 720 brake horse power.

WIDNES Victoria Square was the town's bus station. This 1950 Widnes Corporation all-Leyland bus in cherry red and ivory is standing at the stop outside the Town Hall (off right) on 18 May 1959. St Paul's parish church is on the left. The bus station is now in Vicarage Road behind the church.

WIGAN This picture of Market Place and All Saints' parish church in the summer of 1950 exudes the character of mid-20th-century townscapes with its scarcity of motor traffic and abundance of pedestrians, all properly dressed. A Corporation busman in his white-top summer cap is on his bicycle, and the clatter of clogs and cheerful chatter of mill lasses fills the air. The Market Place was the point where the Warrington-Preston road crossed the Manchester-Southport road and was the hub of the Corporation bus services and previously the tramways.

Wigan was an ancient borough, chartered in 1246. Most of its original timber-framed buildings were lost in the Industrial Revolution, but it was still busy producing coal, iron and cotton in 1950. From late Victorian times to the 1950s all new buildings on the main streets in the town centre were in this Tudor/Elizabethan style with imitation timber framing, but that building tradition was forgotten in the philistine 1960s. The Market Place is now largely pedestrianised with restricted access for delivery vans and short sections of stone wall as windbreaks for public seats. Some new buildings with 'pyjama' stripes pay lip service to the timber-framed tradition. *George Greenwood*

LIVERPOOL
On a winter's dawn on the Mersey the wind tugs at the hand-held camera, causing slight blurring as tugs scurry up and down the river against a red sky in this view from the Birkenhead ferry steamer on 24 November 1962, looking upriver to Dingle Point (centre). Beyond, the river widens to 3 miles between Lancashire (left) and Cheshire (right). We can just make out the silhouettes of the grain silos at Coburg Dock, Liverpool, in the gloom.

LIVERPOOL-bound passengers enjoy the fresh, salty air and close-up views of shipping on the Mersey from the relative shelter of the starboard walkway on the main deck of a Birkenhead ferry steamer crossing the river from Woodside. The three-quarter-mile crossing took 7 minutes and two steamers plied the service. This photograph, from the semi-enclosed seating area outside the main saloon, shows the stairs with their brass handrails to the forward promenade deck and the huge, python-like ropes draped over the bulwarks. Liverpool waterfront lies ahead on the starboard bow and we can see the Royal Liver Building and the steeple of St Nicholas parish church.

LIVERPOOL The two steamers on the Birkenhead ferry passage passed in mid-river at a combined speed of 28 knots. In August 1954 we are bound for Liverpool and, from the aisle across the deck between the gangway gates we glimpse the profile of the other steamer on the service on its way back to Woodside. Cyclists kept their bikes in this aisle between the forward and central saloons. The brass handrail leads upstairs to the promenade deck and mooring ropes casually festoon the bulwarks. In the background are the five-storey Albert Dock warehouses of 1845 and the tower of Liverpool Cathedral.

LIVERPOOL This general view of Liverpool waterfront from Seacombe (Cheshire) on 8 June 1969 shows shipping on the Mersey. The dredger *Peakdale* of Manchester, a sand suction hopper, chugs slowly upriver and the Isle of Man ships *Manx Maid* and *Ben-my-Chree* and the Canadian Pacific liner *Empress of England* are berthed at the landing stage. The dredger was a Dutch vessel built in 1910 as the *Prinses Juliana* and was bought second-hand by Hoveringham Gravels and renamed *Peakdale*; it was the oldest known working dredger when this picture was taken and the last coal-burning steamship on the Mersey. It carried sand, dredged off New Brighton, to docks at Birkenhead, Widnes and Manchester. *Peakdale* was scrapped at Dalmuir on the Clyde in 1970. The *Empress of England* is plying the Canadian Pacific line to Montreal; the company abandoned Liverpool in 1971 and the last ocean passenger liner to leave the Mersey, Elder Dempster's *Aureol* of 1951, sailed for West Africa in 1972.

The soot-black Royal Liver Building, the domed Dock Office and the great Anglican Cathedral still then dominated the Mersey scene here. Left of the Liver Building is the lantern spire of St Nicholas parish church. We also see the first outward signs of the 1960s decade of demolition and reconstruction in the Ravenseft Tower, a concrete chimney (for the heating and ventilation of St John's shopping 'precinct') with a revolving restaurant on top, now occupied by Radio City.

The river is now almost devoid of shipping as container ships dock at Seaforth at the river mouth, although cruise liners occasionally call at the landing stage. Today's city skyline is dominated by towering stacks of concrete and glass in white, black, silver and khaki.

LIVERPOOL This lacy, cast-iron arch and pediment with ball-and-spike finials and a pendant gas lamp, straight out of the cartoons of Rowland Emett, was the gateway for passengers to Birkenhead on Liverpool landing stage. The name 'WOODSIDE FERRY' was stencilled in a rope-framed panel on the lintel, also in cast iron. Two arches like this spanned the access to the two gangways from the landing stage on to the deck of the waiting ferry steamer. The secondary arch, spanned with the lintel painted BIRKENHEAD FERRIES, supports the gangway, lowered by chains on to the deck of the steamer when it has berthed. Dating from the opening of George's Landing Stage in 1876, the ornate arches were each hung with a large, globular lamp before the pendant lamps we see here. Small crown finials on the gangway posts symbolised King Edward III's charter of 1330 to the monks of Birkenhead Priory and their 'successors for ever' for the right of ferry passage and to charge tolls as part of the King's highway from Chester to Liverpool. The poster board in this September 1954 picture is advertising a nightly dancing programme at New Brighton Tower Ballroom, while Liverpool's own song-and-dance entertainer, Frankie Vaughan, was due to appear at the Tower Theatre.

LIVERPOOL This is a general view of the ferry landing stage from a departing Birkenhead ferry, with two Wallasey Corporation ferry steamers berthed at the stage in April 1952. We see the wooden fog bell tower on the stagehands' hut and the Woodside ferry berth with the gangways for the lower and upper decks (right). The two twin-screw steamers in this picture are the *Royal Daffodil II* loading for Seacombe and the *Marlowe*, astern, for New Brighton. *Daffodil* was built by Cammell Laird at Tranmere in 1934, at 591 gross tons; it was a three-decker with a licence to carry 1,995 passengers. She was sunk by a bomb at Seacombe stage in the 1941 blitz, raised and refitted. From 1945 to 1951 she doubled as a cruise ship in Liverpool Bay, and went to the breakers in 1962. The Seacombe and Woodside ferries ran every 10 minutes in peak periods, every 15 minutes in the off-peak, and hourly through the night.

LIVERPOOL The Wallasey Corporation ferry steamer TSS *Marlowe* is on the New Brighton service at Liverpool landing stage, seen from the three-decker *Royal Daffodil II* arriving from Seacombe on Easter Monday 1952. The *Marlowe* and her sister ship *Wallasey* were built in 1927 by the Caledon Shipbuilding & Engineering Company at Dundee, 151 feet long, 48 feet in the beam, with a cruiser stern and twin rudders. Though only two-deckers, at 606 gross tons and licensed to carry 2,233 passengers, the *Marlowe* and *Wallasey* were the largest ferries ever to ply across the Mersey. In their time they served all three Wallasey steamboat stations: Seacombe, Egremont and New Brighton. The *Marlowe* was sold in 1958 to the British Iron & Steel Corporation for scrap. In the background is Liverpool Riverside railway terminus (1895-1971), owned by the Mersey Docks & Harbour Board and used by LNWR/LMSR trains, which ran non-stop between Riverside and Euston for liner passengers. It was also used by troop trains meeting troopships during the wars.

LIVERPOOL The last steam ferry on the Mersey was the *Wallasey* of 1927, seen here dressed overall to mark the centenary of Wallasey Ferries as a municipal undertaking in 1961. She is approaching Liverpool landing stage from Seacombe on 30 May and this view from the deck of a Birkenhead ferry shows four tugs and the Canadian Pacific turbine steamer *Empress of Britain,* from Montreal, berthed further along the stage. In the background are the three chimneys of Clarence Dock power station and, on the left, the distant silhouette of New Brighton Tower Building. The *Wallasey* survived her sister ship *Marlowe*, and six other Mersey ferry steamers built in 1929-34, to retire from service in 1963; she was scrapped at Antwerp in 1964.

LIVERPOOL These passenger liners at Prince's Landing Stage, seen from the Seacombe ferry steamer in 1950, are the Bibby Line troopship *Devonshire* and the Elder Dempster west African liner *Apapa*, both twin-screw motor vessels, together with attendant steam tugs. The *Devonshire* (11,275 gross tons), still in wartime grey, was built as a troopship in 1939 by the Fairfield Shipbuilding & Engineering Company at Govan on the Clyde. Liverpool was the home port for troopships to British overseas posts till 1958, after which sea trooping was continued from Southampton until the end of National Service in 1962, when *Devonshire* was sold to the British India Steam Navigation Company and renamed *Devonia*. She was broken up in 1968. The *Apapa* (11,607gt) was built by Vickers, Armstrong at Barrow in 1947-48 for Elder Dempster's west African service. With a grey hull, green bottom, white superstructure and a plain buff funnel, she plied between Liverpool and west Africa till 1968, when she was sold to Hong Kong to trade as the *Taipooshan* till scrapped in 1975. Her younger sister ship *Aureol* of 1951 was the last passenger liner to leave Liverpool on scheduled service, in 1972.

LIVERPOOL From the bow of a Manx ship we are looking down on the working end of two steam tugs of the Alexandra Towing Company, *Crosby* (right) of 1937 and *North Light* of 1956, triple-berthed at Prince's Landing Stage on 15 June 1964.

LIVERPOOL Mersey tugs are berthed at Prince's Landing Stage on 14 June 1964. The red-funnelled tug is J. H. Lamey's *Anita Lamey* of 1920, and the buff-funnelled tugs around her are (from left to right) the Alexandra Towing Company's *North Rock* of 1956, *North End* of 1957, *Huskisson* of 1934 and *North Quay* of 1956. The *Anita Lamey* had been dieselised in the 1950s with a shorter funnel, while the older tugs have taller funnels. There are more tugs in the background surrounding an Isle of Man 'steam packet'. The customs shed for ocean passengers can be seen behind the covered footbridge linking the stage to the river wall.

LIVERPOOL Against the backdrop of the Royal Liver Building, Liverpool Corporation tramcars shunt around three terminal loops on George's Pier Head, fronting the Mersey. The former George's Dock of 1771 was drained and filled in in 1899-1900 for the site of the Liver, Cunard and Dock office buildings. In this picture, taken in 1950, we see six bogie cars, dating from 1931 to 1937, loading around the south, middle and north loops for lines south, east and north of the city respectively. Pier Head was the destination on most city-bound tramcars as this was the focal point of Liverpool's 97-mile network, connecting with the Mersey ferries to Birkenhead and Wallasey. Motorbuses began to replace the tramcars, route by route, from 1948, Pier Head gradually became a bus station, and the last tram left here in 1957.

The Royal Liver Building, erected in 1908-11, was Britain's first reinforced-concrete, multi-storey building on a steel frame and was clad in grey granite, which was soot-black by the time of this photograph. It was designed by Aubrey Thomas complete with its lantern clock towers fore and aft, 295 feet tall, with 25-foot-diameter clock dials, the largest in England. The 11 storeys housed the offices of the Royal Liver Friendly Society, the district tax offices, Canadian Pacific and many other shipping offices.

Today only sightseeing buses call here, all services now terminating in two new bus stations south and north of the shopping centre. The Liver Building has been cleaned, and the south tramway loop (nearest the camera) has been replaced by an incongruous, three-storey, rhomboid, white concrete building housing a ferry/cruise ticket office, bar, restaurant, two tourist souvenir shops and a Beatles 'museum'.

LIVERPOOL On a wet day at Pier Head in September 1954 passengers are boarding two different types of streamlined tramcars under the web of overhead electric wires below the towering Royal Liver Building. The car on the right is one of the 161, 78-seat, bogie streamliners (or 'Liners') built in 1936-37, loading for route 19 to Kirkby. On the left is one of the 100, 70-seat, four-wheelers ('Baby Grands') of 1937-42 on route 6A to Bowring Park. By this time the north and middle tramway loops on Pier Head had closed, usurped by motorbuses, and the remaining tram routes terminated on the south loop. The 10½-mile line to Kirkby was extended there beyond the city boundary as late at 1943-44 to serve munitions and other factories in the new industrial estate and satellite new town, but the line closed in 1956. Route 6 was one of the last two lines in Liverpool to close, in 1957.

Above: **LIVERPOOL** These noble tramcars graced the wide, open spaces and canyon streets of large commercial and civic buildings of this international ocean terminal, and these cars would still not look out of place today. The Corporation built its own tramcar bodies in the modern workshops on Edge Lane and the last batch was 100 of these streamlined four-wheelers mounted on EMB trucks in 1937-42. These 'Baby Grand' cars were 3-foot-shorter versions of the previous batch of bogie streamliners built in 1936-37 and withdrawn by 1956, and worked the last two tram routes for the last 11 months of the system, route 6A to Bowring Park and route 40 to Page Moss. Here car 289 of 1939 leads a succession of 'Baby Grands' shunting around the south terminal loop in front of the classical Portland stone edifice of the Mersey Docks & Harbour Board offices on Pier Head on 4 August 1957, six weeks before the end of the city's trams.

LIVERPOOL Diesel buses were crowding the remaining electric cars when this picture was taken in September 1954 of streamlined bogie car 964 of 1937 leaving Pier Head under the vast span of overhead rigging as it sets out on its tortuous 10½-mile odyssey to Everton, Walton, Gillmoss and Kirkby. The car is passing alongside a Crossley-bodied Crossley bus of 1949 loading for route 80 to Speke. On the right are the begrimed, Portland stone Cunard Steamship offices (1914-16) and Royal Liver Building (1908-11).

Today the roadway on George's Pier Head is renamed Canada Boulevard and only tourist buses terminate here as river cruises have largely replaced the ferries. On the left are now lawns and a three-storey, white concrete, cruise terminal, bar and tourist souvenir shops. A 1½-mile extension of the Leeds & Liverpool Canal from Stanley Dock to Canning Dock, opened in 2009, now cuts across the open space in a deep, concrete cutting as a cruiseway linking with the Maritime Museum.

LIVERPOOL One of the Corporation's 1962 batch of front-entrance, rear-engined Leyland Atlantean buses from the Metropolitan-Cammell Carriage & Wagon Company looks smart in this photograph on Pier Head against the Royal Liver Building and the Cunard building on 15 September 1963.

LIVERPOOL The Liverpool Overhead Railway ran on this 16-foot-high, colonnaded iron viaduct along the dock side of the dock road for most of its 7 miles from Dingle to Seaforth, and this is Pier Head station behind the Liver Building in September 1954. The front end of one of the original electric trains of 1893, rebuilt wide in 1903, is seen in the station on its way south to Dingle. Passing under the railway is a Liverpool Corporation 1954 Crossley-bodied AEC bus on Water Street on route 79 from Pier Head to Belle Vale. The American automobile turning into the dock road was the Canadian Pacific staff car, a dark blue 1952 Chevrolet, on its way from the company offices in the Liver Building to Gladstone Dock. The Overhead Railway closed at the end of 1956 and the standard-gauge dock railway that ran beneath it between the south docks and the north docks closed in 1971. This section of the dock road is now an eight-lane segment of the city's new ring road.

LIVERPOOL The domed Queen Victoria monument of 1904 dominates this view from St George's Crescent in September 1954. As in Sydney at the other end of her empire, the statue of the Empress of Britain was encircled by a tramway loop, the Castle Street terminus. The two private cars on the left are a 1949 Ford Anglia (left) and a 1952 Sunbeam Talbot. As Corporation buses turn from Lord Street into Castle Street a 'Baby Grand' tramcar on route 6A from Bowring Park lumbers over the junction into Derby Square by the Midland Bank of 1868 to descend James Street to the Pier Head. The domed Town Hall of 1748-1820 terminates the view along Castle Street and architecturally complements the Victoria monument.

LIVERPOOL The tram tracks were still in place when this picture was taken of a 1962 Liverpool Corporation Leyland Atlantean bus in South Castle Street on 15 September 1963, six years after the last tram ran in the city. These tracks in South Castle Street and around the Victoria monument were abandoned in 1949. The Town Hall still terminates the view along Castle Street and the green cabin by the Victoria monument is a Corporation Transport office. South Castle Street behind the camera was bombed off the map in the Second World War. The area has since been redeveloped and this viewpoint is now the site of the Queen Elizabeth Law Courts.

LIVERPOOL CENTRAL station was one of three main-line railway terminals in the city and the headquarters of the Cheshire Lines Committee (CLC) from its opening in 1874 till nationalisation in 1947. In this picture, taken in May 1959, an ex-LMSR 2-6-4 tank engine with a train of ex-LMSR compartment stock in Platform 3 awaits the right-away for all stations to Manchester Central. Two Liverpool Corporation buses stand on the roadway for cabs and mail vans between the main line arrival Platforms 1 and 2, providing Central station's traditional connection with ships at Liverpool landing stage. The station, fronting Ranelagh Street, was approached by rail through a 1,320-yard tunnel from Brunswick Dock goods yard on a rising gradient of 1 in 90. Downstairs was Liverpool Central Low Level station, a dimly lit island platform and terminus of the underground electric Mersey Railway to Birkenhead.

The CLC was a joint system of the Great Northern, Midland and Great Central railways through rival LNWR territory with direct lines from Manchester to Chester and Liverpool. From the 1923 railway Grouping it was operated jointly by the LNER and LMSR, and from 1948 it was part of BR's Midland Region. Central station was host to a variety of locomotives and carriages from all the constituent companies and there were through trains to Matlock and St Pancras, to Nottingham Victoria and Marylebone, and to Sheffield, Hull, Lincoln, Grimsby, Cromer, Great Yarmouth, Cambridge and Harwich. Most of the services ended in the 1960s and the great station closed in 1972. The site was then redeveloped with shopping arcades when the underground station was modernised in 1976-77. Liverpool Exchange station (LYR), for trains north and east, closed in 1977 and all remaining train services to Liverpool are now funnelled into Lime Street (LNWR).

LIVERPOOL The Lord Mayor of Liverpool's coach awakens old echoes as it passes through Rodney Street in the city's Georgian belt on 8 June 1969. Liverpool is one of the few cities in Britain where the Corporation has a state coach for civic occasions. It was built by Gorst & Company in Great Charlotte Street, Liverpool, in 1821. There are double doorsteps that fold up into recesses in the doorcases, and the candle carriage lamps are octagonal with two-tier chimneys. The coachwork is riddled with brass and other fittings, both visible and hidden, all marked with the image of the Liver bird, the emblem of Liverpool. The coach is kept at Croxteth Hall stables and, latterly, livery stables at Tarleton hired out the horses, coachman and footmen when the coach went out, about six times a year, but the Lord Mayor's office has no records of its use since 2001.

LIVERPOOL The original Liverpool University building crowns the top of Brownlow Hill as 'Baby Grand' tramcar 275 of 1938 crests the gradient on route 40 from Pier Head to Page Moss on 4 August 1957, just one month before the tramway system closed. Curved, enamelled steel STOP flags encircle the traction poles on opposite sides of the road supporting the overhead wires. A Crossley-bodied AEC bus of 1950-52 approaches from the opposite direction; these were the first 8-foot-wide buses for Liverpool.

The University building dates from 1887-92 as the Victoria University College and was granted a Royal Charter as Liverpool University in 1903. The building is dressed in hard, red-pressed brickwork and was the original 'redbrick university' in Britain. This and Manchester Town Hall were the masterpieces of the Liverpool-born architect Alfred Waterhouse (1830-1905), although the style and detail of this building, a Victorian Gothic 'tour de force', cannot be appreciated from this distance. Today the Victoria building houses the University senate chamber and theatre while the university extends to more modern buildings in the vicinity.

LIVERPOOL BAY 'The leaving of Liverpool.' The Dutch motor coaster *Kilo* of Amsterdam butts down Crosby Channel past Blundellsands on the Lancashire coast of Liverpool Bay, seen from a passing Isle of Man ship on 26 September 1964. Blundellsands, in the background, is the north end of the built-up area of Liverpool and the sand dunes on the left of the picture stretch along the coast to Southport.

The *Kilo* survived a spectacular fire on 18 November 1963 when, on passage from Liverpool to Amsterdam, she was caught in a force 10 gale between Pembrokeshire and Cornwall. The deck cargo of sodium in drums caught fire in contact with sea water. Coxwain Derek Scott of the Mumbles lifeboat said: 'The drums of sodium were flying into the air tracing arcs of fire through the sky and spilling the flames into the sea.' The fire died down and the *Kilo* put into Swansea Bay and beached at Oystermouth. The fire flared up again and the hatch covers collapsed, but a torrential rainstorm came over and doused the fire in the holds with their cargo of gas cylinders, grease, machine tools and whisky. The Swansea pilot cutter then towed the *Kilo* into port and she got into dock under her own power. She put to sea again after a refit.

LIVERPOOL BAY This was one of the many shipwrecks that littered the sandbanks of the Mersey bar for many years after the war. She was P. Henderson's British & Burmese Navigation line SS *Pegu* of Glasgow, built in 1921. On her regular route from Glasgow to Rangoon via Liverpool she was calling into Liverpool to load textiles when she foundered on the east wall of the Crosby Channel after dark in the evening of 24 November 1939, when the lights of the buoys marking the channel were switched off for the wartime blackout. Her 103 passengers and crew were rescued but the reduced wreckage is still there today, now without its mizzen mast. The picture was taken from a passing Manx ship off Hightown on 15 June 1964. The line of surf marks the top of the 'revetment', a rock embankment that extends for 6 miles retaining the sandbanks along the east side of the dredged shipping channel. The wall along the west side of the channel is 8 miles long. These underwater embankments were laid by the Mersey Docks & Harbour Board in 1923-35 by hoppers dumping rocks from the board's own quarries on the Welsh coast. They extend 40 feet deep under the water and are 200 feet wide at the base and 15 feet wide at the surface.

BURNLEY CENTRAL This is the Lancashire & Yorkshire Railway station, complete with its fleet of hand trolleys for luggage, parcels and mailbags, on 17 April 1960. The station is on a tight curve where the railway from Accrington turns from east to north on the way to Colne and Skipton. Central station is on the north side of Burnley, no more central than Burnley Barracks station on the same line or Burnley Manchester Road on the closed line to Todmorden. It was renamed Burnley Bank Top from 1870 till 1944, when it reverted to Burnley Central. In the 1950s trains ran through here to Skipton, Blackpool, Manchester, Liverpool and Euston. The station was rebuilt by BR in 1964 in an austere, ugly style typical of the period, the track has been singled, the line to Skipton has been cut back to Colne, and trains now run only between Colne and Blackpool via Preston. The trolleys are a feature that has disappeared from British railway station platforms.

PRESTON is only 4 miles north of Leyland, and Lancashire municipalities tended to favour buses built by the local commercial vehicle builder, Leyland Motors. This is an all-Leyland bus, built in 1946 with a Leyland body on a Leyland PD1 chassis, in the maroon paintwork of Preston Corporation before the buses turned blue and cream. Despite the route display, which I selected for the photograph, the bus is on private hire and was pictured outside the swimming baths in Saul Street on 28 May 1962.

SOUTHPORT The smart cream and scarlet paint scheme of Southport Corporation buses was an attractive feature of the street scene in this fashionable seaside resort. This 1952 Weymann-bodied Leyland was 20 years old when pictured loading at the Monument in bosky, red-paved London Square on route 7 from Birkdale to Blowick in September 1972. London Square was the focal point of Southport's tram and bus routes, but buses no longer stop there today because the roadway has been narrowed in favour of pedestrians.

SOUTHPORT Stopping in the shade of the trees on Lord Street, also paved in red tarmac, a Southport Corporation 1952 Weymann-bodied Leyland PD2 is on route 11 running the full length of the 7-mile linear borough from Crossens to Woodvale in September 1972.

SOUTHPORT One of the last few horse-drawn landaus that plied for hire on The Promenade poses for the camera by the Queen Victoria monument at the top of Nevill Street on 27 May 1962. The landaus normally formed a rank along the seaward side of The Promenade. This was the view from the pier entrance and on the right is the Victoria Hotel, built in 1842; the ornate coach portico was added in 1903. The late-1950s Morris Commercial mail van heads a line of parked cars: a Vauxhall, three Fords and an Austin, all of the 1950s. The landaus that took holidaymakers for trots along the seafront disappeared in the 1960s, and the hotel was demolished in 1971 to be replaced by a nine-storey, yellow-brick cube of flats. The Queen Victoria monument has since been turned round to face down the street towards London Square.

Below: **SOUTHPORT** This was Ribble Motor Services' bus and coach station on Lord Street, Southport, from 1954 to 1987. The photograph was taken on 11 July 1958 showing a Leyland Royal Tiger coach with the stylish Burlingham 'Seagull' body of 1950-56 parked at the front of the station advertising an afternoon tour – a practice no longer seen at seaside resorts. This symmetrical Victorian edifice centred on the clock tower was built in 1884 as the terminus and headquarters of the Southport & Cheshire Lines Extension Railway, which connected at Aintree with the Cheshire Lines to Liverpool Central and Manchester Central. The ground-floor façade was fronted by an ample canopy, railway style. The railway closed in 1952 and the station was adapted by the bus company, using the former trainshed as a bus station and garage. The building is now a hotel and the front canopy, which had been removed by the bus company, has been reinstated as an iron and glass colonnade matching the shop colonnades along Lord Street. The station behind it has been demolished and replaced by a supermarket.

Above: **SOUTHPORT** Taking the right-hand fork from Lord Street West into Westcliffe Road, past the public lavatories at the junction, a 1952 Weymann-bodied Leyland bus heads into Birkdale on route 13 from Crossens to Ainsdale Beach in September 1972.

BIRKDALE The Liverpool-Southport line was electrified in 1904 by the Lancashire & Yorkshire Railway with 630-volt DC third rail. Here an ex-LMSR six-car train of 1939 steel saloon stock pulls out of Birkdale station and crosses the main street in July 1969.

AINSDALE On 1 June 1969 two of Southport's 1961-62 batch of Weymann-bodied Leyland PD2s are laying over among the sand dunes at Ainsdale Beach terminus of route 19 from Crossens via Grosvenor Road and route 30 from the Monument via the Coastal Road.

Above left: **MARTON** Blackpool Corporation standard tramcar 48, rebuilt in 1928 from a 1902 car, turns from Whitegate Drive into the forecourt of Marton depot after Promenade service on 13 August 1961. These cars worked the Marton line till they were replaced by modern cars in 1948-52. The depot closed in October 1962 but cars were still stored there till March 1963. Car 48 was the last to leave when some cars were transferred to the central car sheds at Rigby Road for further service; the rest were scrapped on the premises. The depot was sold and converted, symbolically, to a motor garage and petrol station.

Above right: **BLACKPOOL** One of the 'Marton Vambac' cars, renowned for their riding quality, is seen in Whitegate Drive on the Marton line on 13 August 1961. These cars were built by English Electric at Preston in 1939 as semi-open 'sun saloons' with 48 wooden seats for seafront service, but were totally enclosed in 1941 and re-equipped in 1948-52 with modern control and running gear and upholstered seats to replace the old standard trams on the Marton line. Their eight rubber-sandwiched wheels gave a smooth, near-silent ride on the welded tracks newly laid after wartime neglect. Their lightweight bodies, four motors and variable, automatic, multi-notch braking and acceleration control ('Vambac') equipment, housed on the roof under the trolley tower, gave them swift starts and stops as well as their nickname. They provided a 3-minute-interval service on the Marton line from Talbot Square via Devonshire Square and Oxford Square to the Royal Oak. The Vambac equipment later proved to be unreliable. The Marton line closed in October 1962, in the programme of street tramway closures.

BLACKPOOL In Devonshire Square the picturesque tramway waiting room stood on an island in the middle of this three-way road junction and the Old No. 3 & Didsbury Hotel in the background. A Corporation tramcar takes the curve from Whitegate Drive into Church Street on its way from Marton to Talbot Square and pauses to pick up passengers from this stop on the bend, marked by a circular sign on the traction pole reading 'All cars stop here'. The timber-framed passenger shelter with its clock turret and dormer windows also housed an electricity sub-station and public lavatories. Buses from Devonshire Road (left) stopped on the left side of the island on their way to the town centre. The photograph was taken on 28 October 1962, the last day of the Marton tram service. This was the last all-street tram route in Britain and was also on the circular tram tour of Blackpool from 1911 to 1960. These English Electric single-deck cars of 1939, upgraded as 'Vambacs' and dedicated for Marton service, were scrapped in the winter of 1962-63. The passenger shelter was demolished in 1965.

This is now a T-junction with signals and a plain, brick sub-station with a flat roof, and the Old No. 3 & Didsbury Hotel has been renamed The Crown. The inn dates from the late 18th century, and there was another along Devonshire Road called the No. 4. The two are thought to have been loading stages on the pre-railway horse waggon route to Preston and Manchester, Didsbury being a southern suburb of Manchester.

BLACKPOOL A classic Blackpool tramcar by a classic Blackpool landmark. The diminishing number of standard tramcars, built from 1923 to 1929, were still in service until 1966 and during their last few years they became popular for tramcar tours by enthusiasts. Here is car 48, rebuilt by the Corporation in 1928 from a 1902 Hurst Nelson car with British Thomson Houston motors, retaining the original Tudor-arched saloon windows. It is seen on the Promenade by the Tower during an enthusiasts' tour of the system on the closing day of the Marton route, 28 October 1962.

The 519-foot latticed iron and steel tower, a half-size copy of Gustav Eiffel's tower in Paris, was built in 1891-94 by structural engineers Heenan & Froude of Worcester. Unlike the freestanding tower in Paris, Blackpool Tower has a three-storey red-brick building at the base, which then housed a ballroom, circus, zoo, aquarium and cafeteria. (The last three features have been replaced by a play area, coffee bar and 'dungeons'. (The Tower Building was designed by architects James Maxwell and Charles Tuke of Manchester, who also built New Brighton Tower and Tower Building seen in Part 3 of this travelogue.

BLACKPOOL NORTH railway station (LYR, LNWR) was the terminus of the Dickson Road line, the last of the inland street tramways in Blackpool to close, in 1963. This car has just arrived from Fleetwood on 13 August 1961 and the passengers are alighting from the centre door on the nearside and wandering across the road, which is fairly free of motor traffic. Cars reversed here on a single-track stub, and the top of the picture shows part of the triangle in the electric wiring that automatically reversed the trolley as the car left the terminus. This car is one of 20 48-seat 'railcoaches' built in 1937 by the Brush Electrical Engineering Company of Loughborough on EMB bogies with Crompton Parkinson motors and stabled at Bispham depot to work this service to Fleetwood. These 65 cars were the Brush versions of the 45 English Electric 'railcoaches' built for Blackpool in 1934-35 and formed the largest single class of tramcars at Blackpool and the staple workhorses of the system in its heyday. Some were rebuilt later to pull trailer cars and others for one-man operation, and the last of the original 'railcoaches' was retired from service in 1984.

This location is unrecognisable today as the railway has been cut back three blocks to a new terminus further from the town centre. The old North station, in red pressed brick with its clock tower and glazed iron canopy was demolished and replaced by a concrete multi-storey car park.

BLACKPOOL At Talbot Square tram terminus on 5 June 1961 two cars await passengers at the classical stone shelter in the middle of the square, and a third car approaches along Clifton Street in the background. The car on the left is one of the 12 English Electric 'sun saloons' of 1939 that were modernised in 1948-52 as 'Vambac' cars for the inland street line to Marton and Royal Oak; it is destined for Squire's Gate via Marton, an extension of the route via Lytham Road. On the right is one of the fleet of 12 open single-deck 'boat' cars built by English Electric in 1934 with wooden seats for 56. These cars used to stand on this siding to load for the Circular Tour, but that tour ended in 1960 and this car is destined for Royal Oak as if on normal Marton service. The Town Hall is on the right, and in the left-hand foreground is the pitch for a 'shoeshine boy'.

BLACKPOOL With the Tower in the background, an 84-seat English Electric double-deck tramcar of 1934-35 heads a succession of tramcars north along clifftop Claremont Park on 15 September 1963. The 27 streamlined double-deckers were nicknamed 'Balloons' because their bulbous outline made them look as if they were inflated. They had centre doors, twin staircases and a conductor on each deck. Between 1955 and 1980 these cars were rebuilt for 94 seats with single-aspect destination screens. They were useful on the busy seafront line between Pleasure Beach and (Uncle Tom's) Cabin, and from 1958 they began running through to Fleetwood.

BLACKPOOL A trolley-and-trailer-car 'Twinset' leads a succession of trams through Gynn Square on 15 September 1963. Blackpool converted ten of its English Electric 'railcoaches' of 1933-34 into ten traction cars to pull new trailers by Metropolitan-Cammell to form ten of these double-ended 'Twinsets', each with a combined seating capacity of 114 and two conductors. The prototype entered service in 1957 and the rest followed from 1960. Behind the 'Twinset' are two of the original 'railcoaches' and a double-deck 'Balloon' car of 1934-35, all from English Electric. Gynn Square is the point where Blackpool's promenade tramway met the North Station-Fleetwood line.

Cavalcades of trams like this were common on the seafront in mid-century, but since the entire system was renewed in 2009-12 the fleet of 16 five-section, articulated cars with 75 seats and standing room for 150 provides a headway ranging between 10 minutes and 30 minutes between Starr Gate and Fleetwood, with some cars always spare, so there is often not a tramcar in sight. At busy times the service is augmented by the reserve fleet of eight updated 'Balloons' running any distance from Pleasure Beach to points north. This is a far cry from the peak service of 83 cars on the Promenade-Fleetwood line recorded in July 1937.

BLACKPOOL

Standard tramcar 48 was rebuilt from a 1902 Hurst Nelson car with British Thomson Houston motors. The car pauses for its photograph, and for Robin Hogg to board, on Queen's Promenade between Cabin and Gynn Square on 13 August 1961. The former Uncle Tom's Cabin was Blackpool's first amusement house, built in 1850. Part of it fell over the edge of the crumbling cliff and the rest was demolished in 1902. The cliffs were stabilised by the Corporation and the site of what is now just 'Cabin' on the tramway is marked by the 1930s cliff lift tower in the background.

Robin, from Middlesex, is an old friend, and when on leave from RAF National Service in Norfolk we went on tram-hunting holidays to Blackpool, Isle of Man and Glasgow – hitch-hiking overland of course. Robin contributed the photograph of Aberdeen see page 325,

BISPHAM Three different types of Blackpool tramcars are seen on 11 July 1958. On the left is one of 18 clerestory-roofed English Electric single-deckers built in 1928 for the service from North Station to Fleetwood. The double-decker is one of 27 streamlined 'Balloon' cars of 1934-35, and the single-decker on the right is one of 25 'Coronation' cars built in 1952-54. The lattice iron arch over the road was a 'welcome to Blackpool' gateway over Queen's Drive.

CLEVELEYS Stops along the light railway to Fleetwood were marked by railway-style station nameboards like this one at Westmorland Avenue request stop, pictured on 15 September 1963 with an approaching Brush 'railcoach' of 1937 bound for North Station. The circular stop flag was a standard Blackpool design. The line through this housing estate on the north side of Cleveleys has several paved crossings giving access to side streets; otherwise the fenced, 6-mile right of way between Blackpool and Fleetwood is intersected by only three main roads and Rossall Lane. Modern-style station nameboards have been erected along the relaid route since 2012.

ROSSALL On the reserved-track light railway from Bispham to Fleetwood, 1953 'Coronation' car 308 paused at Rossall station on 29 September 1963. The station platform is lit by a quaint lamp post on the DC traction supply. This station was built at Rossall School stop on Rossall Lane in 1925, but was replaced in the 2009-12 renewal of the system with facing platforms and glass shelters. Houses now stretch to the horizon. English Electric had stopped building trams by 1952, when these 25 cars were ordered, and they were built by a railway car builder, Charles Roberts at Wakefield, on Maley & Taunton bogies with Crompton Parkinson motors; they were delivered between 1952 and 1954. The 'Coronations' were 50 feet long and 8 feet wide with 56 seats, the same capacity as the standard double-deck bus of the time. They proved too big for clearances on Blackpool street lines and from 1953 were working the full schedule on the reserved-track coastal route from Starr Gate to Fleetwood. These handsome cars were popular with passengers and crews because they were roomy, comfortable and powerful with all-round visibility, four motors and 'Vambac' control equipment (like the Marton cars), which gave a fast, smooth ride.

BROADWATER The stops along the light railway to Fleetwood were staggered on each side of the road level crossings so that the trams stopped before crossing the road. 'Coronation' car 308 pauses at Broadwater halt, built in 1930, at the skew crossing of the A585 Fleetwood Road on 29 September 1963. This stop, like all the others on the line, has been replaced by facing platforms and glass shelters south of the crossing. The corner newsagent's shop on the left has been replaced by a new building that was at first a grocery shop and is now an estate agency. These 'Coronation' cars, though fast and smooth-riding, were constructed to railway standards and were heavy on the tram track and power consumption, vulnerable to faults and uneconomic to operate, so they were scrapped prematurely between 1968 and 1975, although one survives in the 'heritage' fleet.

FLEETWOOD The segregated light railway from Bispham to Fleetwood ends here where it runs on to Lord Street, the main street of Fleetwood. At this end of the street section a 1937 Brush car stops at the island tramway station at Ash Street (off left) southbound to Blackpool on 29 September 1963. The northbound stop is marked by the classic circular stop flag on the left side of the pedestrian paving in the foreground, where two men are waiting. The station nameboard is on the right. Power cables feed into the overhead wires here, as they did at section breaks about every half mile along the line. The red-brick station building housed a waiting room and toilets under a tiled, pitched and hipped roof, forming a canopy over the loading platform, and sported a clock cupola on top. The siting of this southbound stop was in the tradition of stopping tramcars before road crossings, but the station building was demolished in the 1970s to make way for a new street junction here and the southbound stop was moved across the street to the start of the reserved track in the foreground opposite the northbound stop. It is now called Fishermen's Walk, for the nearby Fisherman's Friend factory that makes throat lozenges, originally for Fleetwood trawlermen.

Left: **FLEETWOOD** was the only town in Britain with a tramway through the main street during the 30 years between the closure of Glasgow tramways in 1962 and the opening of Manchester's new tramway in 1992, and Blackpool trams still roll through the main street for the last mile to the ferry terminus. Towards the end of its 11-mile run from Starr Gate, 'Coronation' car 317 of 1953 drifts quietly through the town centre on 19 September 1965. On its way along Lord Street, the main shopping street, the tram has just left the stop by the circular flag at Church Street crossing and is passing between St Peter's parish church and the District Bank. At Albert Square in the background the line curves half-left into North Albert Street.

The church was built in 1839-41 by Decimus Burton, the architect of the new town of Fleetwood (1836-46), created by Sir Peter Hesketh-Fleetwood of Rossall Hall. From the 1890s to the 1970s Fleetwood was the third busiest deep-sea fishing port of Britain after Hull and Grimsby, but now has no fishing fleet. Albert Square gained a stone clock tower in 1986, and the tramway now runs through a traffic-calmed main street with car parking bays between tram 'pinches'.

Right: **FLEETWOOD** Here is a classic, clerestory-roofed single-deck tramcar on lay-over in Queen's Terrace at the ferry terminus on 11 July 1958, with Fleetwood's grand LNWR/LYR station in the background. Blackpool Corporation ordered ten of these cars from English Electric in 1928, with 48 upholstered seats, two 50hp motors per car and air brakes for the interurban run from North Station to Fleetwood. They also had extra-large platforms for parcels and holidaymakers' luggage and were unusual in having trolley ropes instead of carrying hooked bamboo poles for reversing the trolley. Car 170 was the last of this stock in service, in 1961, when it became a permanent way work car; in 1965 it was rebuilt as one of Blackpool's illuminated feature cars. English Electric produced four more cars like this in 1928 for Liverpool's intended tram subway scheme that never materialised. On the left is the entrance to the ferry across the mouth of the River Wyre to Knott End. The large, yellow-brick railway terminus in the background had a cavernous, 570-foot-long trainshed, 82 feet wide, spanned by a glazed roof supported by very ornate ironwork. The wooden deck of the concourse sloped down to long, wooden platforms. The station was closed in 1966 and demolished in 1969, and the curtailed line to Wyre Dock closed in 1970.

FLEETWOOD Completing the terminal loop around the block at the north end of the 11½-mile tramway from Starr Gate, one of the streamlined double-deck 'Balloon' cars of 1934-35 passes the lighthouse in Pharos Street on its way back to Blackpool on 13 August 1961. The single-track loop ran from North Albert Street via Bold Street, Queen's Terrace and Pharos Street back to North Albert Street. This car, No 247, was one of 13 of this class built in 1934 as 94-seat open-toppers and enclosed in 1941-42. It had since been refitted with a single-aspect destination screen. Observe the long radial pull-off span wires to create the curve in the running wire; they are attached to an anchor post on the left-hand side of the street.

The lighthouse is the taller of two designed by Decimus Burton and commissioned in 1840 to guide mariners into the River Wyre navigation channel; the lower lighthouse stands on The Esplanade. Pharos Street takes its name from the very first lighthouse, built c280 BC on the isle of Pharos off Alexandria in Egypt – pharos is an alternative word for a lighthouse. This one has since been stripped of its Regency stucco veneer to reveal its red sandstone construction.

LANCASTER The passenger barge *Lady Fiona*, berthed at Penny Street Wharf on 12 August 1964, gave cruises along the Lancaster Canal. She was built in 1899 as a horse-drawn barge and dredger for the Lancaster Canal Company, then in 1959 was converted to a diesel passenger launch with seats and half-drop windows from scrapped London trolleybuses and licensed to carry 100 passengers. She remained in passenger service till 2003 and has since been largely restored by British Waterways at Nantwich as a freight barge on the National Historic Ships register.

The Lancaster Canal linked Preston with Kendal, but the last 14 miles at the north end have been cut off by the M6 motorway and that section has been filled in and made into a public footpath. The *Lady Fiona* was licensed to cruise the remaining long, level section from Preston to Tewitfield with no locks through placid countryside, but by no means without interest. There is a branch to Glasson dock on the Lune estuary below Lancaster, and a mile north of the city the canal crosses a handsome stone aqueduct, 600 feet long, over the River Lune. Shortly afterwards it skirts the coast at Hest Bank with sea views across Morecambe Bay.

ARKHOLME The station nameboard and platform lantern were photographed on 2 April 1964, four years after closure of the station on the still surviving line of the former Furness & Midland Joint Railway between Wennington and Carnforth. The closure of intermediate stations on extant passenger routes was part of the Government policy of cutting out stopping trains and speeding up the services; many of the intermediate stopping places had few, if any, passengers by the early 1960s, when there was a big shift from public to private transport. The population of Arkholme then was just under 300.

LANCASTER GREEN AYRE station, pictured on 10 October 1964, was on the Midland Railway route from Leeds and Bradford to Morecambe. Vintage electric multiple unit trains dating from 1908 and 1914 reversed here on a high-voltage AC overhead electric line from Lancaster Castle to Morecambe Promenade and Heysham Harbour. The line from Wennington to Lancaster Green Ayre closed together with the electric railway on 1 January 1966 and Leeds/Bradford-Morecambe trains were diverted via Carnforth, but this pioneer electrification, experimentally upgraded in 1953 to 50 hertz, 25,000 volts AC, set the standard for BR main-line electrification from the 1960s. This station and the railway towards Morecambe have been replaced by a new road, part of the A589 between the two towns.

MORECAMBE Two 1960 Metropolitan-Cammell-bodied Leyland Atlanteans of Ribble Motor Services are seen in Morecambe bus station on 24 February 1963. The front-runner, on the express service X21 from Carlisle to Liverpool, was one of the first batch of Ribble's 'Gay Hostess' double-deckers fitted out by Weymann as coaches with 50 luxury, adjustable seats, a refreshment servery, provision for a hostess or steward, a toilet, extra luggage accommodation and adjustable lighting. The standard Atlantean bus behind is on the limited-stop service X42 from Morecambe to Blackpool. This bus station was on the forecourt of Morecambe Euston Road railway terminus (ex-LNWR), since closed.

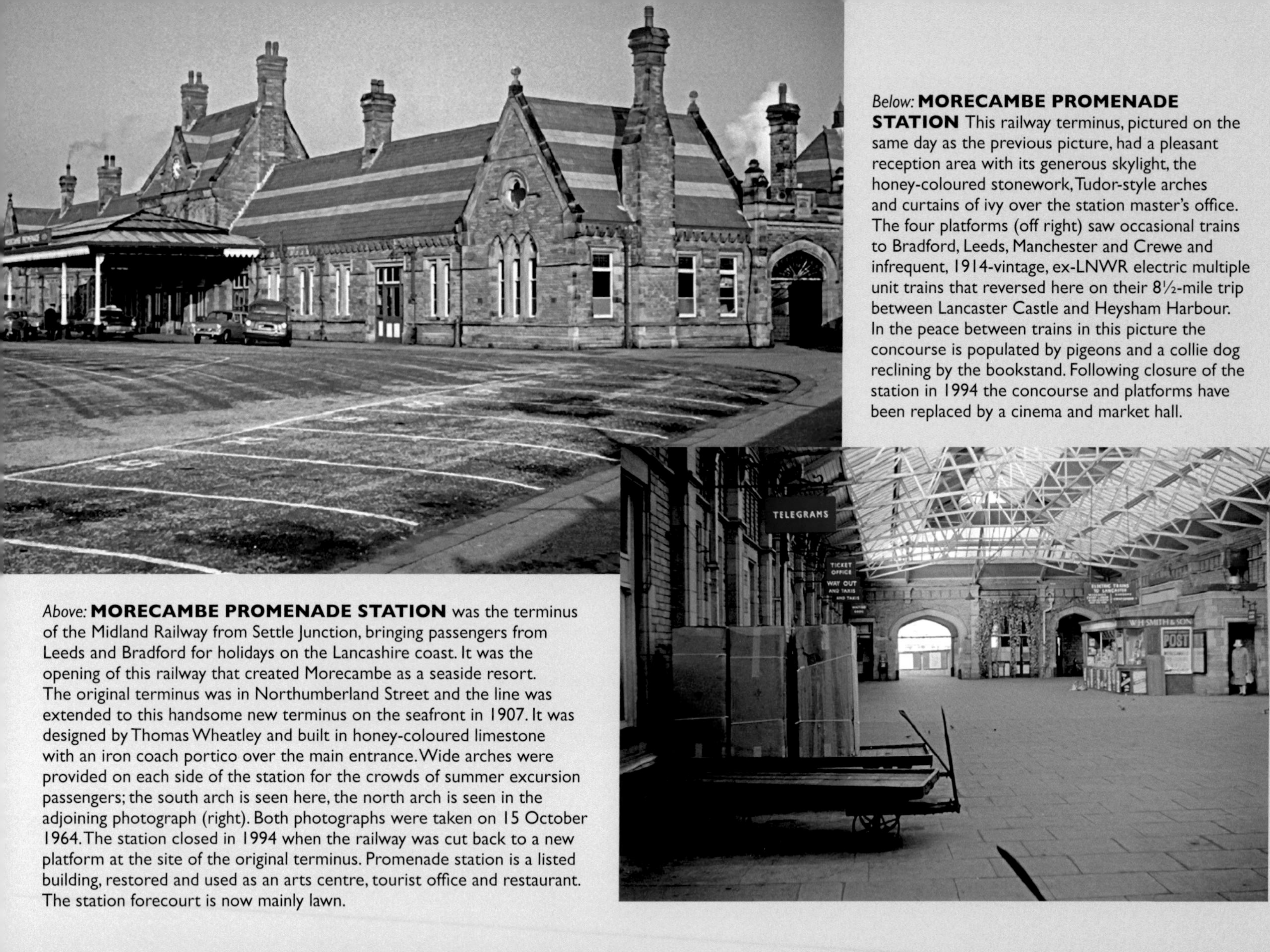

Below: **MORECAMBE PROMENADE STATION** This railway terminus, pictured on the same day as the previous picture, had a pleasant reception area with its generous skylight, the honey-coloured stonework, Tudor-style arches and curtains of ivy over the station master's office. The four platforms (off right) saw occasional trains to Bradford, Leeds, Manchester and Crewe and infrequent, 1914-vintage, ex-LNWR electric multiple unit trains that reversed here on their 8½-mile trip between Lancaster Castle and Heysham Harbour. In the peace between trains in this picture the concourse is populated by pigeons and a collie dog reclining by the bookstand. Following closure of the station in 1994 the concourse and platforms have been replaced by a cinema and market hall.

Above: **MORECAMBE PROMENADE STATION** was the terminus of the Midland Railway from Settle Junction, bringing passengers from Leeds and Bradford for holidays on the Lancashire coast. It was the opening of this railway that created Morecambe as a seaside resort. The original terminus was in Northumberland Street and the line was extended to this handsome new terminus on the seafront in 1907. It was designed by Thomas Wheatley and built in honey-coloured limestone with an iron coach portico over the main entrance. Wide arches were provided on each side of the station for the crowds of summer excursion passengers; the south arch is seen here, the north arch is seen in the adjoining photograph (right). Both photographs were taken on 15 October 1964. The station closed in 1994 when the railway was cut back to a new platform at the site of the original terminus. Promenade station is a listed building, restored and used as an arts centre, tourist office and restaurant. The station forecourt is now mainly lawn.

NEWBIGGIN In the detached part of Lancashire across Morecambe Bay, on the south-east coast of the Furness peninsula, the bodies of some of Barrow Corporation's last tramcars survived as holiday homes. These cars were built by Brush in 1921 and retired at the closure of the tramways in 1932. This car body was being used as a greenhouse when pictured on 1 April 1964. The Corporation trams were painted olive green with cream windows and rocker panels. Hundreds of old tramcar bodies like this survived all over Britain into the second half of the 20th century and many have been restored to working condition, using second-hand or newly made running gear of the right design, for museum operations. The National Tramway Museum at Crich in Derbyshire provides an archive of British tramcar specifications.

Left: **BARROW-IN-FURNESS** Fishing boats sit on the sand at low tide in Walney Channel in this view of Barrow waterfront on 30 May 1962, from Vickerstown on Walney island to the towering cranes on the launching slipways of Vickers Armstrong shipyards and beyond to the cargo cranes on Ramsden Dock. A dredger can be seen on the extreme right, keeping the channel and the port approaches clear of silt. The traditional cargoes in the docks were grain, iron ore, steel and timber.

Barrow shipyard now builds only submarines in a vast hall on Devonshire Dock. The launching slipways in this picture have closed and the characteristic hammerhead cranes have disappeared. The port nearly closed in the 1970s but Ramsden Dock still exports local stone and imports baled woodpulp, sea-dredged aggregates, gas concentrate and waste nuclear fuel (for Sellafield), while the other docks lie empty.

Right: **BARROW-IN-FURNESS** Tramlines, tenements and shipyard cranes are to be seen on Ramsden Dock Road on 1 April 1964. Tramcars have not run along here since 1932, the overhead wires are down, but the 4-foot-gauge tracks remain to this day, paved in granite setts along this road and Michaelson Road, and are now used as a linear, herringbone car park along the middle of the road. The tramline to Ramsden Dock crossed the Furness Railway lines to the docks on the level. Long, 96-seat, double-deck bogie cars were used to carry heavy loads of dockers and shipyard workers at peak times and until 1914 they also carried excursion passengers to connect with Furness Railway steamships from Ramsden Dock to Fleetwood, Blackpool and Douglas. The towering shipyard cranes have gone but the tenements on the right remain, now refurbished and modernised.

BARROW-IN-FURNESS These two Park Royal-bodied Leyland PD2s of 1949 (right) and 1950 (left) front a quartet of Barrow Corporation buses parked in front of the garage in Hindpool Road on 1 April 1964. The fleet colour scheme was then in transition to more cream and less blue, as can be seen on the more modern bus behind.

LAKE SIDE An ex-LMSR 'Black Five' 4-6-0 locomotive, No 44870, built at Crewe in 1945 and stabled at Rugby shed, takes a siesta in the sun at Lake Side branch terminus awaiting the return trip on a day excursion on 1 August 1965, one month before the closure of the line. This was a 9¼-mile branch from Ulverston on the ex-Furness Railway main line from Carnforth to Barrow. Trains connected here with the railway-owned motor yachts that berthed alongside Lake Side station for trips along the 10-mile length of Windermere to Bowness and Ambleside. From 1938 the branch was kept open only for summer passenger service to Lake Side and for goods to Haverthwaite. The last regular passenger trains ran on 6 September 1965 and the last goods on 24 April 1967, but a rail enthusiasts' excursion ran to Lake Side on 2 September 1967. The track was lifted between Plumpton Junction and Haverthwaite in 1971, leaving the Lake Side & Haverthwaite Railway to reopen as a 3½-mile privately preserved railway from 1973. Between Plumpton Junction and Haverthwaite 2¾ miles of the old railway roadbed via Greenodd is now occupied by the improved A590, the main road to Barrow.

CONISTON station was situated at the foot of the Furness Fells, a dramatic terminus to this 9½-mile branch line from Foxfield, opened in 1859. The station buildings, of timber on slate walls, dated from 1862, when the Coniston Railway was taken over by the Furness Railway, being a branch off the main line between Barrow and Whitehaven. The third platform, outside the trainshed, was added in 1896, when the signal cabin was brought from Carnforth Furness & Midland Junction. The single line to the right of the signal cabin was opened in 1860 and led to a wharf for loading copper mined in the mountains. The push-and-pull passenger trains ended in 1958 and the thrice-weekly goods trains in 1962, but the terminus was complete, except for signal arms, when this picture was taken on 13 February 1963. The station was later demolished and the footbridge now spans Ravenglass terminus of the 15-inch-gauge railway into Eskdale. The Furness Railway's elegant and luxurious 42-ton steam yacht *Gondola* of 1859 still plies on Coniston Water after being restored for the National Trust.

SEATHWAITE One of the most scenic bus routes in Britain ran from Ulverston up Dunnerdale to Seathwaite, following the narrow, tortuous road by the River Duddon that formed the boundary between Lancashire and Cumberland. Ribble Motor Services ran three round trips a day on Tuesdays, Thursdays and Saturdays only. In this picture at the Seathwaite terminus by the Newfield Hotel on 3 May 1961 is a Leyland Tiger Cub with Saunders Roe coachwork, one of 50 of these 44-seat buses used by Ribble on country routes from 1954 to 1969. The Ribble company, of Preston, served most of Lancashire, Westmorland and Cumberland; nationalised in 1969, it was split up and sold on privatisation in 1986. There is no bus service up Dunnerdale today.

Part 5, Yorkshire to the Border

Yorkshire

HULL Barges, tugs and a coaster lie in the Old Harbour on the River Hull, seen from Drypool Bridge on 16 June 1970 with the Humber estuary in the background. The dumb barges, or lighters, on the right bank are berthed two or three abreast and the motor tugs *Gillian Knight* and *Hippo D* are berthed alongside them on the left. On the left bank of the river are the motor barges *Polar* and *Vega* and the motor coaster *Moderator* beside the gravel crushing plant. These barges navigated the River Hull as far as Beverley with coal, grain and seed, and up and down the Humber tributaries to and from Lincoln, Nottingham, Sheffield, Leeds and York carrying mainly coal, grain and timber. At this time Hull was the third most important port in Britain and the main base for deep-sea fishing.

The Old Harbour is no longer in commercial use, the Trinity House buoys shed (extreme left) is disused, the gravel plant has disappeared, and the factory beyond has been replaced by a hotel. The warehouse on the right has been converted to flats and the only vessel in the Old Harbour today is Hull's last sidewinding trawler *Arctic Corsair*, preserved by the City Council and berthed on the right bank here as a museum of deep-sea fishing. A tidal flood barrier now guards the mouth of the river.

HULL Brewery Company's horse dray No 5 is delivering ale at the King William Hotel in Market Place on 16 June 1970. Breweries continued to use four-wheel, flat-bed horse waggons, which they called 'drays', for local deliveries long after all other industries had turned to diesel lorries. Railway companies still had four-wheel horse vans with canvas hoods, or 'tilts', into the early 1950s for collection and delivery of parcels and passengers' trunks. Hull Brewery Company, established in 1888, was taken over by a succession of other companies in 1972, 1985 and 1999. The brewery closed in 2002, when production moved to its latest owners in Wolverhampton.

ROTHERHAM

Single-deck trolleybuses were rare in Britain, but Rotherham was served by two trolleybus systems operating all single-deckers for most of the era. The Corporation had an entire fleet of single-deckers from 1912 till 1956, when 14 of these East Lancashire-bodied 38-seaters were rebuilt by Charles Roe of Leeds as 72-seat double-deckers for economies that turned a trading loss into a profit. This bus, No 76 in the fleet, was one of 46 three-axle Daimlers with Crompton Parkinson electric equipment delivered in 1949-50, and one of the 32 vehicles of the batch that were not rebuilt. It is seen on the route to Mexborough and Conisborough on 18 July 1958, a route that was run jointly with Mexborough trolleybuses, also all single-deckers because of low railway bridges. The Mexborough & Swinton Traction Company ceased running trolleybuses in 1961 and Rotherham Corporation followed suit in 1965.

MEADOWHEAD was the southern outpost of Sheffield tramways on the A61 road from Chesterfield. A Sheffield Corporation standard tramcar is loading for the route across the city to Sheffield Lane Top in the north on 2 April 1960. This route closed the following day. The car, No 170, was built in 1933-35 with a 61-seat Corporation body on a Peckham truck. Sheffield painted its trams in ivory with dark blue bands. The tram will exit right, where the trolley will be reversed on a triangular arrangement in the overhead wires. Observe the clock on the traction pole.

NORTON WOODSEATS Inside the upper saloon of the tramcar on the same day approaching Woodseats along Abbey Lane, the passenger reposed on the front seat is Margaret Nicholls from Bishopsbourne, Kent. On a 16-day cycle tour of England and Wales, she had dropped into Sheffield from the High Peak district of Derbyshire and 'changed horses' to get a grandstand view of the city from the comfort and security of a tramcar with its upholstered, leather seats and glassy upper saloon, just as Gladstone recommended seeing London from the top of a bus. The belt line along Abbey Lane formed a loop around the south end of the system linking Woodseats with Beauchief (pronounced 'Beech'f'). It was on a turfed, roadside reservation most of the way from Beauchief but the line closed seven months later. Trams operated a north-south cross-city route in both directions between Firth Park, Woodseats, Beauchief and Vulcan Road, only reversing at the north end.

NORTON WOODSEATS The city of Sheffield lies in a hollow on the eastern edge of the High Peak district of Derbyshire. The tramcar, the stone houses, the gas lanterns, the tram tracks and the moorland backdrop were characteristic of Pennine industrial towns; only the granite setts are missing as Sheffield had paved many of its tramways in asphalt instead. This tram terminus on Abbey Lane was called WOODSEATS on the tramcar destination blinds and car No 244 of 1936 is seen from the upper saloon of another tramcar leaving the terminus on 17 July 1958. The cross-city route from Woodseats to Wadsley Bridge closed on 3 October 1959.

NORTON WOODSEATS

This 69-seat, Roe-bodied Leyland PD3 bus of 1959 looks smart in Sheffield's ivory and dark blue paint scheme without the dark grey roof of earlier Sheffield buses. It is on Abbey Lane at Woodseats tram terminus on 17 July 1958. Route 63 circled around Woodseats and Beauchief and crossed the city centre to terminate at Shirecliffe in the northern suburbs. Tramcar No 161 of 1935 has just arrived at the terminus and passengers are alighting. It is about to reverse over the crossover and the route blinds have already been reset for the return journey to Wadsley Bridge via Shoreham Street. The trolley reverser can be seen in the overhead wires beyond the car. This picture represents the transition from tramcars to motorbuses in Sheffield in 1952-60.

BEAUCHIEF Two more modern classes of tramcars in Sheffield are seen on the reservation alongside Abbeydale Road South at Beauchief terminus on 19 May 1959. Car No 513 was one of 35 built by Charles Roberts of Wakefield in 1950-52 to match the Corporation's prototype of 1946. The tramcar in the background is one of 81 rather trim standard cars with slightly arched roofs, built by the Corporation in 1936-44.

SHEFFIELD Kerbside loading at the Town Hall takes place on a three-track section of the tramway in Pinstone Street on 2 April 1960. Car No 68 is a standard 61-seater of 1930 built by the Corporation on a Peckham truck. The centre track was used by cars on another route that stopped elsewhere. It was unusual to see tramcars loading at the kerb in Britain, although there was no reason why the track should not loop into the kerbside as it does here. Some systems built passenger loading islands in the middle of the road. The Town Hall, with its 180-foot clock tower, was built in 1891-96 to a design by Edward Mountford. The private car on the left in a 1949 Ford Anglia.

SHEFFIELD Even in the eighth year of Sheffield's tramway scrapping programme, tramcars still dominated the city centre. In this view of Fargate on 19 May 1959 are three tramcars and three private cars. A 1948 Austin A70 is pulling out of Leopold Street and tramcar No 191 of 1934 is being tailed by a 1948 Austin Princess and flanked on its nearside by a 1955 Standard. Two more modern tramcars of 1950-52 are passing each other halfway down the street. The *Sheffield Telegraph* office terminates the view. Sheffield's last tram ran through Fargate on the route from Vulcan Road to Beauchief on 8 October 1960.

The Yorkshire Penny Bank stands on the corner of Surrey Street (right). It was founded at Leeds in 1859 as a savings bank for 'the working men of the West Riding' and branches extended through midland and northern England. The 'penny' dropped from the name in 1959. Fargate is now a pedestrian precinct with restricted access for loading vehicles.

SHEFFIELD The clean outlines of Sheffield Corporation's standard trams were complemented by their smart, ivory paintwork, trimmed with dark blue bands and simple but neat ochre lining-out of the panels, the city coat of arms and no lettering or advertising. Standard car No 161 of 1933 is loading at the island stone shelter in Fitzalan Square on its way from Woodseats to Wadsley Bridge on 19 May 1959. This route closed on 3 October that year. The standard trams had six route screens: a destination and 'via' screen at each end and a destination screen on each side.

SHEFFIELD Trams to Vulcan Road, Brightside and Sheffield Lane Top divided after passing under the Wicker Arches, the viaduct carrying the electrified lines of the ex-Great Central Railway. This picture shows standard car 115, one of 68 cars built in 1930-33, southbound from Vulcan Road to Beauchief. In the background a northbound standard car forks left for the climb to Sheffield Lane Top. The route from Vulcan Road, Tinsley, to Millhouses and Beauchief was the last tram route in Sheffield and closed on 8 October 1960.

The railway, also with overhead electric wires, was on the route from Manchester London Road to Sheffield Victoria via Penistone, and was the only British railway electrified at 1,500 volts AC. Electrification was completed to Sheffield in 1955 and extended for freight to Tinsley in 1965, but the route closed to passengers in 1970 and to freight in 1981. All trains between Sheffield and Manchester are now routed by the non-electric ex-Midland line via Dore and Chinley.

BRIGHTSIDE was the ironically named tram terminus among the grim, industrial steel works along the Don valley north-east of the city, but on this day, 17 July 1958, it looks brighter in the presence of a shiny, ivory tramcar glinting in the sunlight. Car 527 was one of the 36 post-war tramcars of this type, all with 62 seats, built by Charles Roberts on Maley & Taunton trucks. The last of these cars were delivered after the Corporation had decided to replace the trams with buses and they were prematurely scrapped after a minimum of only eight years, in contrast to the 30 years of some of the other cars still in service.

LEEDS Entering the city from the south-east on the top deck of a tramcar in Hunslet Road we meet the standard Leeds Corporation tramcar of the period bound for Hunslet and passing a 1954 Foden lorry waiting to reverse into a side street on 15 July 1958. The 'Horsfield' tramcars were designed by the tramways' General Manager, Mr R. L. Horsfield; the first four were built in the Corporation workshops and another 100 by Brush of Loughborough, all on Peckham trucks, in 1930-31. They were 60-seat cars with two 50hp motors per car and air brakes. From 1938 Leeds used bow collectors instead of trolley poles for a more secure contact with the overhead wire, as trolley wheels and skids could dewire at junctions. The Hunslet line closed on 18 April 1959. This view was taken from an ex-London 'Feltham' class car inbound from Middleton.

LEEDS trams were augmented by these second-hand 'Feltham' class cars from London Transport for the last 10 years of the system. A total of 90 'Felthams' arrived in Leeds in 1950-52 although only 83 were adapted for service there. These large, speedy cars with centre entrances were contemporaries of the native 'Horsfield' trams, having been built in 1930-31, but while the 'Horsfield' car was a standard 60-seat four-wheeler, the 'Feltham' was a high-powered bogie car with 70 seats in sumptuously furnished and heated saloons, and gave a smooth, steady ride, although they were heavy on the tracks. They were built by the Union Construction Company at Feltham on EMB bogies for London United Tramways and Metropolitan Electric Tramways, and were inherited by LT in 1933. On its outward, clockwise journey around the Middleton circular route south of the city on the last day of service, 28 March 1959, car No 546 drifts down Lower Briggate under the railway bridge just east of Leeds City station and pauses at the signals at the junction with Swinegate (left) and the line to Swinegate car sheds and workshops.

LEEDS Kirkgate was the city terminus of the last two tram routes. A Leeds 'Horsfield' car and an ex-London 'Feltham' car, both of 1931, are on lay-over in Kirkgate on 19 September 1959, less than two months before closure. The Corn Exchange was nominally the city terminus, but for the last eight months of operation the trams were relegated to this single-line loop around the block east of the exchange. The trams unloaded and took their lay-over here, then followed the granite-paved turnout into New York Street to reload there. Kirkgate leads to the parish church of St Peter, towering in the background, and the bridge carried the former NER line east to Hull and York. The 'Horsfield' car is operating route 22 to Temple Newsam and the 'Feltham' is on route 18 to Cross Gates, both east of the city. Two Leeds Corporation buses, both Roe-bodied Leylands, can be seen behind the trams. Leeds buses and trams were previously blue and cream, but from 1950 the trams were repainted crimson and cream and the buses two-tone green.

LEEDS A reflex right turn out of Kirkgate brought the trams into New York Street, where 'Horsfield' car No 198 loads at the stop flag on the left, framed between the grimy, four-storey buildings as it sets forth on its run east to Temple Newsam on 19 September 1959. New York Street, York Street and York Road carried the last two tram routes out of the city, dividing at Halton Dial for Cross Gates and Temple Newsam. The Yorkshire Penny Bank, which was founded in Leeds in 1859, is on the right, and next door is the other side of Scarr's department store, which we saw in Kirkgate.

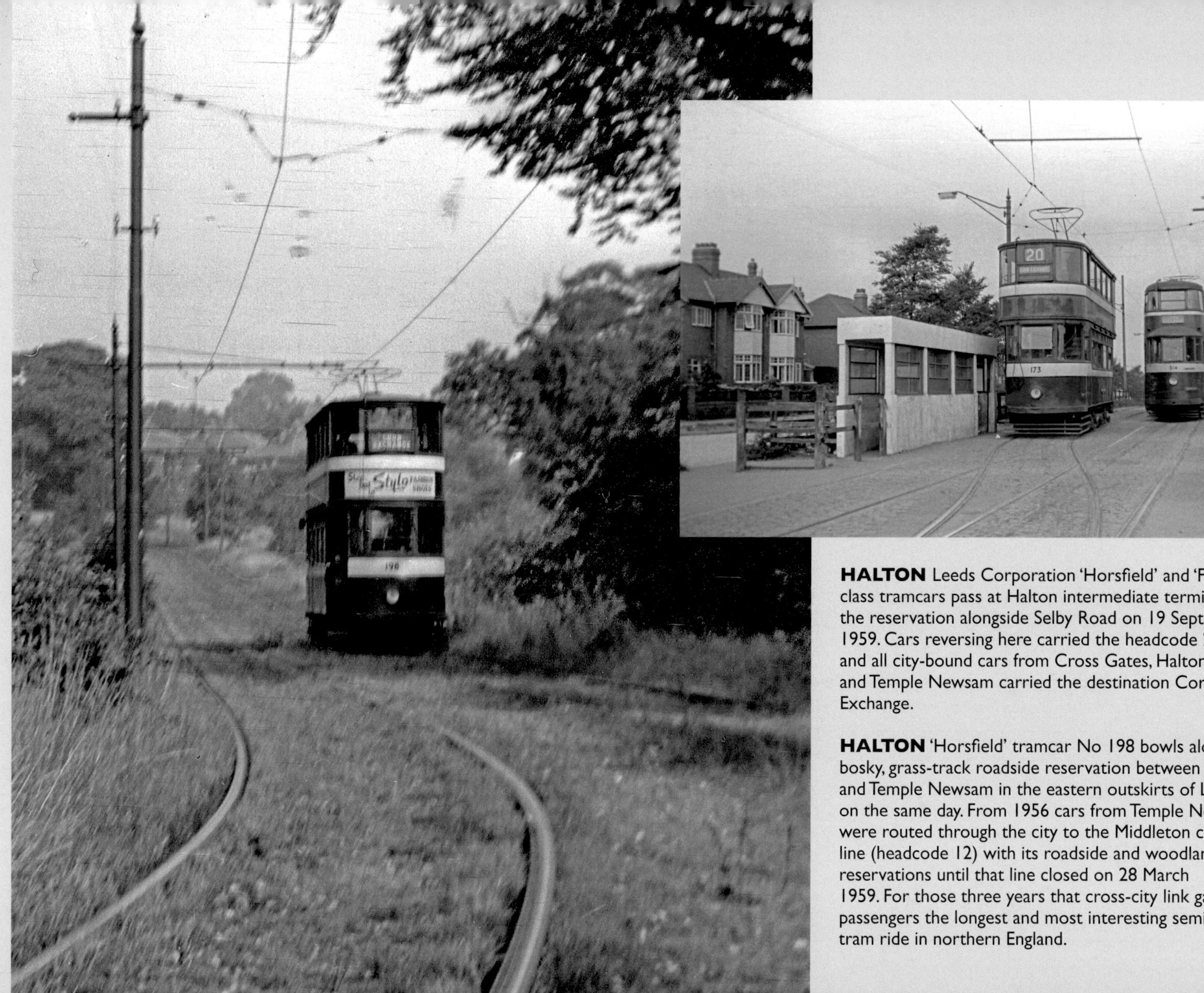

HALTON Leeds Corporation 'Horsfield' and 'Feltham' class tramcars pass at Halton intermediate terminus on the reservation alongside Selby Road on 19 September 1959. Cars reversing here carried the headcode 20 and all city-bound cars from Cross Gates, Halton and Temple Newsam carried the destination Corn Exchange.

HALTON 'Horsfield' tramcar No 198 bowls along the bosky, grass-track roadside reservation between Halton and Temple Newsam in the eastern outskirts of Leeds on the same day. From 1956 cars from Temple Newsam were routed through the city to the Middleton circular line (headcode 12) with its roadside and woodland reservations until that line closed on 28 March 1959. For those three years that cross-city link gave passengers the longest and most interesting semi-rural tram ride in northern England.

TEMPLE NEWSAM The end of the line: 'Horsfield' tramcar No 198, built by Brush in 1931, stands at the bucolic terminus on the edge of the woods at Temple Newsam (headcode 22) on 19 September 1959. This was on the edge of Temple Newsam Park, with gardens and golf courses surrounding Temple Newsam House, a 16th-, 17th- and 18th-century mansion with one of the finest collections of paintings, furniture and porcelain in Britain. The Temple Newsam and Cross Gates lines were the last two tramways in Leeds and closed together on 7 November 1959.

BRADFORD and Leeds shared the distinction of running the first electric trolleybus services in Britain in 1911. While Leeds abandoned trolleybuses in 1928, Bradford, with its steep hills, retained an extensive system of trolleybuses, which were masters of the hills, unlike the diesel buses that succeeded them. The last new vehicles arrived in 1951 and 11 older ones were rebodied until 1963. As other trolleybus systems closed down, Bradford collected an eclectic fleet of second-hand vehicles from Notts & Derby, Llanelly, Darlington, St Helens, Brighton, Hastings, Doncaster and Mexborough. Bradford went on to run Britain's last trolleybuses in 1972. The last two routes were the east-west route 7 from Thornbury to Thornton and the 8 from the city centre north-west to Duckworth Lane, each with its own depot, at Thornbury and Duckworth Lane. Route 8 started here in the commercial heart of the city on a loop around this square in Tyrrel Street, and here we see No 703 waiting for the green signal to turn right into Sunbridge Road on 5 October 1971. It has a 1959 East Lancashire body on a 1945 Karrier chassis with Metropolitan Vickers electric equipment. The Yorkshire stone buildings in this scene had all been cleaned since the era of steam woollen mills and still stand today, though most of them have changed their original use. This is now a pedestrianised conservation area with flush paving and restricted access for loading vehicles.

BRADFORD trolleybus No 703 is seen again, leaving Duckworth Lane terminus city-bound on the same day. No 711, of the same type, has taken its place on the terminal loop.

THORNTON On the east-west route 7 Bradford trolleybus No 731, another East Lancashire-bodied Karrier, is passing the Great Northern Railway Hotel at Thornton, eastbound to Thornbury depot on 5 October 1971. Bradford's routes 7 and 8 were the last two trolleybus routes in Britain and closed prematurely on 5 March 1972 as a result of a national coal strike that reduced coal stocks at the power stations and caused 20 days of blackouts in that strike-bound decade.

TEESSIDE trolleybuses were promoted in 1912 by the Cleveland Iron & Steel Works to take men to and from the work sites along the south bank of the River Tees near Middlesbrough. The overhead and depot were ready by 1915, but the Kaiser war deferred operations till 1919, when they were run by a joint board of Eston UDC and Middlesbrough Corporation. Roe-bodied Sunbeam trolleybus No 6 of the Teesside Railless Traction Board leads a Bristol Lodekka motorbus of United Automobile Services along Eston Road between South Bank and Grangetown on 28 March 1970. Bolckow Terrace (left) was named after Henry Bolckow, who founded the iron and steel industry on Teesside. The firm of Bolckow, Vaughan, which initiated the trolleybus system, was taken over in 1929 by Dorman, Long, which built the great steel arch bridges at Newcastle in 1928 and Sydney in 1932. The steel works supplied the 550-volt traction current till 1955, when it was switched to the National Grid. The Grangetown route was extended in three stages from 1951 to 1968, linking Grangetown and Normanby via Eston in a loop for circular operation in 1968. This was the last trolleybus extension in Britain. The trolleybuses were repainted from dark green to turquoise when Teesside Borough Transport took over later in 1968. This was Britain's last but one trolleybus system to close down, in 1971, one year before Bradford's.

All the elements of this scene have disappeared: the iron and steel works, the railways serving them, Bolckow Terrace and Eston Road, which has been intercepted by the Grangetown bypass.

RIBBLEHEAD station at the head of Ribblesdale is 1,025 feet above sea level on the Settle-Carlisle section of the former Midland main line, serving a remote hamlet and farming community. Behind it, Whernside rises to 2,419 feet, the highest peak in Yorkshire. 'Black Five' No 44898, built at Crewe in 1945, has stopped with a Carlisle to Bradford train on 25 September 1963. The station waiting room doubled as a chapel with a harmonium for Sunday services until 1956, the stony station approach road was used as a sheep market, and from 1938 to 1970 the railway station was also the highest weather station in England as the station master and his wife recorded and reported wind speeds and rainfall for the Air Ministry, the RAF and the river authorities for Yorkshire and Lancashire.

The quarry sidings and signal cabin closed in 1969 and the station closed in 1970, but the up platform reopened as a halt for southbound trains in 1986 and a new down platform was built south of the up platform in 1993. This station is now used mainly by fell walkers. The Settle & Carlisle Railway Trust restored the derelict up-side buildings as a Midland Railway period station and visitor centre, which opened in 2000. The former quarry is now a nature reserve and new sidings have been laid opposite the up platform and behind the down platform for the shipment of timber from nearby plantations.

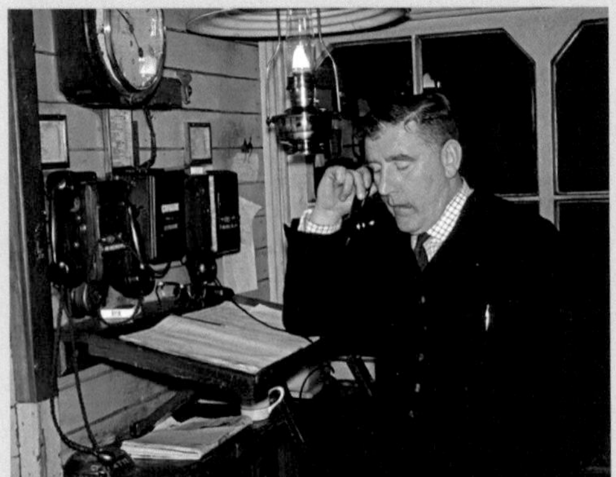

RIBBLEHEAD Bill Sharpe was the last station master and weather observer at Ribblehead, from 1960 to 1967; the station was then made an unstaffed halt so Bill lost his job. He turned down an offer to be an assistant station manager at Appleby and reverted to signalman, becoming a relief at all cabins on the line from Horton to Ais Gill, so he was able to stay in the station master's house at Ribblehead. He was on duty in Ais Gill cabin at the summit of the line when the 'Farewell to Steam' excursion train passed on its way back to Liverpool on 11 August 1968.

Bill was born in Leeds and lived in the dales country from the age of 14, when he started work on a farm at Ingleton. At 19 he went to work in the granite quarry at Ingleton, then the limestone quarry at Ribblehead. He joined the railway at 27 and stayed at Ribblehead station through three grades of work: porter for 12 months, signalman for eight years and station master for seven years. His son Geoffrey was a signalman at Milnthorpe on the LNWR main line in Westmorland. Bill is pictured on the phone to 'control' at Carlisle on relief signal duty on 7 December 1967.

DENT HEAD The 'Long Drag' north of Settle reaches its first summit 1,151 feet above sea level inside Blea Moor Tunnel, 500 feet under the moor. The tunnel is 1½ miles long, dank, smoky and spooky, and conditions were bad for footplate and maintenance men in steam days. Now over the crest and gathering speed on a downhill run, it will be a relief for the engine crew on 'Black Five' No 45131 (Armstrong Whitworth, 1935) with a northbound freight as it emerges from the north portal of the tunnel into the sunshine and verdant beauty of Dentdale on 12 October 1967.

DENTDALE The former Midland Railway Settle-Carlisle main line over the 'roof of England' is viewed from Blea Moor on 19 June 1965. The wisp of steam marks a southbound passenger train crossing Dent Head Viaduct, and we can see steam from a previous train pothering out of the north portal of Blea Moor Tunnel below our location. In December 1963 the line was blocked by snow for a week, mainly by a 60-foot drift over the north portal of this tunnel. The railway cuts a ledge along the side of Widdale Fell (right, 2,203 feet), and Baugh Fell (2,216 feet) rises in the background.

DENT In the late-afternoon sunlight on 20 September 1963, an ex-LMSR 'Jubilee' Class 7P locomotive, with a van and four coaches, stops in Dent station at 5.54pm on a Bradford-Carlisle service. Dent signal cabin and Dent Head Viaduct can be seen in the background with Blea Moor on the right. This station, at 1,145 feet, is 5 miles from and 700 feet higher than the village of the same name. The access road from the valley bottom, first metalled in 1954, climbs 450 feet in three-quarters of a mile, starting with hairpin corners on a 1 in 5 gradient. Dent station is still open as a halt and the station house on the right is now in private use.

DENT With light snow on the ground and its steam backlit by the sun, a 'Black Five', fitted with a small snowplough, brings a Bradford to Carlisle stopping train into Dent station, the highest in England, on 19 January 1966.

DENT The streamlined 1959 Morris Minor car parked here looks out of place in the quaint main street, named simply The Street, on the road through Dentdale on 1 June 1961. The street is roughly paved with cobbles (not granite setts) the full width of the street between the buildings with no footpaths. On the right is a drinking fountain, roughly hewn from red Shap granite, in memory of Adam Sedgwick (1785-1873) of Dent, one of the founders of the science of geology. The Sun Inn stands at the top of the street where it zigzags out of the village towards Sedbergh, the nearest town, 5½ miles north-west.

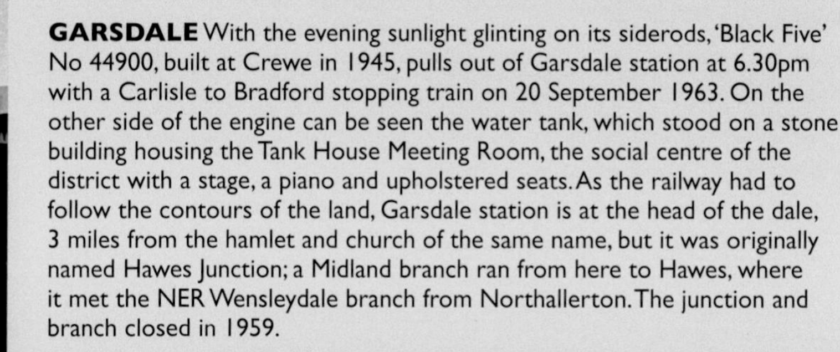

GARSDALE With the evening sunlight glinting on its siderods, 'Black Five' No 44900, built at Crewe in 1945, pulls out of Garsdale station at 6.30pm with a Carlisle to Bradford stopping train on 20 September 1963. On the other side of the engine can be seen the water tank, which stood on a stone building housing the Tank House Meeting Room, the social centre of the district with a stage, a piano and upholstered seats. As the railway had to follow the contours of the land, Garsdale station is at the head of the dale, 3 miles from the hamlet and church of the same name, but it was originally named Hawes Junction; a Midland branch ran from here to Hawes, where it met the NER Wensleydale branch from Northallerton. The junction and branch closed in 1959.

AIS GILL The former Midland Railway main line to the north reaches the 1,169-foot summit on the watershed and county boundary with this view north from Yorkshire into Westmorland. Here a big BR Standard 9F 2-10-0 locomotive crests the summit with a heavy load of anhydrite southbound from Long Meg Quarry in Cumberland to Widnes on 19 January 1966. It was the coldest day since the notorious winter of 1947, with a maximum temperature of 28 degrees F (-2½ degrees C), and the smoke and steam shows up boldly in the cold air. The four-track layout here provided loop sidings for slow, loose-coupled goods trains to stand by for fast, continuous air-braked freight and passenger trains to pass. The standard MR signal cabin was built in 1900 and is now preserved at the Midland Railway Centre, Butterley, Derbyshire. The stone bothy is a platelayers' hut. In the background is Wild Boar Fell (2,324 feet), below which the railway curves right over Ais Gill Beck and past Aisgill hamlet, the nearest habitation, as it descends into Mallerstang.

MALLERSTANG 'Long Meg' on the 'Long Drag': another hulking, grimy 9F plods slowly up Mallerstang with the heavy, metallic clank-clank of its coupling rods as it toils up final stretch of the steady 1 in 100 gradient for 16 miles on the northern ascent to Ais Gill summit on 9 June 1967. This train, like the one we saw opposite, was known as 'Long Meg', a twice-daily load of anhydrite from Long Meg Quarry to Widnes chemical works and the heaviest train on the 'Long Drag'. In latter years it was always hauled by a 9F, this one being No 92208. As it approached this location the exhaust echoed against the escarpment of Wild Boar Fell high above the line on the west side, and on a still day the laboured beat of the steam exhaust could be heard for 2 minutes into the distance towards the summit. Mallerstang is a wide, U-shaped, glaciated valley cradling the headwaters of the River Eden, which flows by Appleby and Carlisle into the Solway Firth.

MALLERSTANG British Railways' last steam excursion train, the 15-guinea 'Farewell to Steam', ran from Liverpool via Manchester to Carlisle and back on 11 August 1968, one week after the end of regular steam traction on the national railway system. On the return journey two 'Black Fives', Nos 44871 and 44781, are seen double-heading the 13-coach train and storming the gradient up Mallerstang in record time. All the locomotives for this trip, including 'Black Five' No 45110 from Liverpool to Manchester and 'Britannia' Class No 70013 *Oliver Cromwell*, from Manchester to Carlisle, were stabled and prepared at Carnforth shed, which closed the next day. When *Oliver Cromwell* ran light over the line, after the excursion train, on its way to temporary retirement in Norfolk, it was thought to be the last steam engine over the 'Long Drag'; however, after a short ban on steam over BR metals, this scenic route has become a favourite for privately organised steam excursions.

DALLAM railway viaduct over the River Bela and its water meadows was a dramatic feature of the landscape between Milnthorpe and Sandside. This 300-yard viaduct on 23 stone arches and three steel arches carried the 5-mile single-line branch of the Furness Railway from Arnside to Hincaster, where it linked with the LNWR main line. Intermediate stations were at Sandside and Heversham. The link was built mainly to carry coke trains from County Durham that went via Tebay to the iron and steel works in Furness. It was also used by stopping passenger trains from Grange-over-Sands to Kendal, excursion trains, and a fortnightly special train carrying Durham miners to a convalescent home at Conishead near Ulverston. Passenger services on the branch ended in 1953 but coke trains and excursions continued to use it till it closed on 9 September 1963, one month before this photograph was taken, following the demise of the Furness iron industry. The viaduct was demolished in 1966 but the line from Arnside to Sandside quarry remained open for stone trains till 1971. Here the River Bela flows into the River Kent estuary, seen beyond the viaduct, with Whitbarrow (706 feet) in the background.

LONSDALE The trail of steam along the far fellside is from a northbound goods train on the former LNWR West Coast Main Line hugging the slopes of Dillicar Common between Grayrigg and Tebay on 15 August 1963. The line swings east from Kentdale to Lonsdale to take advantage of the gap cut by the River Lune through the fells linking the North Pennine Moors to the east with the Cumbrian Mountains to the west, giving trains an easier assault on the climb to 916 feet over Shap Fells. The Lune rises in Ravenstonedale and flows south by Kirkby Lonsdale and Lancaster to the sea. Dieselisation of BR saw the last ordinary steam passenger and freight trains pass through these fells in December 1967. The M6 motorway opened in 1970 with a two-tier ledge along the fellside above the railway, then in 1974 the railway was electrified with overhead gantries and catenary.

Right: **LONSDALE** This sheep's-eye view shows a 'Black Five' leading a southbound freight through the Lune gap at Carlin Gill, the 'witch's ravine' in the background between the green pastures of Westmorland and the brown moors of Yorkshire, on 1 May 1963. Above the railway is High Carlingill Farm on the route of the Roman road from Lancaster to Carlisle, and at the top of the picture is Uldale Head (1,533 feet). The M6 motorway now runs along the slopes in the foreground on two levels.

Left: **GRAYRIGG** After cresting Grayrigg bank on the climb from Oxenholme, 'Black Five' No 45481 heads a northbound freight between the up and down loop sidings at Grayrigg on the West Coast Main Line between Lancaster and Carlisle on 1 May 1966. The remains of the former Grayrigg station, which closed in 1954, still lay just out of sight beyond the signal cabin in the rear of the train.

OXENHOLME station on the former LNWR main line, seen here on 29 May 1962, was the junction for the branch to Kendal and Windermere. The covered bay platform and sidings on the left were for branch traffic. From here northbound trains on the main line begin the ascent of Grayrigg bank, the first part of the climb to Shap summit, and steam freight and passenger trains could whistle up a banking engine from the sidings behind the camera if they needed a push up the side of Hay Fell. Oxenholme, with its engine shed, freight yard, signal cabin and station offices, was a railwaymen's village, but it was in decline at this time together with the railways. The engine shed closed in 1962 and the goods and banking engine sidings were lifted in 1969.

In 1973 the main line was electrified as part of the West Coast route to Scotland, the Windermere branch was singled, the signal cabins closed and the semaphore signals were replaced with colour lights. The sidings on the left have been replaced by a car park and the island platform buildings have been demolished, but the overall canopy remains and the station looks much the same today, although it has been fancifully renamed Oxenholme (The Lake District), even though it is not in the Lake District; the National Park boundary is 5½ miles down the Windermere branch.

OXENHOLME station by gaslight, looking north along the down main platform on 16 February 1968. The picture shows the porter/ticket collector's cabin, the destination boards, the clock and the stonework of the station buildings. This station was the scene of a murder at 3.15am on 10 February 1965 when three policemen were shot – one fatally, one seriously injured – when they cornered a gunman in the waiting room on the up main platform (right). The man was wanted for using a gun when police searching for a burglar stopped a stolen van. There followed an armed manhunt over the fells south-east of the station at daylight when four farmers chased a man one of them spotted running across the fields, and joined in the hunt with their shotguns as police from three counties converged on the area with 30 rifles and 100 revolvers. After a 1½-mile chase over The Helm ridge and across fields, a shot in the leg from a farmer and a grazed temple from a police shot brought him down near Blease Farm and he was arrested.

OXENHOLME This two-car diesel multiple unit, seen on a siding at Oxenholme station, was one of the second batch of BR Derby lightweight units with AEC engines built in 1954-55 for services between Carlisle, Penrith and Whitehaven. This set worked on the Carlisle-Silloth branch from 1954 till the line closed in 1964. These sets later saw service between Carlisle and Skipton and on 18 April 1966 they inaugurated a diesel service on the Windermere branch, operating between Windermere and Carnforth. They were ideal for passengers viewing the scenery through the large, observation-style windscreens with glazing between the passenger saloons and the motorman's cab instead of the opaque partitions on later DMUs. The yellow warning panel replaced the original cream 'moustache' on the dash panels of these early DMUs. Hundreds more steam trains ran on the Windermere branch in the next two years because of frequent breakdowns of diesel locomotives and multiple units, and these ex-west Cumberland DMUs were scrapped in 1967-68.

44963

KENDAL An all-LMSR passenger train, headed by a class 4MT tank engine, running alongside Castle Road, Kendal, forges out of town up the 1 in 80 gradient to Oxenholme on a local stopping train from Windermere to Lancaster in March 1965.

Left: **KENDAL** 'Black Five' No 44963 (Horwich, 1946) climbs the 1 in 80 gradient out of Kendal towards Oxenholme with the early-afternoon freight to Carnforth on 14 February 1968.

KENDAL Driver Joe Wilson of Carnforth shed is in the cab of BR Standard 9F No 92009 shunting Kendal goods yard on 15 February 1968.

KENDAL After shunting the goods yard (left), 'Black Five' No 44894 (Crewe, 1945) is running around its train (which is just out of sight) on the running lines at Kendal before taking it away to Carnforth at 2.25pm on 1 August 1968, two days before the end of steam on BR. Most steam engines were neglected and filthy in the last months of steam traction, so No 44894 had been cleaned by a band of railfans for photography. The parcels van sidings are on the right; the vans will be loaded with parcels and mailbags in Kendal station platform later in the day.

KENDAL The crimson Ribble buses add colour to the main street of the 'Auld Grey Town' (their paintwork has been rendered lighter by Kodachrome film). In this picture on 5 March 1962 a 1950 low-bridge double-decker is at the stop by the Town Hall on Highgate on the 55-mile route 68 from Keswick to Lancaster. This is an all-Leyland bus as both the chassis and the body are by Leyland Motors; it is also advertising Leyland Paints, made in the same town in south Lancashire. Low-bridge buses were used on this route to negotiate the railway bridge at Carnforth. The Ribble single-decker passing the Town Hall is a 1951 Weymann-bodied Leyland Olympic on a town service.

Today this is a one-way street, with northbound traffic turning right or left at the signals by the Town Hall, and the street over the brow is a pedestrian zone with limited access for motor vehicles. The Town Hall was built piecemeal from 1825 to 1897 and the clock tower of 1861 strikes the hours and the quarters and a carillon plays a different folk tune for each day of the week every three hours from 9.00am to 6.00pm. The Town Hall was home to Kendal Municipal Borough Council till 1974, when five local councils were amalgamated to form South Lakeland District Council, now based here.

STAVELEY The last steam freight to Windermere, headed by 'Black Five' No 44709 (Horwich, 1948) runs tender-first west of Staveley on 2 August 1968, two days before the end of regular steam workings on British Railways. This was the last steam engine to shunt Kendal goods yard, on Saturday 3 August, and as there was no freight on Sundays it was the last steam engine on the branch. On the left are the slopes of Hugill Fell; on the right is Karl Greenwood, aged 3.

WINDERMERE 'Shovelling white steam over her shoulder', an ex-LMSR 4MT 2-6-4 tank engine lifts a passenger train out of Windermere on its way to Lancaster on 25 February 1965. Steam lingers in the crisp air, almost obscuring the panoramic view of the Cumbrian Mountains with snow on the peaks.

WINDERMERE Privately owned steam launches like this were owned by landed gentry, industrialists, railway companies and wealthy merchants with homes around the English lakes in the 19th century, and many of these vessels were salvaged and restored to working order in the mid-20th century. This is *Dolly*, 41 feet long by 6ft 6in beam, built about 1850 for an owner on Ullswater. She sank when crushed by ice in the big freeze of 1895 and lay on the bed of the lake, which preserved her timber, till discovered by the Furness branch of the British Sub-Aqua Club in 1960 and raised in 1962. The hulk was moved to Windermere and restored by the late George Pattinson, a Bowness builder with a sand and gravel wharf on Rayrigg Bay, where the vessel is seen in steam on 18 September 1965 for the first time since it was recovered.

Mr Pattinson saved many old Cumbrian lake craft and founded the Windermere Steamboat Museum, which opened here on Rayrigg Bay in 1975. The museum closed in 2006 for a larger building to be constructed to cover the growing collection and the dock and to restore more vessels. The charity Lakeland Arts reopened the museum in spring 2018 as the Windermere Jetty Museum of Boats, Steam and Stories. *Dolly* is on display there but no longer on the water.

LADY OF THE LAKE

ULLSWATER The motor yacht *Lady of the Lake* is one of the oldest vessels afloat, dating from 1877, and is seen arriving at Howtown pier on 1 August 1964. The Ullswater Navigation & Transit Company plies a cruise and ferry service along the length of the lake between Glenridding, Howtown and Pooley Bridge all the year round. The *Lady of the Lake* was built by T. B. Seath at Rutherglen, Glasgow, as a single-screw steam yacht, 97 feet by 15 feet by 2ft 5in, 45 gross tons and licensed to carry 110 passengers. She was taken in three sections by train to Penrith and by horse waggon to Ullswater for reassembly, and entered service as a Royal Mail steamer carrying mails as well as passengers between the lakeside communities she served. Her sister, the *Raven*, was built by T. B. Seath in 1889. Both vessels were converted from steam to diesel motor yachts in 1935 and are still in service together with more modern vessels, thanks to a change of command in 1954 when Sir Wavell (later Lord) Wakefield of Kendal bought a majority share in the company to save it from closing down. The year after this photograph was taken, the *Lady of the Lake* was badly damaged by fire from a shed blaze while she was on the slipway near Pooley Bridge and she was out of service for 14 years before being restored with a new engine and relaunched in 1979.

Ullswater is on the boundary between Westmorland and Cumberland; Glenridding and Howtown are in Westmorland while Pooley Bridge and the background to this photograph are in Cumberland. Donald Campbell broke the world water speed record on Ullswater in his jet *Bluebird K7* in 1955 with an average speed of 202.32mph over the measured mile. In 1983 a speed limit of 10mph came into force on the lake.

MILLOM Ironworks were situated at the southern tip of Cumberland with Black Combe (1,969 feet) in the background. A vast internal railway system served the iron works and the nearby Hodbarrow iron ore mine and connected with the Furness Railway main line between Barrow and Whitehaven. The mine supplied pure haematite iron ore to iron works in Furness for 11 years before the first blast furnace was built here in 1866 between Hodbarrow and the nearby village of Holborn Hill; it subsequently grew into the boom town of Millom (meaning 'at the mills') with terraced houses and public buildings. Hodbarrow mine was on the coast and the mining company built a sea wall in 1900-05 to stop the sea flooding the workings. Eventually the iron ore ran out. This picture of the iron works was taken on 22 October 1967, the year before the mine and works closed down. The two sites have been cleared, except for the slag heaps, and are now wildlife reserves. Millom, the former boom town, is now a depopulated ghost town.

MILLOM Ironworks 0-4-0 saddle-tank engines *Prince John*, built by Andrew Barclay at Kilmarnock in 1918, and No 10, built by Peckett at Bristol in 1934, are pictured outside the engine shed on 22 October 1967.

Right: **DALEGARTH** is the upper terminus of the 7-mile, 1ft 3in-gauge Ravenglass & Eskdale Railway. The locomotive *River Irt*, an 0-8-2, built by the RER in 1928, has turned round on the turntable at the end of the line to run round its train, and the guard is checking and selling tickets for the return run to Ravenglass on 4 June 1961. The railway opened in 1875 as a 3-foot-gauge line terminating a quarter of a mile further up the dale at the village of Boot to carry haematite iron ore from the mines to the Furness Railway main line at Ravenglass. It also carried passengers from 1876 to 1908, but closed in 1913. Then in 1915-17 the model engineer W. J. Basset-Lowke and Narrow Gauge Railways Ltd relaid the track to 1ft 3in gauge from Ravenglass to the present terminus at Dalegarth on a short spur off the original steep route to Boot. This was a passenger railway but it also carried granite from the quarry at Beckfoot to Murthwaite crushing plant from 1922 to 1953. During that period three miles of mixed-gauge track from Murthwaite to Ravenglass allowed standard-gauge locomotives and waggons to straddle the miniature railway to collect ballast for the main line. The RER was put up for sale in 1960 and saved from closure by the RER Preservation Society with financial backing from Sir Wavell (later Lord) Wakefield of Kendal, saviour of the Ullswater Navigation & Transit Company, and stockbroker Colin Gilbert. Today the railway and the Ullswater company are owned by the Lake District Estates Group controlled by the late Lord Wakefield's descendants.

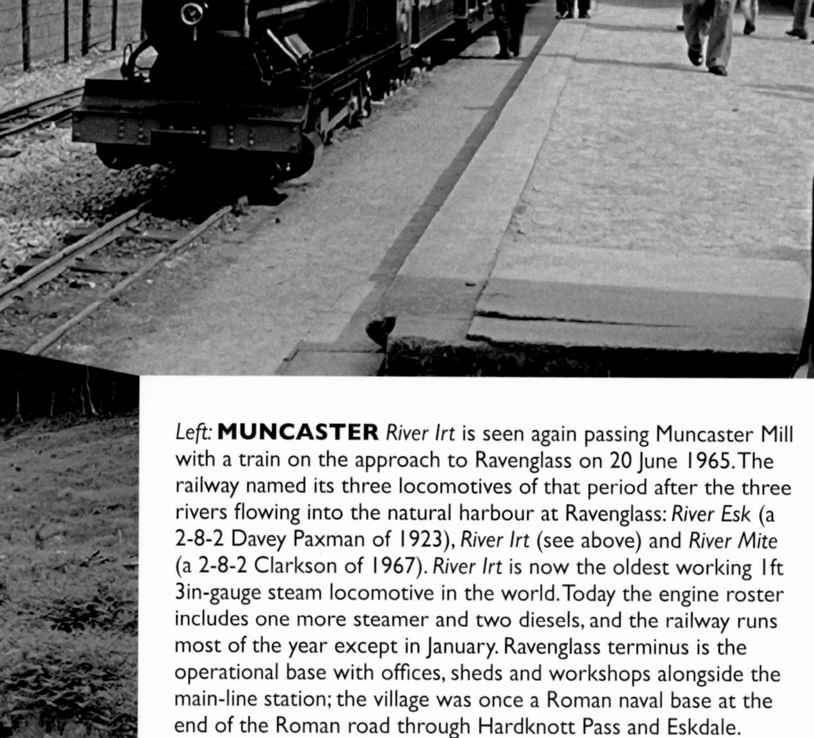

Left: **MUNCASTER** *River Irt* is seen again passing Muncaster Mill with a train on the approach to Ravenglass on 20 June 1965. The railway named its three locomotives of that period after the three rivers flowing into the natural harbour at Ravenglass: *River Esk* (a 2-8-2 Davey Paxman of 1923), *River Irt* (see above) and *River Mite* (a 2-8-2 Clarkson of 1967). *River Irt* is now the oldest working 1ft 3in-gauge steam locomotive in the world. Today the engine roster includes one more steamer and two diesels, and the railway runs most of the year except in January. Ravenglass terminus is the operational base with offices, sheds and workshops alongside the main-line station; the village was once a Roman naval base at the end of the Roman road through Hardknott Pass and Eskdale.

WHITEHAVEN Haig Colliery was the last coal mine in Cumberland, employing 1,800 men in the 1960s. In this picture on 19 June 1969 we see a train of National Coal Board tip wagons being loaded with coal at the coal screening plant, which sorted the coal into different sizes. In the background are two pithead winding frames to work the lifts underground and the colliery main building housing the boilers, engine room, ventilation plant, stores and offices. In the foreground the junk heap of scrap iron and old railway sleepers would be called modern sculpture today. The colliery closed in 1986 as a result of a dangerous geological fault, but the main building and one winding frame survives as the Haig Colliery Mining Museum. The rest of the buildings and the railways have gone. The mining museum closed in 2016 but the building is scheduled as an ancient monument for its winding engine

WHITEHAVEN Noise, coal dust and steam surround the coal screening plant as railway wagons are loaded with coal sorted by size, and an 0-4-0 saddle tank engine stands by the control room on 5 May 1969.

WHITEHAVEN
Industrial steam: the fireman of NCB 0-4-0 saddle tank *Solway*, built by Hudswell Clark in 1948, is cleaning out his fire grate at Haig Colliery on 5 May 1969 with two colliery winding frames in the background.

WHITEHAVEN Three of NCB saddle tank engines stand at Haig Colliery on 19 June 1969, including two 0-6-0s with narrow Giesl ejectors designed to reduce coal consumption. In the right foreground the fireman of 0-6-0 locomotive *Revenge* is cleaning his smokebox and burying the track in cinders and soot. On the left the 0-4-0 *Solway* is backing down on to a train of loaded coal wagons. The brick hut was the weighbridge house. These two 0-6-0s with Giesel ejectors were built by Hunslet at Leeds in 1950 and one of them, the middle engine of the trio, named *Repulse*, now pulls passenger trains on the Lakeside & Haverthwaite Railway.

WHITEHAVEN *Solway* on the Solway: the NCB 0-4-0ST runs along the clifftop on the brink of the Solway Firth on 19 June 1969 with a train of empty trucks from the harbour to the washing plant at the former Ladysmith Colliery, 1½ miles south, to be loaded with more washed coal for the harbour. On the left is the west pier and lighthouse, built by John Rennie in 1823-38 to protect the harbour entrance. To the left of the locomotive we see the top of the chimney of 1840 on the disused engine house of the former Wellington Colliery.

WHITEHAVEN On the same day *Solway* makes its way south along the cliffside from Haig Colliery with empty trucks from the harbour for Ladysmith washing plant, with St Bee's Head in the right background.

WHITEHAVEN This 1 in 5 cable incline called Howgill Brake, was the link for coal wagons between Haig Colliery and Whitehaven harbour. The cable was worked by an electric winding engine house at the top and the weight of the loaded wagons descending (pictured) was offset by the empties from the harbour hooked on to the other end of the cable. In this view from the top of the incline we see the harbour laid out below with trucks of coal lining the piers awaiting shipment. We also see the Quaker Oats mill on the east pier, the gas works and a disused colliery at the foot of the cliffs north of the harbour. The mill closed in 1972 and in the same year Howgill Brake stopped working because of a landslip and the railway trucks used Corkickle Brake instead till 1975, when the coal went by road.

CARLISLE Seven main-line railways converged on the border city of Carlisle in pre-Grouping days and the city is surrounded by a network of freight lines avoiding Citadel main-line passenger station. Here, from St Nicholas Bridge on the southern approaches, we see ex-LMSR 'Black Five' No 44792 (Horwich, 1947) with a northbound freight on 10 April 1964.

CARLISLE CITADEL station (left) was named after the Citadel (right), both forming two sides of Court Square and pictured here on 28 May 1961. The twin circular towers flank the English Gate in the south wall of the city; the Scotch Gate was on the north wall. The original Citadel towers of 1541-53 were rebuilt in red sandstone in 1804-11 as the Law Courts, which they were at the time of this photograph; they are now the head office of Cumbria County Council. The statue is that of William, first Earl of Lonsdale, who initiated the rebuilding of the Citadel to the Law Courts. The railway station was built in 1847 in neo-Tudor grey stonework by Sir William Tite, architect to both the Lancaster & Carlisle Railway and the Caledonian Railway, the original joint owners of the station. The east front is non-symmetrical with a buttressed, lantern clock tower and an arcaded stone portico to the left. We can also see the transverse ridge-and-furrow, glazed overall roof spanning the platforms. Sir William also designed Lancaster and Penrith stations, to match the adjacent castles. Before the Grouping, Carlisle was the junction of the London & North Western Railway, the Caledonian Railway, the Midland Railway, the North Eastern Railway, the North British Railway, the Glasgow & South Western Railway, and the Maryport & Carlisle Railway. At the time of this photograph it was the meeting place of British Railways' Midland, North Eastern and Scottish Regions.

PHILADELPHIA, with its loco sheds and workshops, was the hub of the former Lambton Collieries' 70-mile network of railways serving a group of mines between Durham and Sunderland. It was on the line from Herrington Colliery to the BR exchange sidings at Penshaw on the Durham-Sunderland line and the colliery engines had running powers over BR (ex-NER) to deliver the coal to the staiths on the River Wear at Sunderland. The cabs of the locomotives were tapered to fit a small-bore tunnel on the way. In this picture two NCB 0-6-0 saddle tank steam locomotives stand at the coaling stage at Philadelphia on 28 March 1968. The drop-bottom wagons on the ramped pier dropped coal down chutes to the locomotive bunkers in the same way as ships were loaded at the staiths on the river. Behind the ramp is the winding frame for the Dorothea pit.

PHILADELPHIA NCB locomotive No 8 propels a train of empty coal wagons around the curve at Philadelphia Bank Top Junction on its way from Penshaw marshalling yard to Houghton Colliery on the same day. The third leg of this triangular junction led to Philadelphia Works and Herrington Colliery. Steam engines pottered around Philadelphia for only one more year before they were replaced by ex-BR 0-6-0 diesel shunters in 1969. The locomotive repair shops closed in 1987 and the general workshops in 1989. County Durham had 127 mines employing 108,000 colliers when the National Coal Board took over in 1947. The last mine to close was at Monkwearmouth in 1994.

NEWCASTLE is a city of dramatic, high-level bridges. Less photographed than those spanning the river is this stone-arch railway bridge leaping high over The Side at its junction with Dean Street, from which this picture was taken on 28 March 1970. Dean Street was built in the 1780s to succeed the steep and narrow ascent of The Side on the Great North Road route from the old Tyne bridge to the city centre at a time when packhorses were giving way to horse-drawn waggons. The bridge in this picture was built in 1848-49 to carry the York, Newcastle & Berwick Railway, now part of the East Coast Main Line. The bridge was widened in 1893-94. The prominent building in the background is the Moot Hall, built in 1810-11 for the Northumberland County Courts.

NEWCASTLE At the top of Grey Street, by now with clean buildings, one of the Tyneside PTE's Alexander-bodied Leyland Atlantean buses of 1965 pauses at the signals beside the Earl Grey monument on 28 March 1970. The word 'lonnen' on the destination blind is from a dialect word for a 'lane', which is at Fenham; the word is 'loan' in Scotland. Newcastle buses were blue and white from 1912 until 1949, when they began to be repainted in yellow and cream. The trolleybuses were yellow with brown/maroon bands from 1935, so when nine Bournemouth trolleybuses were loaned to Newcastle from 1942 to 1945 they merged unobtrusively into the fleet. The brown bands disappeared from 1949 and the yellow paintwork went through an orangey phase before reverting to yellow as seen here.

BERWICK The border at Berwick was also the border between the territories of English and Scottish bus companies, but they shared the same premises. Here is the joint bus station and garage of United Automobile Services of Darlington and the Scottish Motor Traction Company of Edinburgh, photographed on 29 May 1959 with buses of those two companies respectively left and right. On the left is a 1949 Eastern-bodied Bristol L loading for Ord, Horncliffe and Norham in Northumberland, and on the right is a 1956 Alexander-bodied AEC Reliance destined for St Abbs via Eyemouth on the Berwickshire coast. Berwick was the last outpost of the Bristol L type on United in 1966. The bus station has since been replaced by a new library and three shops fronting Marygate, and Berwick has no bus station today.

United started bus operations at Lowerstoft in 1912 with a route to Southwold and in the same year it operated its second bus route from Bishop Auckland to Durham! The company gradually expanded its services through much of the east side of England from Suffolk to Northumberland, ultimately concentrating services in the area from Filey to Berwick. In the process it created in its wake the Eastern Coach Works at Lowestoft, Eastern Counties Omnibus Company, of Norwich, East Midland Motor Services of Chesterfield and a legacy of services in Lincolnshire and East Yorkshire. The company standardised on Bristol chassis with Eastern coachwork as seen here.

Part 6, Wales, Man and Scotland

Glamorgan

MUMBLES Pier was the outer terminus of the Swansea & Mumbles Railway, which ran 5½ miles around the shores of Swansea Bay. Here, on 2 August 1959, we see one of the double-deck tramcars dating from electrification in 1929. The line was electrified at 650 volts DC with double overhead wires to feed the 120hp motors of the big cars running at high speed, sometimes as two-car multiple units. The 278-yard-long pier was opened in 1898 and, after periodic closures for restoration, remains open today with a lifeboat station in place of the former landing stage and visitor amenities at the pier entrance.

MUMBLES This is the interior of the upper saloon of Swansea & Mumbles car No 10 at Mumbles Pier on 2 August 1959. These 45-feet-long double-deckers were the largest tramcars in Britain, with 106 seats. They were double-ended, so the seats, which were upholstered in leather, were reversible as on normal tramcars.

Right: **MUMBLES** Car No 10 of 1929 rocks along the 1898 extension of the Mumbles Railway from Southend to Mumbles Pier on the same day. The town of Oystermouth in the distance was the original terminus of the line, opened in 1807 as the horse-drawn Oystermouth Tramroad. The extension had to be cut out of the cliffside of Mumbles Head and was retained by a sea wall. The cars had doors on the inland side only as all the stations and halts were on that side of the line. The centre rails, laid along most of the single-line sections, were bonded to the running rails to increase the negative return current to the power station. Two months after this photograph was taken this section of the line closed for conversion to a motor road for buses to take over the entire route five months later.

WEST CROSS In this view from a Mumbles tramcar, Swansea-bound, we see West Cross Halt, where the line ran close to the high-tide mark with a low sea wall around the shores of Swansea Bay. A cycle path now follows the track of the railway from Swansea to Mumbles.

SWANSEA terminus of the Mumbles Railway was at the town end of Oystermouth Road. On 2 August 1959 we see car No 10 again, one of the 106-seat, 120hp electric cars built by the Brush Electrical Engineering Company in 1928-29, when the former steam railway was electrified. Sometimes they ran coupled together as two-car multiple unit trains to carry the crowds at busy periods. The line from Swansea to Southend closed on 5 January 1960.

Left and above: **SWANSEA** Rutland Street car shed housed the fleet of 13 electric cars at the Swansea terminus of the Mumbles Railway. These huge Brush bogie cars were painted crimson and cream.

Right: **SWANSEA** The Mumbles Railway is viewed from the top of a tram as it enters Swansea along the seaward side of Oystermouth Road with the former London & North Western Railway (right) that led to Swansea Victoria station and the docks. The end of St Helen's Road (left) was the St Helen's tram terminus of the Swansea town system, the Swansea Improvements & Tramways Company, which closed in 1937; the depot was just off left in St Helen's Road. All these lines have disappeared and Oystermouth Road has been widened across both railway trackbeds to seaward; the Bay View Hotel survives.

DOLGOCH A narrow chimney on the narrow gauge. By the water tower at Dolgoch station on the 2ft 3in-gauge Talyllyn Railway is engine No 4, with a train from Towyn to Abergynolwyn on 13 May 1960. This engine worked on the former Corris Railway from 1921 to 1947. It came to the Talyllyn Railway in 1951 and was named *Edward Thomas*, who was the former 'traffic manager' and general factotum for 53 years. The engine was fitted with this experimental 'Giesl ejector' blastpipe and fishtail chimney in 1958 but that failed to reduce coal consumption or improve performance and did nothing to improve its appearance either, so the engine was refitted with a conventional chimney in 1969. The engine is still in service on the railway following a major overhaul in 1976 and a new boiler in 2004. Passengers alight here at Dolgoch to see the nearby waterfalls.

DOLGOCH The track of the Talyllyn Railway through the woods on the upper half of the line on 13 May 1960. The original track, dating from 1865, had been relaid by the Talyllyn Railway Preservation Society with the help of Territorial Army engineers during the 1950s. The railway traverses the escarpment along the south side of the Afon Fathew valley and passes through woods of slender, grotesquely bent and curly trees that look like a setting for a fairy tale. Passengers view the trees down the escarpment below the railway (on the left) at treetop level, which reminds me of the cartoonist Rowland Emett's 'branch line' through the treetops in the story book *Anthony and Antimacassar,* written by his wife Mary. His cartoons in *Punch* (1939-53) often featured and fantasised quaint, narrow-gauge railways. He visited the Talyllyn and created the Far Tottering & Oyster Creek Railway, which carried passengers in Battersea Park for the 1951 Festival of Britain. He went on to exhibit sculptures of whimsical machines.

ABERGYNOLWYN This was the charm of the dormant Welsh narrow gauge that attracted preservationists and started the restoration movement in the late 1940s. This was the disused line of the Talyllyn Railway beyond the passenger terminus at Abergynolwyn to Bryn Eglwys slate quarries on 13 May 1960. The slate quarries were abandoned in 1946, but in 1976 the Towyn-Abergynolwyn passenger service was extended over this part of the disused quarry line for 1 mile to Nant Gwernol.

Abergynolwyn is half a mile beyond its station but this extension to Bryn Eglwys quarries gave access to a cable incline from this section of the line down to the village in the valley below, where waggon turntables led to storage sidings serving the coal yard, the writing slate factory, the houses, the school and the chapel!

MARFORD Abandoned, rusty and forgotten, this 0-6-0 saddle tank engine, bereft of builders' plates and nameplates, was a relic of a standard-gauge industrial railway at the disused Rossett Sand & Gravels quarry. The engine could be seen at close quarters from the GWR main line between Wrexham and Chester and was standing on parallel exchange sidings buried in sand. The quarry was situated at Springfield Lane, Marford, near Rossett, where a spur off the main line between Gresford and Rossett stations led to four sidings of GWR and LMSR trucks, shunted by the quarry company locomotive. Rossett Sand & Gravels Ltd opened this quarry in 1927 initially to supply sand for concreting the Mersey road tunnel. This 0-6-0 inside-cylinder saddle-tank engine, *Netherton*, built in 1903 by Manning Wardle at Leeds, was bought second-hand from the construction contractors Sir Lindsey Parkinson & Company at Winwick Quay, Warrington, in 1943. The sand quarry closed in 1948 and *Netherton* was scrapped a few months after this photograph was taken in 1952, when the quarry was reopened by the United Gravel Company, using lorries to remove the mountain of sand. The quarry closed in 1971 and this is now a Site of Special Scientific Interest owned by the North Wales Wildlife Trust.

CEFN-Y-BEDD was a rustic station on the former Great Central/LNER triad of lines from Wrexham Central to Chester Northgate and Seacombe ferry, which divided at Hawarden Bridge. The view is looking south towards Wrexham on 10 July 1958. These ex-GCR stations, with their brick buildings, gardens and oil lanterns, are now unstaffed halts with new shelters and electric lights. The station had no footbridge and passengers crossed the line to the opposite platform by the timber barrow crossing in the foreground, they still do.

CAERGWRLE CASTLE & WELLS was another station on the Wrexham leg of the triad of GCR/LNER lines to Chester and Seacombe via Hawarden Bridge. A locomotive and goods brake van pause outside the signal cabin during shunting on the daily pick-up goods duty. Trains to Seacombe ferry were diverted to New Brighton in 1960 and now terminate at Bidston, connecting with electric trains to Liverpool. The Chester leg of the triad closed in 1968, and today Caergwrle station has lost its suffix 'Castle & Wells'.

AFON WEN Two coaches from Merseyside on a day excursion to Snowdonia are parked outside the Pwllgwyn Hotel on the A541 road between Mold and Denbigh in August 1951. A day trip by coach was the highlight of the year for those who could not afford to spend all their fortnight's holidays in a seaside resort or holiday camp. Coach hotels such as this were licensed to open in the mornings to cater for outward-bound coach parties taking their mid-morning break. These coaches, owned by Harding's of Birkenhead, are in a tasteful colour scheme of grey trimmed with smoky blue. The leading coach is a 1947 Burlingham-bodied Leyland and the rear coach looks like a 1938 Harrington-bodied Leyland. In those days all coaches carried the company name, address and telephone number in stylish signwriting on the back (now they show only the Internet web address in sans-serif, lower-case, adhesive vinyl lettering).

Harding's coach company dated from 1891 when Alfred Harding began running horse-drawn waggonettes. Coaches still ply from a depot at Grange Road West, Birkenhead, but they are mainly white and the name has changed to Selwyn's.

LLANDUDNO The Great Orme Railway terminus at the foot of Old Road, Llandudno, on 11 May 1960. This 3ft 6in-gauge cable tramway climbed 650 feet in just over 1 mile to the summit of the Great Orme headland (Y Gogarth in Welsh) with a maximum gradient of 1 in 3½ from this terminus up Old Road. The tramway was operated in two sections with a winding station halfway, where passengers changed cars. The centre slot between the grooved running rails is the cable conduit on the street section. The upper section is laid on sleeper track across rough grass with a maximum gradient of 1 in 10.

LLANDUDNO Great Orme Railway cable-car No 5, seen here in the terminal station fronting Church Walks, Llandudno, on the same day, is one of the four bogie passenger cars that have operated the line since its opening in 1902 (car No 4 was wrecked in a runaway). They were built by Hurst, Nelson & Company at Motherwell. There were also three four-wheel vans from 1902 to 1911 used for carrying coke to the winding station, supplies to the summit hotel and occasionally coffins for burial at St Tudno's Church on the Great Orme.

Two cars, one up, one down, are fixed to the cable on each section with a maximum speed of 5mph. The trolleypole and the overhead wire were used for telegraph communication between the cars and the winding station, but these were replaced by an electronic induction loop when the line was closed for a complete refit in 1999-2000. The couplers on these cars might have been used with the vans but are not known to have been used for passenger train operation. The cars were painted plain dark blue and carried the name Great Orme Railway from 1935 till 1977, but the line has since reverted to its original title, the Great Orme Tramway, and the cars are in a mid-blue with bold, ornate lining and lettering in cream and white. The line has been owned and operated in turn by the Great Orme Tramways Company, Great Orme Railway Ltd., Llandudno Urban District Council (1949-74) and, now, by Conwy County Borough Council.

LIVERPOOL-DOUGLAS Liverpool -bound Isle of Man turbine steamer *Lady of Mann*, built by Vickers Armstrong at Barrow in 1930, is seen over the stern of the Douglas-bound TS *Manxman* (Cammell Laird, Birkenhead, 1955) as they cross halfway on the Irish Sea passage on 19 September 1964.

DOUGLAS Gulls circle overhead as the Isle of Man turbine steamship *Ben-my-Chree*, built by Cammell Laird at Birkenhead in 1927, loads at King Edward VIII Pier, Douglas, for Liverpool on 20 June 1964. The *Ben-my-Chree* was the progenitor of 11 passenger ships of this design built for the Isle of Man Steam Packet Company until 1955. Three of them were lost in the evacuation of Dunkirk in 1940 and replaced after the war. These handsome vessels, looking like small Cunard liners, began to be replaced by car ferries from 1962, and the *Ben* was retired from service in 1965. The Steam Packet Company operated motor vessels from 1972 and was taken over by Sea Containers Isle of Man in 1996.

DOUGLAS This profile of Douglas Corporation crossbench horse tram No 46 of 1908 at Victoria Pier terminus is set against the backdrop of Douglas Bay and Onchan Head on 9 June 1961. The tramway dates from 1876 and it has been the only horse tramway in the British Isles since the one at Fintona, County Tyrone, closed in 1957; those at Morecambe and Pwllheli ceased in 1926 and 1927. The service originally ran all year round, but since 1927, when the Corporation put buses on the promenade, the horse tramway has run only in the summer holiday season, currently from April to November.

DOUGLAS The 3-foot-gauge horse tramway runs for 1¾ miles along the promenade around Douglas Bay. Here, a crossbench car pauses at a stop to pick up a passenger on 15 June 1964. The tramway terminates at the north end of the promenade, where it meets the Manx Electric Railway. In the 1950s there was a fleet of 32 cars and a stud of 80 horses providing a peak service every 1½ minutes in August, but the service has declined since then, now with only 13 cars (including three saloons for inclement weather) and 21 horses (all Clydesdales and Shires). The future of this tramway is a subject of debate and controversy. The lofty white building high among the trees was the Falcon Cliff Hotel, which had its own cliff railway from the promenade; the hotel has since been converted to offices.

DOUGLAS station, with its substantial, glazed redbrick buildings, four platforms and extensive canopies, was the central terminus of the Isle of Man Railway's three lines to Peel, Port Erin and Ramsey. On 7 June 1961 the Peel train in the station is headed by 2-4-0 tank engine No 11 *Fenella* of 1894, in the Indian red locomotive colour of the period 1944-65. The Isle of Man Railway Company, which operated mainly in summer with skeleton services in winter, closed down in 1965. The Marquis of Ailsa and friends leased and operated the three lines for the summers of 1967 and '68 but at great financial loss. The Peel and Ramsey lines were finally closed and the track was lifted. Lord Ailsa, now with a modest Government grant, continued to operate the Port Erin line in 1969-71, but still at a loss. The IMR Company, with a bigger Government grant, resumed operation of the Port Erin line in 1972. The railway was eventually nationalised by the Isle of Man Government in 1980 and the summer service still runs on the 15½-mile Douglas-Port Erin line today, the carriages now repainted in dark brown and white. Since the closure of the Peel and Ramsey lines, Douglas station has lost its canopies and half its platforms, which have been replaced, symbolically, by a bus depot and car park.

DOUGLAS Derby Castle is the name of the joint terminus where the Douglas promenade horse tramway meets the 550-volt Manx Electric Railway, on the same 3-foot gauge, for onward travel along the east coast of the island to Laxey and Ramsey, a journey of 17¾ miles. The horse trams terminated under the freestanding cast-iron canopy in the background, demolished in 1980. On 9 June 1961 the electric train in the foreground – trolleycar, crossbench trailer and 6-ton van – dates entirely from 1899, built throughout by G. F. Milnes & Co at Birkenhead, as was most of the stock on the line. Derby Castle was the name of a castellated hotel with a dance hall and variety theatre, later replaced by the intrusive, concrete Summerland leisure centre, which was demolished after a fire. The joint tram terminus is still called Derby Castle today. Many generations of the Earls of Derby held office as Lords of Man on behalf of the British Crown from 1405 to 1736.

GROUDLE GLEN The Manx Electric Railway (MER) is a roadside and cross-country interurban line winding around the headlands, hills and wooded glens along the east coast of the island. Here, trolleycar No 20 tows a crossbench trailer car up the 1 in 24 gradient out of Groudle Glen southbound to Douglas on 18 June 1964. Car 20 is one of four 'winter saloons' that were built by Milnes for the Laxey-Ramsey extension in 1899 and provide the basic service. The original Milnes bogies on cars Nos 19 to 22 were replaced in 1904 by J. G. Brill bogies from Philadelphia to give a better-quality ride.

GROUDLE GLEN The 2-foot-gauge Groudle Glen Railway, built in 1896, runs for three- quarters of a mile through the wooded glen and along the clifftop high above the sea. Two Bagnall 2-4-0 tank engines, *Sea Lion* of 1896 and *Polar Bear* of 1906, were named after the menagerie of animals enclosed in the sea-washed coves, once viewed from footbridges beyond the terminus. The polar bears were released in 1914 and the sea lions in 1939, when the railway closed for the two world wars. In the 1940s metal thieves and vandals postponed post-war reopening till 1950, with *Polar Bear* only; saboteurs again put the railway out of action from 1959 to 1961, when it reopened for two seasons. A green *Polar Bear* is seen here with a train arriving at the glen terminus on 17 August 1961 with its train of crossbench coaches built in 1896-1905 by G. F Milnes at Birkenhead, the same firm that built cars for the MER during the same period. Vandal havoc closed the railway again after the 1962 season and the two engines went to England.

The railway was restored for reopening in 1986. The locomotive *Sea Lion* is back in its original light green paintwork, supplemented by other restored narrow-gauge engines. *Polar Bear* is now working at Amberley Chalkpits Museum in Sussex. The original Milnes coaches have been rebuilt and accompany both engines at Groudle Glen and Amberley.

ESKADALE North of Groudle Glen the railway runs alongside the country road to Baldrine. Here we see trolleycar No 5 of 1894 towing winter saloon trailer car No 59 southbound on 16 June 1964. Six of these trolleycars were built by Milnes for this extension of the line from Groudle Glen to Laxey and the start of the year-round service in 1894, and four of them survive today. Cars Nos 5, 6, 7 and 9 have recently been refitted with one-piece windscreens. Trailer car No 59 is one of only two saloon trailers on the roster, built in 1904 by the Electric Railway & Tramway Carriage Company at Preston with an open platform or veranda at each end; they are rarely used in service.

MANX ELECTRIC RAILWAY The original car No 1 on the MER is pictured running southbound between Eskadale and Halfway House in unlined crimson and white with a crossbench trailer on 18 June 1964. It was the first of three cars of this type built by G. F. Milnes at Birkenhead for the opening of the line from Douglas to Groudle Glen in 1893. Their original Milnes bogies were replaced by Brush bogies in 1902. Car No 3 was destroyed in the Laxey car shed fire in 1930, but the surviving cars Nos 1 and 2 are the oldest electric railway or tramway cars still in public service anywhere in the world. For many years they were used as work cars with ladders slung under their rocker panels, but since the centenary of the railway in 1993 they have been restored for passenger service in smart, Victorian-style, lined-out paintwork and lettering.

HALFWAY HOUSE-BALDRINE Protected by the two-aspect highway signals, a crossbench trolleycar with a crossbench trailer crosses the Douglas-Ramsey main road southbound between Scarff's Crossing and Halfway House on 18 June 1964. It was a rare treat to ride on the front seat beside the motorman on these crossbench trolleycars but it could be breezy. There were no seats outside the bulkheads on the trailers. Car No 32, seen here, and sister car No 33 were built in 1906 by the United Electric Car Company at Preston on Brill bogies with General Electric motors, and were the two fastest cars in the MER fleet. There were originally nine crossbench trolleycars in the fleet by different makers dating from 1898 to 1906, but only five are still on the roster and usually only appear in service when traffic exceeds the capacity of all the other serviceable stock.

The overhead line equipment on the MER is unusual with centre poles and copper running wires suspended from brackets on each side, about 16 feet high (higher at road crossings) and aligned for fixed-head trolley wheels for more reliable high-speed operation. The steel poles are buried 5 feet in the ground and are more closely spaced on the curve here than on the straight line beyond. The rail joints are copper bonded to complete the electric circuit to the power substation.

GARWICK GLEN A southbound electric train pauses at Garwick Glen station 'for the beach, smugglers' caves and tea garden' on 16 June 1964. Garwick Glen then had its own station master. The train consists of a 'winter saloon' trolleycar, a crossbench trailer of 1899 and a 5-ton van of 1904. The wooden station buildings, dating from 1895, were demolished in 1979, when the glen and the hotel were closed to the public.

LAXEY MER 'winter saloon' car No 21 and a crossbench trailer, both of 1899, run along the clifftop south of Laxey Bay on 18 June 1964.

LAXEY With Laxey Glen and Snaefell (2,034 feet) in the background, car No 22 of 1899 awakens the echoes as it drones up the 1 in 40 gradient along the south side of the glen towards South Cape with a crossbench trailer and van in tow on 18 June 1964. Laxey village nestles in the glen below. Car No 22 was rebuilt by Manx craftsmen with replica coachwork after an electrical fire in 1990, and re-entered service in 1992.

LAXEY The interior of MER Milnes car No 20 of 1899 on 16 June 1964. These cars have 48 upholstered, transverse, reversible seats in two saloons, originally for smokers and non-smokers, with a panelled wooden partition and a Tudor-arched pane in the door. Cars Nos 19 to 22 were built with wooden seats, which were replaced with upholstered seat cushions and backrests in 1932; they have since been reupholstered.

LAXEY station, with its rustic wooden buildings in a glade of cawing rooks, is seen on 16 June 1964 – and not a passenger in sight. The through line of the 3-foot-gauge MER is on the right and on the left is the lower terminus of the 3ft 6in-gauge Snaefell Mountain Railway. This 4½-mile line to the summit was built and electrified in seven months ready for opening in 1895, and the MER took it over in 1902. Snaefell cars Nos 1 and 6, seen here, are two of the fleet of six cars of 1895, again by Milnes of Birkenhead. In the centre MER car No 20 of 1899 pauses southbound from Ramsey to Douglas.

LAXEY Electric railway cars of two gauges meet here to exchange passengers for scenic journeys up Snaefell and along the coast to Douglas and Ramsey. Car No 4 on the left was one of six built in 1895 for the opening of the 3ft 6in-gauge Snaefell Mountain Railway, which starts here and runs 4½ miles up Laxey Glen on a ruling gradient of 1 in 12 to a terminus at 1,990 feet, just below the 2,034-foot summit viewpoint. The Snaefell cars picked up the overhead current with a bow collectors, one on each end of the car, instead of a trolley, to cope with high winds on the fells.

Car No 21 on the right was one of four built for the extension of the 3-foot-gauge Manx Electric Railway from here to Ramsey in 1899. The two types of car are pictured side by side on 17 August 1967 awaiting passengers for Snaefell and Douglas. Car No 21 sports an impressive array of front-end equipment: two electric headlamps, an oil marker lamp, a coupler and cowcatcher, together with the usual cornerwise steps for passengers boarding and for the conductor to serve the trailer car in transit.

Left: **DHOON GLEN** This is a typical Manx Electric Railway landscape, in Dhoon Glen on the 1899 extension from Laxey to Ramsey. Following the contours of the land as far as possible, the line loops around the glens along the way. In this picture on 17 August 1961 the double track crosses the bottom of the picture with one rusty traction pole and one new pole supporting the overhead electric wires. Past Dhoon Glen station (off left) it recrosses the picture between the hedgerows in the background, and a southbound two-car train can be seen approaching in the distance in the upper background of the picture.

BALLASKEIG BEG The great hills ranging from Snaefell (2,034 feet) to North Barrule (1,860 feet) form the backdrop to the Manx Electric Railway between Laxey and Ramsey, seen here with northbound trolleycar No 7 of 1894 towing a crossbench trailer car on 17 August 1961.

RAMSEY The only section of the MER that looks like a street tramway is this 100-yard section alongside Walpole Drive, which has side traction poles and was originally laid with grooved rail. When the line was built in 1899 the Ramsey Commissioners planned to pave the full width of Walpole Road incorporating the tramway, but the ballasted track still runs along a natural roadside reservation of compressed soil and stones and is only paved across side streets. In this picture car No 22 of 1899 has stopped to drop passengers at the corner of Queen's Drive on 17 June 1964. The line continues along a private right of way behind the houses on Waterloo Road to the terminal yard on Albert Street.

RAMSEY Trolley and trailer cars on the MER change places by power and by gravity at crossover points in the track at Douglas, Laxey and Ramsey stations, where trainsets reverse for return journeys. The ritual was recorded here at Ramsey terminus on 6 June 1961. Trolleycar No 22 has uncoupled from the trailer car, run forward on the down line and reversed over the crossover to the up line. The station master has released the handbrakes on the trailer car to run by gravity down the slope beyond the crossover. The conductor waits to turn the trolley pole around car No 22 to reverse over the crossover and back on to the trailer. Both these cars were built by Milnes at Birkenhead in 1899. Laxey station has two crossovers in the track for the reversal procedure there. The building on the left was the former Plaza cinema, named on the timetable as the Ramsey terminus.

RAMSEY Queen's Pier was built by the Isle of Man Harbour Board in 1881-86 for Irish Sea ferries calling here on their way between Douglas, Belfast and Ardrossan without the need to berth in the harbour. As the pier was 717 yards long – nearly half a mile – the 3-foot-gauge construction tramway was retained to carry passengers' luggage on hand trucks to and from the pier head. Here at the pier entrance on 17 June 1964 we see the 10-seat petrol tram of 1950, while in the siding is the 1937 diesel locomotive with a passenger coach and flatcars waiting for the next ship.

RAMSEY The 10-seat Wickham petrol tram of 1950 negotiates the passing loop halfway along Queen's Pier on the same day. The last ship called here in 1970, the tramway closed in 1981, and the pier closed in 1991. The derelict structure, which has lost its deck buildings and railings, is now under restoration.

RAMSEY The Isle of Man Railway started the Isle of Man Road Services in 1930, when it bought out the two bus companies on the island and coordinated all bus services with the railway, with joint publicity and ticket availability. All the island's bus garages doubled as bus stations with waiting rooms and offices. This is Ramsey bus station on the corner of Queen's Pier Road and Prince's Road on 18 June 1964. The island bus services were worked entirely by single-deckers until 1946, and the three Leyland buses on the forecourt date from 1947. The two double-deck PD1s also had Leyland bodies, which were unusual in having odd ventilator windows at the front of the upper saloons.

RAMSEY harbour was the home of the Ramsey Steamship Company, which carried bulk cargoes around the Irish Sea. At Ramsey it exported lead from Foxdale mines until 1960 and imported coal from Whitehaven, building materials and animal food. On 17 June 1964 the motor coaster *Ben Vooar*, built in 1950, is berthed at the East Quay. Beyond it is the Market Place with St Paul's parish church, and on the right is the West Quay with its agricultural merchants and ships' stores. The Isle of Man Railway, which served the lead mines, ran a harbour branch from Ramsey station via Derby Road and along the West Quay until 1954.

The Albert Tower on the hill in the background, Llergy Frissel, commemorates an informal visit to that spot by Queen Victoria's consort, Prince Albert, in 1847. The Royal Yacht anchored in the bay and the Prince went ashore early next morning for a walk. He asked the first man he met, the town's barber, to show him the way up the hill and the barber led him to the top. The Ramsey Steamship Company was 101 years old when it was wound up in 2014, but its ships, now with other companies, can still be seen in Ramsey and around the British Isles.

RAMSEY The afternoon train hobbles slowly through the grass and weeds along the uncertain track into the derelict-looking terminus station at the north end of the Isle of Man Railway system on 16 August 1967. This was the first summer of Lord Ailsa's era of operation after the whole system had been closed for one year. The locomotive, 2-4-0 tank engine No 11 *Maitland* of 1905, is in the green paintwork of the Ailsa era. The building alongside is the two-road carriage shed with timber walls and a corrugated-iron roof. The line in between led to the one-road, two-engine shed built of the local slaty stone. The Ramsey line was opened by the Manx Northern Railway in 1879, was amalgamated with the Isle of Man Railway in 1904, and finally closed at the end of the 1968 summer season.

RAMSEY Pictured outside the engine shed on 16 August 1967, No 11 *Maitland* is an example of the standard 2-4-0 tank engine built for the Isle of Man Railway by Beyer Peacock at Gorton foundry, Manchester, to a similar design built by that company for 3ft 6in-gauge railways in Norway. The green paint scheme of the Lord Ailsa era was a revival of the original IMR scheme carried from 1873 to 1939. Until 1954 the Ramsey train engine ran beyond the station and along Derby Road to shunt the harbour sidings during the terminal lay-over.

KIRK MICHAEL On the indirect railway journey from Douglas via the west coast to Ramsey on 20 June 1964, 2-4-0 tank engine No 12 *Hutchinson* of 1908 takes time out to uncouple from its train, shunt these two coaches out of the down siding and add them to the front of the train. The handsome, rock-faced, red sandstone station building, off left, has been preserved as a private house.

ST JOHN'S A summer idyll on the Isle of Man Railway on 20 June 1964: 2-4-0 tank engine No 5 *Mona* of 1874 simmers in the sunshine while the driver takes his lunch break in the stone-based signal cabin, built by the former Manx Northern Railway in 1879. This was the point where the 16½-mile MNR line to Ramsey joined the IMR line from Douglas to Peel. The signalman has left his lady's bicycle leaning against the ladder up the ex-MNR wooden, slotted-post, semaphore signal, which is the up main starter. When the line was clear the signal dropped vertically into the slot and the oil lamp on top of the post turned to show a green light. The water tank is on the left.

PEEL IMR 2-4-0 tank engine No 4 *Fenella* of 1884 and its two-coach train stand at Peel terminus alongside the harbour with the castle in the background on 7 June 1961. The 11½-mile line from Douglas to Peel was the first of the three lines of the IMR, opened in 1873 and closed in 1968. The station has been replaced by a car park. Only the 15½-mile line from Douglas to Port Erin, opened in 1874, survives today and there is an IMR museum in the old bus garage next to Port Erin station. The ruins of the 14th-century castle and the 13th-century cathedral beyond it within the castle bailey stand on St Patrick's Isle, connected to the mainland by a causeway that is an extension of the harbour west quay. The isle was the one-time seat of the Norse kings of Man and the Isles (including the Hebrides, Kintyre, Arran and Bute) from 1079 till 1263, when it passed to the Scottish crown. The isle of Man later passed to the English crown. The Norse colonists of the island established the Tynwald, the Manx Parliament, which, dating from c977, is the oldest continuous parliament in the world.

Dumfries-shire

DUMFRIES Three red buses of the Western Scottish Motor Traction Company animate this High Street scene on 31 May 1962. The bus on the right is a Northern Counties-bodied Guy of 1945-46. The buses complement the ruddy-brown sandstone buildings, notably the Town House and Mid Steeple (1705-07) and the burgh church of St Bride (1868). The Victorian fountain with cherubs and dolphins celebrates the public water supply to Dumfries. The Town House was the old town hall and prison and on the facing wall is a cast-iron plate showing the cattle drovers' mileages to Annan, Castle Douglas, Carlisle, Edinburgh, Glasgow, Portpatrick, Huntingdon and London. The two buses on the left, advertising 'Shop at Binns', are loading outside Binns's emporium. Binns was a chain of large department stores, founded by George Binns at Sunderland in 1811, with many branches in towns from Middlesbrough to Edinburgh, and the bold 'Shop at Binns' advert was displayed on the front and back of buses in that area.

This lively picture of the town centre contrasts with the rundown scene today. High Street is now a pedestrian zone and most of the shops have now changed ownership and uses. The Binns buildings is now divided into small shops; today you can only 'shop at Binns' in Darlington.

EDINBURGH The contours of the 'old town' give rise to adjacent buildings on different levels and there are five places in the city where streets bordered by tall buildings bridge high over other streets in deep canyons of tall buildings. Examples are South Bridge and King George V Bridge over Cowgate in the old town, and here, where Regent Bridge, built in 1815, carries Waterloo Place over Calton Road in an eastern extension of the Georgian 'new town'. This bridge was designed by Archibald Elliott as a Napoleonic War memorial comprising screens of Ionic colonnades with central arches of the Corinthian order. The front door of the Head Post Office (left) was on the fourth storey, fronting Waterloo Place. Late-1950s Morris Commercial mail vans are parked on the right of Calton Road and a 1939 Morris 10 fronts a line of parked cars under the bridge in this picture on 15 April 1963. The Head Post Office has since moved elsewhere.

EDINBURGH The concealed radiator was the new look of 1953, when this Edinburgh Corporation bus was built with a Metropolitan-Cammell 'Orion'-style body on a Leyland PD3 chassis. It was photographed at a stop on the ascent of Dundas Street, Edinburgh, on route 27 to Oxgangs on 15 April 1963. Oxgangs is an old measure of arable land.

EDINBURGH My favourite Edinburgh bus photographs are these two 'bus-scapes', featuring buses in action in townscape settings. Although the pictures were taken beyond the period of this book, they feature Alexander-bodied Leyland Atlanteans that entered service in Edinburgh from 1965. The first picture shows a 1969 model passing St Giles Cathedral in High Street on 31 May 1980. The second picture is of a similar type turning the corner from York Place into North St Andrew Street with the Firth of Forth and the hills of Fife in the background on 10 July 1981.

Edinburgh took delivery of 588 of these Alexander-bodied Leyland Atlanteans from 1965 to 1981 and the last one was retired from service in 2000. These stylish buses were bow-fronted with high domed roofs and panoramic windows. They still carried the madder (dark red) and white colours of the trams that buses replaced in 1950-56, and the front overhang of these rear-engined buses gave them some resemblance to the trams in their motion as they pitched along and belatedly swung around corners.

Edinburgh City Transport was renamed Lothian Region Transport in 1975 and Lothian Buses in 2000. It is the largest of the 11 remaining municipal bus companies in Britain since the deregulation of bus operations in 1986. It is owned 91 per cent by Edinburgh City Council and 9 per cent by Midlothian, East Lothian and West Lothian County Councils. The fleet colours are still madder and white, with exceptions for special services.

Lanarkshire

UDDINGSTON On this old cast-iron fingerpost in Glasgow Road on the A74 trunk road from Carlisle, photographed on 21 May 1959, a black hand in low relief points the way to Glasgow while the sign to Bothwell and Hamilton is a wooden board with hand-painted lettering. It stood at the junction with the A721 New Edinburgh Road. Solidly built dormer bungalows in red sandstone with parkland gardens overlooked this location, where Glasgow tramcars passed on their way to Main Street, Uddingston, until 1948, when line 29 was cut back to Broomhouse Zoo, the first of the Glasgow tramway closures.

The signpost has now gone and the bungalows are masked from view by a jungle of rhododendrons in the front gardens. The M74 motorway, which has eclipsed the A74 from Carlisle, crosses under Glasgow Road immediately south of this junction.

DALMARNOCK A Glasgow Corporation 'Coronation' car of 1939 drones through the grim canyon of four-storey tenements, like a street through a prison; the streets are paved with granite setts the full width of the roadway. This is Dalmarnock Road at Davidson Street (right) on 8 March 1962, and the tramcar is on line 26 bound for Scotstoun via Partick. The Corporation built 146 of these 'Coronation' cars on EMB bogies from 1937 to 1941 and another six were built in 1954. All the buildings in this view have been cleared and the scene is now a semi-urban desert.

BRIDGETON A standard Glasgow tramcar seen against standard Glasgow tenements on Dalmarnock Road on 27 May 1961. Car No 76, built by the Corporation on Brill trucks in 1920, has had its broken lifeguard tied up with string by the motorman in a city traffic jam after noisily dragging it over the granite setts from Argyle Street to Clydebank and back. The happy crew held up following tramcars for the photograph before reversing into Ruby Street and Dalmarnock depot for repair. These hexagonal-dash tramcars were built over the period from 1910 to 1924. Line 26 from Farme Cross to Clydebank was replaced by motorbuses on 2 June 1962.

BRIDGETON A Glasgow Corporation 'Cunarder' class tramcar of 1949 glides past the wide open plain of granite setts at the junction of Dalmarnock Road (left) and Old Dalmarnock Road (right) on line 26 from Farme Cross to Clydebank on 27 May 1961. Glasgow built 100 of these tramcars on Maley & Taunton bogies from 1948 to 1952 and they were nicknamed after the great Cunard ocean liners built by John Brown's shipyard at Clydebank.

The telephone kiosk on its island in the middle of the junction has a distinct lean to the left owing to subsidence. There are many pedestrians about but few motorcars, characteristic of a city of tenement dwellers; the car on the right is a 1939 Morris 8. Dalmarnock gas works dominates the background in Old Dalmarnock Road.

All the residential and industrial buildings in this picture have gone and been replaced with pleasant, modern housing only two or three storeys high. The forked road junction has been replaced by a landscaped, triangular green, making a T-junction of the two roads. Since the tramways closed in 1962 the durable granite sett-paved streets have been replaced by asphalt in a constant, execrable state of erosion with cracks, patches and potholes ever since, giving all road users a rough ride.

BRIDGETON Cross was a five-way tramway junction in the east end of Glasgow with London Road across the background. A 'Coronation' tramcar of 1939 is about to turn into Dalmarnock Road (right) on line 26 to Farme Cross on that same May day. Trolleybus overhead wires turn into James Street (left). The ornate cast-iron bandstand-like structure was built and donated by George Smith's Sun Foundry of Glasgow in 1875 to shelter the unemployed, and was called 'The Umbrella'. It was accompanied by a police telephone kiosk, a tramway inspector's kiosk and railed steps to underground lavatories. The domed corner building on the right is the Olympia cinema of 1911, part of the ABC circuit from 1924 till closure in 1974.

All the buildings in this picture still stand today, cleaned and restored, but all the shops have changed hands and half of them are now empty and shuttered. 'The Umbrella', then painted black, has been repainted in two-tone blue with white spandrels and gold details on the clock tower, but the public seats and lavatories have been removed. Bridgeton Cross today is not the busy community centre it was then and this viewpoint is now screened by trees.

GOVANHILL Trolleybuses came to Glasgow in 1949, late in the trolleybus era, to begin replacing the tramcars. This was Britain's last and only post-war trolleybus installation (apart from the short Teesside extensions in 1951-68) and Glasgow was the only city in Scotland with trolleybuses except for Dundee's experiment with them in 1912-14. Only six trolleybus routes were installed in Glasgow, and from 1958 the Corporation began to replace tramcars with motorbuses instead. Consequently tramcars, trolleybuses and motorbuses were all running at the same time in Glasgow from 1949 to 1962 – and single-deck trolleybus added to the mixture. Then in 1965 the trolleybus routes began to be replaced by motorbuses too. This 1962 Crossley-bodied BUT trolleybus, No 123, is speeding along Aikenhead Road, Govanhill, on route 102 from Riddrie to Polmadie on 17 April 1966. The route closed later the same year and this trolleybus was the last to run in Glasgow, for a photo-call on 28 May 1967, the day after the closure of trolleybus services.

GOVANHILL This 1958 Crossley-bodied BUT trolleybus is in Cathcart Road on 17 April 1966, and the two uniformed busmen on the right are a conductor and driver from the nearby Larkfield garage, which was shared by motorbuses and trolleybuses. This route, the 105, was the last trolleybus route in Glasgow, closing on 27 May 1967, and the quiet hum of electric traction, so appropriate to this empty Glasgow Sabbath scene, was replaced by diesel buses. Govanhill looks much the same today, but all the shops along Cathcart Road have changed and many have been closed and shuttered. The prominent barber's shop pole sign on the left has also disappeared.

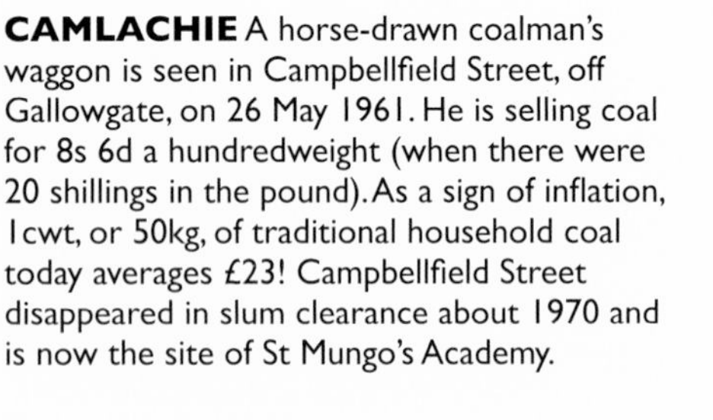

CAMLACHIE A horse-drawn coalman's waggon is seen in Campbellfield Street, off Gallowgate, on 26 May 1961. He is selling coal for 8s 6d a hundredweight (when there were 20 shillings in the pound). As a sign of inflation, 1cwt, or 50kg, of traditional household coal today averages £23! Campbellfield Street disappeared in slum clearance about 1970 and is now the site of St Mungo's Academy.

CAMLACHIE Glasgow 'Coronation' car No 1155 of 1939 and a Central SMT all-Leyland low-bridge bus of 1948 are city bound along Gallowgate, also on 26 May 1961. The tramcar is on line 15 from Baillieston to Anderston Cross.

CALTON London Road, half a mile east of Glasgow Cross, is viewed from the top of a tramcar on 2 September 1962. Air brakes hiss as oncoming 'Coronation' car No 1243 of 1939 stops to pick up a passenger on its way to Auchenshuggle. Glasgow's official last service car had run the previous evening, but it looked like normal service for the next three days when the Corporation ran a special short working of line 9 between Anderston Cross and Auchenshuggle with eight cars running alongside the replacing buses for those who wished to take a last tram ride.

26

Left: **GLASGOW CROSS** station on the underground steam railway is on the right of this photograph of Trongate with a 1951 'Cunarder' car and two pre-war 'Coronation' cars on 1 June 1962. The policeman in a white coat is on 'point duty' regulating traffic at the junction with Saltmarket (left). The red sandstone station was on the Caledonian Railway's 3-mile cut-and-cover tunnel under the main streets from Dalmarnock Road to Stobcross Street. The Glasgow Central Line, as it was called, closed in 1964 and reopened in 1979 as the electric Argyle Line with a new station a quarter of a mile west in Argyle Street, leaving an uneven spacing of stations between Bridgeton Cross and Glasgow Central. Glasgow Cross station was not demolished till 1977; its site is now a triangular, paved pedestrian island in the east fork of Trongate.

Above: **POLLOKSHIELDS** Two Glasgow Corporation work cars are seen in Barrland Street permanent way yard on 1 September 1962. On the left is water tank car No 19, built in 1907, used for washing and brushing the tracks. On the right is welder car No 21, built in 1905 with a shortened body from an 1898 bogie single-deck passenger car remounted on an electrified horsecar truck. These cars were normally seen out on track work only at night when no trams were in service.

Left: **GLASGOW CROSS** Steam rises from the low-level railway station in this view of Trongate from a tramcar emerging from London Road on 21 December 1960. Pedestrians are clad in long overcoats and the white-coated policeman is on point duty where the single overhead wires for the trams crossed the double overhead wires for the trolleybuses passing between Saltmarket (left) and High Street (right). Ahead, a lightly laden lorry follows a Corporation 'Kilmarnock bogie' tramcar of 1927-28, almost in silhouette, on line 26 from Burnside to Scotstoun, about to converge with tramcars from Gallowgate. The two motorcars on the right are a 1956 Wolseley 680 and a 1960 Rover 90. Glasgow Cross station (right) occupied a triangular site in the middle of this five-way junction of main streets in the old city centre. The streets were still paved with granite setts across their full width, but have since been repaved with asphalt. All the overhead wires have gone and some of these shops have closed as the focal point of city life has moved west and Glasgow is no longer busy with through traffic.

GLASGOW Old tramcars built from 1900 to 1928 still haunted the streets of Glasgow and outnumbered the more modern cars throughout the city when this picture was taken in Argyle Street, the main axis of the tramway system, on 22 May 1959. The two four-wheel standard tramcars on the left are eastbound on line 29, Maryhill to Tollcross, although the leading car is on a short working to Glasgow Cross, where it will turn back. The private car sandwiched between them is a 1956 Morris Minor estate car with a timber frame at the back. Leading the line of oncoming tramcars is a 'Kilmarnock bogie' of 1928-29 on line 9 from Auchenshuggle to Dalmuir West.

The tramlines and granite setts have been replaced with asphalt and Argyle Street is no longer a through route for road traffic to Trongate, being blocked by a pedestrian precinct from Queen Street to Glassford Street. Most of the buildings in this picture are still there today with only a few glass-faced blocks merging unobtrusively into the building line and general elevation.

GLASGOW Two gaunt old standard tramcars on line 15 meet on Argyle Street on 22 May 1959. Car No 311 was built in 1909 and is westbound to Anderston Cross, while car No 927, of 1900, emerges from beneath Central station bridge, eastbound to Baillieston. Central station, terminus of the old Caledonian Railway, spans the street for 130 yards, and acts as a sounding board for the tramcars, echoing the ghostly drone of the electric motors, the sound of the wheels drumming over the rail joints and the hiss of the air brakes. At this crossroads just east of the station the two tramcars are about to hammer across the tracks linking Jamaica Street (left) with Union Street (right).

Since the electrification of the main line, Central station has been cleaned and attractively repainted with the name 'Central Station' in relief serif lettering across the lintel of the bridge, and advertising has been removed.

GLASGOW On the west side of the bridge carrying Central station over Argyle Street an eastbound 'Cunarder' car pauses while a 'Coronation' car turns north into Hope Street on 27 May 1961.

HOT

Left: **GLASGOW** In the commercial heart of the city 'Coronation' car No 1194 of 1938 descends Hope Street, jangling through the trailing junction with the line along Bothwell Street (left) and passing the corner of Gordon Street by the Central Station Hotel (right) on 27 May 1961. Hope Street rises up the north slope of Clydesdale in a series of terraces, levelling out at intersecting streets, drops across the defile of Sauchiehall Street, and rises again to Cowcaddens. A ride on a tramcar down this switchback was a fascinating experience.

This scene is substantially unchanged today. All the buildings have been cleaned, showing the ruddy brown sandstone facades. Hope Street is now one-way, uphill, for northbound buses, taxicabs and bicycles only. The wider street section in the foreground is now divided by parallel lines of railings marking off a cab lane on the right and a bus bay on the left. Following the withdrawal of the electric tramways and the increase in motor traffic, Hope Street is now said to be 'the most polluted street in Scotland'.

GLASGOW The Victorian Gothic pile of the Christian Institute and other buildings dwarf 1939 'Coronation' car No 1185 as it drifts down Bothwell Street on line 18A from Springburn to Shawfield on 26 May 1961. This service closed eight days later. The Christian Institute filled the block from West Campbell Street to Blythswood Street and was built in three sections by two architects in one unifying style: the Christian Institute (John McLeod, 1878-79), the Bible Training Institute, and the Young Men's Christian Association (R. A. Bryden, 1895-98). The YMCA was a 189-bed hostel and restaurant providing lodgings at reasonable prices for young men working in the city.

Owing to rising maintenance costs and new fire regulations the building was demolished in 1980 and replaced by a soaring glass skyscraper. The rest of Bothwell Street and the west side of the city centre has been transformed with many modern, high-rise office blocks.

GLASGOW On its way from Scotstoun West via Great Western Road, standard tramcar No 95 of 1923 passes through Sauchiehall Street, Glasgow's main shopping street, destined for Dennistoun in the east end on 22 May 1959. Wellington Street is on the left. This section of Sauchiehall Street is now a pedestrian precinct and the buildings on the left have been replaced by a modern shopping complex called the Sauchiehall Centre.

COWCADDENS A frequent service of cars on line 29 to Maryhill is seen at the top of Hope Street in the Cowcaddens district of Glasgow on 27 May 1961, only five months before the closure of this service and 14 months before the last tram in the city. The 29 was then the only tram service operating up this end of Hope Street, where the cars turned left into Cowcaddens Street, which terminates the view. 'The Cowcaddens Equitable Loan' is signwritten across the first floor of the building in the background.

ANDERSTON There are six Glasgow tramcars in this picture of Anderston Cross on 25 May 1961, three on lines 9 and 26 along Argyle Street (right) and three on the double-track stub sidings in Stobcross Street (left), the terminus of line 15 from Baillieston. It seemed as if Glasgow trams would roll on forever, but line 15 closed in March 1962 and line 9, Glasgow's last tram service, from Auchenshuggle to Dalmuir West, was cut back to Anderston Cross (Stobcross Street) on 2 September; the last car ran from here on the 4th. The two-storey building on the curve into Stobcross Street is Anderston Cross station on the steam underground railway from Dalmarnock to Finnieston, designed by local architect John Burnet for the Caledonian Railway. The station closed in 1959 and the train service ceased in 1964. Anderston Cross was the centre of this township, which was a separate burgh from 1824 to 1846. The stone cross that once stood here was called the 'stob' and Stobcross Street once led to Stobcross House, the mansion of the Anderson family. The town that grew here became Andersonstown, which evolved into Anderston. Stobcross House was demolished to make way for Queen's Dock.

The entire town centre was wiped out by a massive road junction with slip roads and footbridges, completed in 1971, as seen here from the same viewpoint and looking in the same direction on 30 June 2012. Here, the M8 motorway on a concrete viaduct crosses the Clydeside Expressway that flattened Stobcross Street and replaced the westward continuation of Argyle Street, which has been blocked by new housing between here and Finnieston. The photograph was taken when the Clydeside Expressway was clear of the normal streams of traffic to show the complete environment. Down a hole under this concrete jungle is a new railway station, now named only Anderston, on the central low-level line that was reopened in 1979 as part of Glasgow's extensive suburban electric railway system, and which now enjoys the highest percentage patronage of the local population of any British city. Queen's Dock, which replaced Stobcross House, was closed to shipping in 1970 and partly filled in for car parking.

POSSILPARK Glasgow 'Coronation' car No 1170 of 1939, on line 18, passes the gates of Macfarlane's Saracen Foundry in Hawthorn Street on 27 May 1961, seven days before the line closed. Line 18 crossed the city from Burnside in the south-east to Ruchill in the north-west, then turned east across the north of the city via Possilpark to Springburn. The tower of Ruchill Hospital can be seen in the background. The junction in the overhead wires here marks the turnout into Saracen Street on the former line 27 from Springburn to Shieldhall, closed in 1958.

Scotland was the home of ornamental iron foundries, Glasgow was the capital of the industry, and Macfarlane's was the largest in the city. These foundries produced the ornate cast ironwork that graced British and colonial towns, such as market halls, porticos, conservatories, bandstands, shop colonnades, shelters, drinking fountains, gates, lamp posts, railings and brackets. Macfarlane's was taken over by Allied Ironfounders in 1965 and demolished in 1967; it has been replaced by a modern industrial estate.

GOVAN A Glasgow trolleybus adds to the kaleidoscope of colour at Govan Cross on 2 June 1962 with gay bunting for Govan Fair, the red police and public telephone booths, and the gilded drinking fountain combining to brighten up this setting dominated by soot-stained, brown sandstone buildings. The Burgh of Govan was incorporated into the City of Glasgow in 1912. The trolleybus is on route 106, which replaced tram line 7 from Bellahouston to Millerston in 1958; the trolleybuses on this route were themselves replaced by motorbuses in 1966 and the last trolleybuses ran through here on route 108 from Shieldhall to Mount Florida in 1967. The tram tracks and trolleybus wires in Govan were also used by Fairfield shipyard trains, with electric, steeple-cab locomotives, collecting steel, forgings and timber from Govan railway goods yard (off left), an operation that ceased in 1966.

The drinking fountain is a memorial to John Aitken, physician and surgeon, former Medical Officer to the Burgh, Govan Police and the collieries at Ibrox and Drumoyne. It has since been moved to the right and repainted crimson. The two telephone booths and the underground lavatories have gone. The British Linen Bank is now the Bank of Scotland and Govan railway goods yard is now the bus station. The shops and tenements on the left have been replaced by the redbrick, three-storey Govan Shopping Centre. Like Bridgeton Cross, Glasgow Cross and Anderston Cross, Govan Cross is now only a ghost of a once busy community centre.

GOVAN The original *Queen Mary* is seen steaming down the Clyde past Govan on a day excursion 'doon the watter' on 2 June 1962, watched by passengers and crew on the small Govan passenger ferry at its berth. On the right are some of the cranes of Harland & Wolff's seven-berth shipbuilding yard, which closed the following year. Astern of *Queen Mary* a cargo ship is berthed at Yorkhill Quay. The passenger ferry closed in 1966 and reopened in 2012. Merchant shipping retreated downriver to larger docks at Sheildhall and Greenock in the 1970s.

The *Queen Mary* was built by William Denny & Brothers at Dumbarton in 1932-33, and at 871 gross tons was the largest of Williamson Buchanan's famous fleet of fast, quiet and comfortable turbine steamers with two funnels and black and white paintwork. She was billed as 'Britain's finest pleasure steamer' and plied day trips from Glasgow Bridge Wharf to Dunoon, Rothesay and Largs. She was renamed *Queen Mary II* when the Cunard ocean liner *Queen Mary* was launched at Clydebank in 1935. The Williamson Buchanan fleet amalgamated with the LMSR's Caledonian Steam Packet Company in 1939. During the Hitler war *Queen Mary II* was painted grey and worked the Greenock-Dunoon ferry and tendered troopships in the firth, including the *Queen Mary*. In 1957 she was reboilered as an oil-burner with one funnel as seen here. After a refit in 1971 she went on the routes to Campbeltown and Inveraray.

The Caledonian and MacBrayne fleets amalgamated in 1973 and *Queen Mary II* had her original name restored in 1976 when the Cunarder retired from service to Long Beach, California – but the Clyde queen had only one more year to run. When laid up she was sold to Glasgow District Council for a maritime museum that never materialised, and was then towed to Chatham for a cosmetic refit to restore her two-funnelled, black and white appearance, she then served as a floating restaurant at Savoy Pier, Westminster, from 1988 to 2009, before languishing in Tilbury docks. Friends of TS Queen Mary bought the ship in 2015 and had her towed back to Greenock in 2016 for preservation on the Clyde.

GOVAN The vehicular ferry at Govan was one of the strangest craft afloat. Others of this design worked Finnieston ferry and Whiteinch ferry and there was one relief vessel, all operated by the Clyde Navigation Trust. In 1912 this elevating-deck ferry replaced the former chain ferry on the passage between Water Row, Govan, and Ferry Road, Pointhouse, and coped with the 14-foot tidal range by raising and lowering the vehicle deck to align it with the loading bays on each side of the river. They were double-ended vessels with twin screws at each end to save turning round in the busy, narrow fairway, and the wheelhouse was centrally situated on top of the central gantry. This vessel was No 4 in the fleet, built in 1937, 275 gross tons, 82 feet long and 44 feet wide. The ferry ran day and night carrying not only vehicles but also foot passengers working at the shipyards on both sides of the river here and the mills at Partick. This picture was taken from beside the Govan landing bay on 2 June 1962. On the opposite bank is Pointhouse, on the confluence of the rivers Clyde and Kelvin, site of the former shipyard of A. & J. Inglis, who built Britain's last three paddle steamers: *Lincoln Castle* (1941) and *Waverley* (1947) for the LNER and *Maid of the Loch* (1953) for BR. Both Govan ferries, vehicular and passenger, closed in 1966, two years after the opening of the second bore of the Clyde road tunnel a short way downriver. All the industrial buildings and cranes at Pointhouse have been cleared and this is now the parkland site of the spectacularly modern Riverside Museum of Transport, which saw the reopening of Govan passenger ferry in 2012.

GOVAN The vast hulls of new ships under construction on the stocks of the Fairfield Shipbuilding & Engineering Company at Govan are seen on 2 June 1962. Govan was the centre of shipbuilding on the Clyde, starting with wooden ships in 1841. Fairfield was the name of the farm on the site of the shipyard opened in 1864 by Randolph, Elder & Company. John Elder was the marine engineer who invented the fuel-efficient compound steam engine, which allowed for longer voyages. The Fairfield company was founded in 1888 and this Govan yard grew to be the largest and busiest shipbuilding yard in Britain. In its heyday it employed more than 5,000 men building freighters, passenger liners and warships. Shipbuilding was heavy, noisy and dangerous work, carried out in the open in all weathers and there were many accidents with loss of limbs and life. British shipyards were still using 19th-century equipment and working practices after the Hitler war, there was a different trade union for almost every trade in the yard, and the industry was plagued by job demarcation, union disputes and late delivery, losing orders to competitive German, Swedish and Japanese shipyards, which had modernised equipment and methods after the war. The Fairfield company was bankrupt in 1966 but the yard kept going under receivers and a succession of new managements: Upper Clyde Shipbuilders (an amalgamation with four other yards), Lithgow's, the Norwegian firm Kvaerner, BVT Surface Fleet and now, since 2009, BAE Systems Surface Ships. This firm also owns the former Yarrow shipyard at Scotstoun and specialises in building ships for the Royal Navy. These are the only two shipyards left on the Clyde today and have been transformed with modern equipment and construction slips housed in huge sheds. They are allied to BAE Systems Submarine Solutions at Barrow.

ABERDEEN Corporation gasworks railway 0-4-0 saddle tank engine No 3, built by Andrew Barclay in 1926, trundles two oil tank wagons along Miller Street, passing the corner of Baltic Place, in June 1962. On the left a man up a ladder is repainting a gas lamp in Corporation green and on the right is a road sweeper's metal handcart. The gasworks in Cotton Street can just be seen in the far background and this short line connected the gasworks with the harbour and British Railways on Waterloo Quay. The engines also served a siding into a chemical works.

These were all tram engines with side skirts covering the motion for street running and they were repainted from Corporation green to Scottish Gas Board blue after gas nationalisation in 1948. The steam engines were replaced by diesels in 1964 and the railway was lifted in stages after the closure of the gasworks in 1975 and the chemical works in 1985. Three steam engines and two diesels have been preserved, and No 3 is now under a canopy at the Grampian Transport Museum, Alford. It has been restored to full working order and is occasionally operated on the Royal Deeside Railway. *Robin Hogg*

Inverness-shire

AVIEMORE Back to the 1890s: ex-Caledonian Railway 0-4-4 tank engine No 55173, dating from 1895, is seen by Aviemore signal cabin, built in 1898, on the former Highland Railway main line between Perth and Inverness, with the Cairngorm Mountains in the background, in August 1956. The engine is at rest while the crew take a break on the trackside. Most of these engines were fitted with 'stovepipe' chimneys as seen here.

AVIEMORE This 1929 Cowieson-bodied Albion motorbus was used as a motor caravan with a travelling fair when photographed alongside a 1936 Ford V8 car at Aviemore in August 1956. Both Albion and Cowieson were Glasgow firms and Scotland's leading bus-builders in their time. Albion produced the largest-capacity engines on the British bus market. The large steering wheel seems almost to fill the cab and the steering column projects through the dash panel to the steering mechanism on the front axle. The bus was new to Northern General Motors of Arbroath, which served the area between Dundee and Aberdeen. That company was taken over in 1930 by W. Alexander & Sons of Falkirk, serving much of central and eastern Scotland, and this bus was sold out of service in 1939 to Banff County Council and finally to Mr A. Dick, the showman, of Fochabers. Its top speed was about 20mph, which was the legal limit when it was new. In the background are the braes of the Monadh Liath ranged along the west side of Strathspey.

MALLAIG, the end of the road and the main fishing port on the west coast of Scotland, is noted for its herring and kippers. It occupies a rocky headland between the sea and a sheltered bay. This view across the harbour to the village of Courteachen on the other side of the bay was taken on 23 May 1959. Mallaig is at the end of the old 'Road to the Isles' that goes 'by Tummel and Loch Rannoch and Lochaber'. It is also the terminus of the scenic West Highland Extension Railway, 45 miles from Fort William, opened by the North British Railway in 1901, the last main-line extension in Britain, albeit single track, for services from Glasgow Queen Street. With the Grouping of railways in 1923 Mallaig became one of the remote western outposts – together with Seacombe, Silloth and Southport – of the LNER, which otherwise served the eastern side of Britain. From here one boards a ferry to 'the tangle of the isles' (Muck, Eigg, Rum and Canna) or 'over the sea to Skye', all of which boldly crown the horizon west and north of Mallaig. In 1959, when this picture was taken, the road from Fort William to Mallaig was still a tortuous, single-lane route with passing places, reminiscent of the old Khyber Pass, an adventure to drive along. Since then the road has been further blasted out, straightened and widened through the rocky landscape and rebuilt as a less arduous, two-lane carriageway, but it has lost its romance and sense of adventure. Fish from Mallaig now goes by road instead of by rail. The railway was dieselised in the 1960s but special steam trains run from Fort William in the summer holidays and the growth of tourism has altered the character of this workaday fishing port.

Acknowledgements and References

My thanks for making this album possible go to those who printed my black and white photographs:

Ian Breckin of Silvertone, Leeds
CC Imaging Photo Lab, Leeds
Steve Howe of the Black & White Picture Place, Chester
the late Ken Tyhurst of Canterbury

Thanks also to those who processed my colour slides and prints:
Fujifilm Laboratories, Warwick
CC Imaging Photo Lab, Leeds

In writing the introductory text and captions I am indebted to the following people for information and assistance:
David Anderson of Cheltenham Borough Council planning office
Roy Andrews, berthing manager, Mersey Docks
Lewis Baron of the Douglas Bay Horse Tramway
Michael List Brain of Preston near Canterbury, owner of the tug *Cervia* at Ramsgate
Noreen Chambers of the Medway Queen Preservation Society
Garry Cowans of Margate Civic Society
Paul Crampton of Canterbury, local historian
Maurice Cullan, senior engineer, Volk's Electric Railway, Brighton
Carol Donelly, a Carlisle city guide
Graham Fairhurst of Southport, a transport historian
Barry Fuller, manager of Volk's Railway, Brighton
Ted Gadsby of Walsall: old buses and buildings in Birmingham and Wednesbury
Martin Garside, publicity officer, Port of London Authority
Steven Hannibal, Network Rail local operations manager, Boston
Michael Hunt, curator, Ramsgate Maritime Museum
Bryan Lindop, customer services manager and head of heritage, Blackpool Transport
Chris Lines, Lord Mayor's Officer, Liverpool City Council
Barrie McFarlane, hon Historian, Volk's Electric Railway Association, Brighton
Stuart McKenzie, British Waterways harbour master on the River Ouse
The late Bruce Maund of Birkenhead, transport historian
Nigel Mussett and Peter Shaw, Friends of the Settle & Carlisle Railway
Glynn Parry of Bromborough, local history lecturer
Geoff Price, of Halton-on-Lune, a tramway archivist
Peter Roach, operations manager, Paignton & Dartmouth Steam Railway
Pat Rudrum of Holt, Norfolk, my Internet intermediary
Robert Sawyers, relief harbour master, Hull
Alan Scarth, curator of ship models, Merseyside Maritime Museum
Catherine Spiller, assistant collections curator, Dumfries Museum
Joy Thomas, Wrexham Local Studies librarian
Paul Tritton of Maidstone: general reference on east Kent
Tom Turner of Wallasey: help in identifying and dating motor vehicles
Danny Witherington, British Waterways' north-west office, Wigan.

I am also indebted for information to the staff of :
Associated British Ports at Barrow, Fleetwood and Hull
Banbury tourist office
Barrow town planning office
Blackpool Tower
BAE shipyards at Barrow and Govan
Canterbury City Council and Museum
Conwy County Borough Council
Peter Donaldson, volunteer, Grampian Transport Museum, Alford
Exmouth tourist office
Greenwich Borough Council
Haig Colliery Mining Museum, Whitehaven
Hastings tourist office
Hull Maritime Museum
Manx Electric Railway, Douglas
Mersey Ferries; Seacombe
Mitchell Library, Glasgow
National Waterways Museum, Ellesmere Port
New Holland Bulk Services
Newquay tourist office
Norfolk County Libraries for computer services at Holt
Office for National Statistics, Newport (Mon)
Oxford tourist office

Peel Ports (Mersey Marine Section)
Penzance tourist office
Polperro Heritage Museum of Fishing & Smuggling
Rachel Roberts, curator, Windermere Jetty Museum of Boats and Steam
Salter's Steamers, Oxford
Seaton & District Electric Tramway
Swanage tourist office
Teesside Archives

References

The following is a list of books, magazines and newspapers I have consulted for information, almost all of which are in my own library and collections at home:

The ABC of Midland Red Vehicles, In Allan, 1950
A-Z of British Bus Bodies, by James Taylor, 2013
About Brighton, by Antony Dale, 1965
The Ancient and Historic Monuments of the Isle of Man, by the Manx Museum and National Trust, 1981
The Ancient City of Canterbury, by the Chamber of Trade and City Corporation, 1900
Anglo-Saxon England, by Professor F. M. Stenton, 1943
The Banbury to Verney Junction Branch, by Bill Simpson, 1978
The Birkenhead Railway, by T. B. Maund, 2000
Birkenhead's Docks and Railways, by Ken McCarron, David Marks and Paul Rees, 1997
Blackpool: a Tradition of Trams, by J. A. Garnham, 1976
Blackpool by Tram, by Steve Palmer and Brian Turner, 1968;
Blackpool and Fleetwood by Tram, by Steve Palmer, 1988
Blackpool's Century of Trams, by Steve Palmer, 1985
Blackpool to Fleetwood, by Brian Turner
The Book of Oxford Buses and Trams, by Stephen Jolly and Nick Taylor, 1981
Bowaters' Sittingbourne Railway, by Arthur Wells, 1962
Bradshaw's Railway Guide for Great Britain and Ireland (timetables), June 1949
The Branch Lines of Cornwall, by Lewis Reade, 1984
Branch Lines to Newquay, by Vic Mitchell and Keith Smith, 2001
The Bridges of Britain, by Eric de Maré, 1975
Britain's Light Railways, by Anthony Burton and John Scott-Morgan, 1985
British Bus Fleets: Yorkshire Municipal, by P. J. Marshall and Basil Kennedy, 1957
The British Bus Story, 1946-1950, A Golden Age, by Alan Townsin, 1983
British Bus Systems, No. 2: Ribble, by Eric Ogden, 1983
British Electric Trains, by H. W. A. Linecar, 1946
The British Motor Bus, by Gavin Booth, 1986
BR timetables: Midland, winter 1950; Southern, summer 1951; Western, summer 1952
Bygone Central Newcastle II (St Nicholas to Percy Street), by Frank Manders, 1995
Canals and Waterways, by Michael Ware, 1987
The Canterbury & Whitstable Railway, by Brian Hart, 1991
Chronicle of the 20th century, by Chronicle Communications and Longman Group, 1988
Classic British Steam Locomotives, by Peter Herring, 2000
Clayton's of Oldbury (canal carriers), by Alan Faulkner, 1978
Cosens of Weymouth, 2001, by Richard Clammer
Daily Express and Daily Mail, 2-13 February 1953 (east coast floods)
Daily Express, 11 February 1965 (armed manhunt at Oxenholme)
Daily Mail, 2-12 January 1952 (SS *Flying Enterprise* saga)
Date a Number (guide to motor vehicle registrations), by Autobus Review Publications
The Definitive Guide to Trams (including funiculars) in the British Isles, by David Voice
The Directory of British Tramways, by Keith Turner, 1996
East Coast Sail, by Robert Simper, 1987
The Great Railway Conspiracy, 1994, by David Henshaw
East Kent (a history of the East Kent Road Car Company), by Frank Wordworth, 1991
Electric Trains, by Robin Jones, 2010
Glory Days: East Kent, by Glyn Kraemer-Johnson and John Bishop, 2005
East London Line, by Vic Mitchell and Keith Smith, 1996
Echoes of Steam and Vintage Voltage, by Cedric Greenwood, 2015
Ellesmere Port, 1795-1960, by T. W. Roberts, 1995
Ellesmere Port: The Making of an Industrial Borough, by P. Aspinall and D. Hudson, 1982
Estuary and River Ferries of South West England, by M. Langley and E. Small, 1984
Farewell to North-west Steam, by Ivo Peters, edited by Mac Hawkins, 1992
50 Years of Teesside Trolleybuses, 1919-1969, by the National Trolleybus Association, 1969
The Five Minute Crossing (the Tilbury-Gravesend ferries), by John Ormston, 1992

Folkestone-Boulogne, 1843-1991, by John Hundy
The Furness Railway, by K. J. Norman, 2001
Forgotten Railways: Vol. 7, East Anglia, by R. S. Joby, 1985
Glasgow's Railways, by W. A. C. Smith and Paul Anderson, 1993
Glory Days: Southdown, by Glyn Kraemer-Johnson and John Bishop, 2001
The Golden Age of Buses, by Charles Klapper, 1978
Great British Tramway Networks, by Wingate Bett and John Gillham, 1957
Great Railway Stations of Britain, by Gordon Biddle, 1986
The Groudle Glen Railway, by Tony Beard, 2001
Hampton and Studd Hill, by Harold Gough, Bygone Kent magazines, February and March, 1996
Heritage Railway Magazine 256 ((news of *Invicta's* move to Whitstable)
The History of the British Trolleybus, by Nicholas Owen, 1974
Holborn Viaduct to Lewisham (the railway), by Vic Mitchell and Keith Smith, 1990
Horse Tram to Metro (100 Years of Local Public Transport) by Tyne & Wear PTE, 1978
The Humber Crossing, by Hull Junior Chamber of Commerce & Shipping, 1974
The Humber Ferries, by Alun A. D'Orley, 1968
An Illustrated History of Liverpool's Railways, by Paul Anderson, 1996
Industrial Locomotives of North Wales, by V. J. Bradley, 1992
Isle of Man, Ward Lock's Red Guide
Isle of Man Railway, by J. I. C. Boyd, 1967
Kendal and Windermere Railway, by Julian Mellentin, 1980
Kent Messenger newspaper, 13 February 1953 and 31 December 1954 (east coast floods)
The Lakeside & Haverthwaite Railway Visitors Guide
The Lambton, Hetton & Joicey Railway, by Glen Kilday, Back Track magazine, May 2017
The Last Berth of the Sailorman, 1996, by the Society for Sailing Barge Research
Leicester's Trams, by Geoff Creese, 2000
Lightweight DMUs, by Evan Green-Hughes, 2012
The Line Beneath the Liners (100 years of the Mersey Railway) by John Gahan, 1983
Liverpool, City of Architecture, by Quentin Hughes, 1999
LNER Branch Lines, by C. J. Gammell, 1993
The L&NE in Wales and the Wirral, by Bennington Marsh, Railway World magazine, April 1961
LMS Branch Lines, by C. J. Gammell, 1988
The Long Return (Oxford to Cambridge Railway), by Bill Simpson, 2017
London Bus File 1933-39, by Ken Glazier
London Bus File 1950-54, by Ken Glazier
London Railways, by Edwin Course, 1962
London's Historic Railway Stations, by John Betjeman, 1972
The London, Tilbury & Southend Railway, volume 6: The Gravesend Ferry, by Peter Kay, 2017
Looking Back at British Tugs, by Andrew Wiltshire, 2007
Manx Electric, by Mike Goodwyn, 1993
Mechanical Horses, by Bill Aldridge, 2000
The Mersey Estuary, by J. E. Allison, 1949
Mersey Ferries, Volume 1, Woodside to Eastham, by T. B. Maund, 1991
Mersey Ferries, Volume 2, Wallasey, by T. B. Maund and Martin Jenkins, 2003
Merseyside: The Indian Summer, by Cedric Greenwood, 2007
Midland Red Buses & Coaches, Ian Allan ABC, 1954
Midland Red, by John Banks and G. H. F. Atkins, 2003
Narrow Gauge Railways of Britain, by F. H. Howson, 1948
Narrow Gauge Railways: Wales and the Western Front, by Humphrey Household, 1996
A Nostalgic Look at Leeds Trams since 1950, by Graham Twidale, 1991
A Nostalgic Look at Sheffield Trams since 1950, by Graham Twidale, 1995
A Nostalgic Look at Liverpool Trams, 1945-1957, by Steve Palmer and Brian Martin, 1996
The Oldest Passenger Railway in the World (Mumbles), by the South Wales Transport Co, 1954
Oxford Mail, 4 February 1952 (death of King George VI)
Pleasure Steamers, by Bernard Cox, 1983
Rail Centres: Oxford, by Laurence Waters, 1986
Rail News, September 2019 (tramway extension in Birmingham)
Rails to Port and Starboard (Mersey dockside railways), by John Gahan, 1992
Railway Adventure, by L. T. C. Rolt, 1977
The Railway Heritage of Britain, by Gordon Biddle and O. S. Nock, 1990;
Railway Stations in the North West, by Gordon Biddle, 1981
Railway Stations of Wirral, by the Merseyside Railway History Group
Railway Stations in the North West, by Gordon Biddle, 1981
Railways in the Isle of Man, by Martin Bairstow, 2002
Ribble Bus Services timetable, Northern Area, 1965-66 and 1969-70
Railway Stations in the North West, by Gordon Biddle, 1981
River Ferries, by Nancy Martin, 1980
Roads and Rails of Birmingham, 1900-1939, by R. T. Coxon, 1979

The Roman Forts of the Saxon Shore, by Leonard Cottrell, 1964
Rossett, Marford & Gresford, by Helen Maurice-Jones, 2002
Royal River Highway, by Frank Dix, 1985
Sailing Barges, by Martin Hazell, 2001
The Sailing Barges of Maritime England
Seaside Piers, by Simon Adamson and Anthony Dale, 1977
Settle-Carlisle Railway, by W. R. Mitchell and David Joy, 1966
Seventy-five Years on Wheels (Barrow-in-Furness trams and buses), by Ian Cormack, 1960
Ships of the Isle of Man Steam Packet Company, by Fred Henry, 1967
Ships of the Mersey and Manchester, by H. M. Le Fleming, 1959
Sir Edward Watkin, 1819-1901, the last of the railway kings, by John Greaves, 2005
South of the Solway, by David Joy, Back Track magazine, May 2017
Southdown Fleet and Routes, by the Southdown Enthusiasts' Club, 1949
Southdown Album 1954-1979, by the Southdown Enthusiasts' Club, 1979
Southern Main Lines: Sittingbourne to Ramsgate, by Vic Mitchell and Keith Smith, 1991
The Splendid and Romantic History of the Kent Barge, Kent Messenger, 31 December, 1954
Steam Days at Birkenhead, by Stanley Jenkins, Steam Days magazine, February, 2010
Steam Railways in Industry, by Colin Gifford and Horace Gamble, 1976
Steamers of the Lakes, vol 2: Coniston, Derwentwater, Ullswater, by Robert Beale, 2011
The Story of Cornwall's Ports and Harbours, by Cyril Noall, 1970
The Story of the Medway Queen, by the Paddle Steamer Preservation Society, 1974
Sunday Express, 3 February 1953 (Stranraer-Larne ferry *Princess Victoria* sinking in storm)
Superlative Newcastle upon Tyne, article by Ian Nairn, The Listener, 28 July 1960
Swanage Pier, by L. Cade, magazine of the Medway Queen Preservation Society, winter 2007
Thanet Advertiser & Echo, 6 February 1953 (Margate lighthouse toppled in sea floods)
Thanet's Tramways, by Robert Harley, 1993
Too Many Boats (British Waterways), by Robert Wilson, 1980
Tramways Remembered: West and South West of England, by Leslie Oppitz, 1990
Tramway Twilight, by J. Joyce, 1962
Transport in Britain from Canal Lock to Gridlock, by Philip Bagwell and Peter Blyth, 2002
Trolleybus Trails, by J. Joyce, 1963
Tynwald, Symbol of an Ancient Kingdom, by David Craine
United, A Short History of United Automobile Services Ltd., 1912-1987, by Nigel Watson, 1987
Visitors' Companion to the Isles of Scilly, by F. Gibson
Volk's Railway, Brighton, 1883-1964, by Alan Jackson
The Wallasey Bus, by T. B. Maund, 1995
The Waterways of Britain, by Anthony Burton, 1983
Whitstable Harbour Memories, by Paul Tritton, 1997
Who's Who in British History, edited by Juliet Gardiner, 2000
Yesterday's Britain, by Reader's Digest, 1998

Videography

Manx Trains and Trams, a Duke Video, 2001
Marsden Rail 40, Yorkshire and Lancashire, A Cine Rail video, 1968
Riding a Regency Regent, by Independent Transport Videos (notes by Brian Jackson and Geoff Smith), 2017

Index

Bus and coach stations

Berwick 270
Brighton 62
Birkenhead Woodside 141
Cambridge 112
Canterbury 30
Cheltenham 89
London Bridge 49
Morecambe 210
Newquay 104
Oxford 79-83
Ramsey (IOM) 300
Seacombe 152, 153
Southport 192

Canals

Wolverhampton 127
Ellesmere Port 137
Lancaster 208

Docks and harbours

Barrow 213
Birkenhead 140, 146-150
Bristol 89
Conyer Creek 42
Exeter 94, 95
Exmouth 97, 98
Folkestone 16
Hastings 57
Hull 217
Liverpool 173, 176
Mallaig 327
Newhaven 61
Newquay 105
Penzance 107
Polperro 106
Ramsey 300
Ramsgate 17-19
St. Ives 106
Seacombe 151, 154
Whitehaven 265
Whitstable 41

Ferries and excursion steamers

Birkenhead – Liverpool 144 – 147, 172, 174
Dartmouth – Kingswear 100, 101
Dorset coast 71
Douglas to Liverpool 286
Exmouth - Starcorss 98
Firth of Clyde 323
Govan – Pointhouse 324
Hull – New Holland 118-120
Rock Ferry 139
Scilly isles 108, 109
Sussex coast 61
Thames and Isis 75
Thames estuary and Medway 39-40
Tilbury – Gravesend 44
Ullswater 258
Wallasey – Liverpool 152, 174-176
Woolwich – North Woolwich 45

Horsedrawn vehicles 185, 191, 218, 312

London River 3, 4, 44, 45, 51, 52

Lorries and vans 14, 31, 33, 140, 156, 160, 229,

Motor buses and coaches 9, 10,

Barrow 214
Birkenhead 141-143, 156
Birmingham 124
Black & White 89
Bournemouth 68-70
Brighton 62
Brighton, Hove & District 64
Bristol 82
Central SMT 312
Chester 134
Crosville 82, 141
Devon General 99
A. Dick, Fochabers 326
Eastbourne 60
Eastern Counties 112
East Kent 23, 28-32, 34, 35, 37
Edinburgh 306, 307
Exeter 95
Harding's, Birkenhead 283
Isle of Man 301
G. Julian, Grampound Road 105
Liverpool 181-183
London 34, 47. 49, 53, 56,
Midland 88, 123
Newcastle 269
Nottingham 131
Oldham 163
Oxford 73, 74, 76-81, 88
Premier Travel 112
Preston 190
Ribble 121, 142, 210, 216
SMT 270
Scout 121
Sheffield 222
Southdown 60, 83
Southern Vectis 67
Southport 190-192, 194
Standerwick 121
Oxford 73, 74, 76-81, 88
United 238, 270
United Counties 112
Wallasey 152, 153, 157, 160
West Bromwich 125
Western National 93, 104
Western Scottish 304
Widnes 168

Paddle steamers 8-9, 38-40, 45, 61, 71, 119, 120

Private cars 10, 22, 26, 65, 96, 100, 243, 326

Private steam launch 257

Railways 9, 12, 13,

BR Eastern 54. 110, 113-116, 118
BR Midland 72, 131, 133, 134, 135, 139, 140, 141, 155, 158, 164, 169, 184, 193, 211, 214, 215, 239-254, 256, 266
BR North Eastern half title, 4, 227, 269
BR Scottish 326
BR Southern 24. 36, 66, 93, 96
BR Western 98, 99, 102, 103, 104, 126, 128, 129, 130, 134, 135, 140, 141, 148
Cliff railways 57
Groudle Glen Rly. 290
Industrial railways 43, 136, 148, 151, 156, 238, 259, 260, 262-265, 267, 268, 280, 325
Invicta locomotive 27
Isle of Man Rly. 288, 301-303
Liverpool Overhead 182
GCR/LNER in BR Midland 133, 158, 85, 281, 282
London Underground 46, 48
Ramsgate Tunnel Rly. 20. 21
Settle – Carlisle line 239-245

Ravenglass & Eskdale 261
Talyllyn Rly. 277-279

Railway landscapes *half title*, 4, 98, 241, 246-248, 256, 261, 290, 293-295, 297

Railway stations and halts

Anderston Cross 321
Arkholme 208
Banbury Merton Street 87
Birchington-on-Sea 24
Birkdale 193
Birkenhead Woodside 140-141
Bolton Trinity Street 169
Britannia halt 103
Brocklesby 117
Burnley Central 189
Carlisle Citadel 266
Chester General 135
Church Stretton 129
Coniston 215
Douglas (IOMR) 288
Douglas (MER) 289
Ellesmere Port 135
Euston 55
Glasgow Cross 314, 315
Garwick Glen 293
Ironbridge & Broseley 130
King's Cross 54
Kingswear 102, 103
Lancaster Green Ayre 209
Laxey 296
Liscard & Poulton 158
Liverpool Central 184
Morecambe Promenade 211
Old Hill 126
Oxenholme 249-251
Oxford General 86
Oxford Rewley Road 84, 85
Pier Head 182
Newton Abbot 99
Newton Poppleford 96
Nottingham Midland 131
Oxford General 86
Oxford Rewley Road 84, 85
Peel 303
Preston 6
Ramsey (IOM) 301
Rock Ferry 139
Rotherhithe 46
Seacombe & Egremont 155
Shipton-on-Cherwell 87
Wapping 48
Wolverhampton High Level 129
Wolverhampton Low Level 128

Shipping and shipbuilding 44, 146, 149-152, 154, 172, 176, 177, 187, 188, 213, 286, 323, 324

Steam road locomotives 33, 160

Street scenes and general views

Aberdeen 325
Banbury 88
Barrow 213
Birmingham 124
Blackpool 196, 197, 199, 205-207
Bradford 235-237
Bridge 25
Bridgeton 310
Brighton 64, 65
Buxton 132
Burnham Market 111
Calton (Glasgow)313
Camlachie 312
Carlisle 266
Cheltenham 90

Chester 134
Chilham 26
Cliftonville 22
Dalmarnock 308,
Dent 243
Douglas 287
Dumfries 304
Eastbourne 60
Edinburgh 305, 306
Glasgow 315, 317-319,
Govan 322
Ironbridge 130
Kendal 255
Leeds 229, 230-232
Leicester front cover, 2, 122
Liverpool 179, 183, 186
New Brighton waterfront 159
Newcastle 269
Newport (IOW) 67
Norton Woodseats 221
Oldham 163
Oxford 77
Ramsey (IOM) 298, 300
Seacombe 156
Sheffield 225, 227, 228
Southport 191
Stepney 47
Teesside 238
Wallasey 157
Wapping 48
Warwick 123
Wednesbury 125
West Kirby 161, 162
Widnes 166
Wigan 170

Then and now (scene changes)

Burnham Market 111
Ellesmere Port 137
Anderston (Glasgow) 321

Tramways and cars 10-12, 14,

Barrow 212.213
Blackpool 195-207
Brighton (Volk's) 62, 63
Douglas 287
Eastbourne 58-60
Glasgow 309-322
Great Orme 284, 285
Grimsby & Immingham 115, 116
Leeds 229-234
Leicester front cover, 2, 122
Liverpool 179-181, 186
Manx Electric 289-298
Ramsey pier 299
Seaton 91, 92
Sheffield 220-228

Transporter Bridge, Widnes 165-167

Trolleybuses 12,

Bradford 235-237
Brighton 62
Glasgow 311, 322
Rotherham 219
Teesside 238

Tugs 44, 45, 95, 138, 149, 152, 159, 171, 176-178, 217

A page for your own personal memories...